Aeolian
Islands

**NORTHEASTERN
SICILY**
Pages 154–187

MESSINA ●

NORTHEASTERN
SICILY

Catania ●

Enna
●

●TERN
Y

● Caltanissetta

SOUTHERN
SICILY

Syracuse ●

RAGUSA●

**SOUTHERN
SICILY**
Pages 128–153

| 0 kilometres | 25 |
| 0 miles | 20 |

DK TRAVEL GUIDES

SICILY

DORLING KINDERSLEY *TRAVEL GUIDES*

SICILY

DORLING KINDERSLEY
LONDON • NEW YORK • SYDNEY • MOSCOW • DELHI
www.dk.com

A DORLING KINDERSLEY BOOK

www.dk.com

Produced by Fabio Ratti
Editoria Libraria e Multimediale
Milan, Italy

PROJECT EDITOR Giovanni Francesio
EDITOR Elena Marzorati
SECRETARY Emanuela Damiani
DESIGNERS Studio Matra–Silvia Tomasone, Lucia Tirabassi
MAPS Oriana Bianchetti

Dorling Kindersley Ltd
PROJECT EDITOR Fiona Wild
DTP DESIGNERS Maite Lantaron, Lee Redmond
PRODUCTION David Proffit
MANAGING EDITORS Fay Franklin, Louise Bostock Lang
MANAGING ART EDITOR Annette Jacobs
EDITORIAL DIRECTOR Vivien Crump
ART DIRECTOR Gillian Allan
PUBLISHER Douglas Amrine

CONTRIBUTORS
Fabrizio Ardito, Cristina Gambaro
Additional tourist information by Marco Scapagnini

ILLUSTRATORS
Giorgia Boli, Silvana Ghioni,
Alberto Ipsilanti, Nadia Viganò

ENGLISH TRANSLATION
Richard Pierce

Film output by Graphical Innovations, London
Reproduced by Lineatre Service, Milano
Printed and bound by L. Rex Printing Company Limited, China

First published in Great Britain in 2000 by
Dorling Kindersley Ltd,
9 Henrietta Street, London WC2E 8PS
Copyright 2000 © Dorling Kindersley Ltd

ISBN 0 7513 1178 2

**The information in every
Dorling Kindersley Travel Guide is checked annually**.
Every effort has been made to ensure that this book is as up-to-
date as possible at the time of going to press. Some details,
however, such as telephone numbers, opening hours, prices,
gallery hanging arrangements and travel information are liable to
change. The publishers cannot accept responsibility for any
consequences arising from the use of this book.
We value the views and suggestions of our readers very highly.
Please write to: Editorial Director, Dorling Kindersley Travel Guides,
Dorling Kindersley, 9 Henrietta Street, London WC2E 8PS.

◁ The Temple of Hera in the Valle dei Templi at Agrigento

CONTENTS

Female bust sculpted in the 5th
century BC (see pp28–9)

INTRODUCING
SICILY

Backcloth, Museo delle Marionette
in Palermo (see pp48–9)

PALERMO
AREA BY AREA

Castellammare del Golfo *(see p92)*, one of many fishing villages on the Sicilian coast

TRAVELLERS' NEEDS

A cheese vendor at Catania open-air market *(see pp210–11)*

Ancient theatre mask, Museo Eoliano *(see p186)*

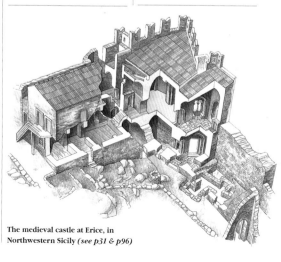

The medieval castle at Erice, in Northwestern Sicily *(see p31 & p96)*

HOW TO USE THIS GUIDE

THIS GUIDE will help you to get the most out of your visit to Sicily. It provides detailed practical information and expert recommendations. *Introducing Sicily* maps the island and sets Sicily in its historic, artistic, geographical and cultural context. *Palermo Area by Area* and the four regional sections describe the most important sights, with maps, floor plans, photographs and detailed illustrations. Restaurant and hotel recommendations are described in *Travellers' Needs* and the *Survival Guide* has tips on everything from transport to hiring a surfboard.

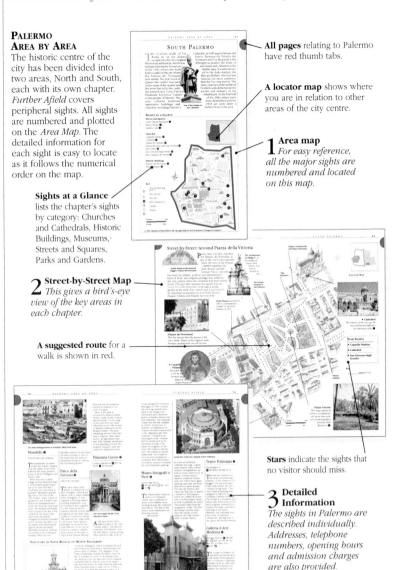

PALERMO AREA BY AREA

The historic centre of the city has been divided into two areas, North and South, each with its own chapter. *Further Afield* covers peripheral sights. All sights are numbered and plotted on the *Area Map*. The detailed information for each sight is easy to locate as it follows the numerical order on the map.

Sights at a Glance lists the chapter's sights by category: Churches and Cathedrals, Historic Buildings, Museums, Streets and Squares, Parks and Gardens.

1 Area map *For easy reference, all the major sights are numbered and located on this map.*

All pages relating to Palermo have red thumb tabs.

A locator map shows where you are in relation to other areas of the city centre.

2 Street-by-Street Map *This gives a bird's-eye view of the key areas in each chapter.*

A suggested route for a walk is shown in red.

Stars indicate the sights that no visitor should miss.

3 Detailed Information *The sights in Palermo are described individually. Addresses, telephone numbers, opening hours and admission charges are also provided.*

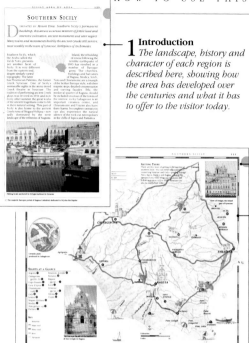

1 Introduction
The landscape, history and character of each region is described here, showing how the area has developed over the centuries and what it has to offer to the visitor today.

SICILY AREA BY AREA

Apart from Palermo, Sicily has been divided into four regions, each with a separate chapter. The most interesting towns, villages and sights to visit are numbered on a *Pictorial Map*.

Each area can be identified by its own colour coding.

2 Pictorial Map
This shows the road network and gives an illustrated overview of the whole region. All the interesting places to visit are numbered and there are also useful tips on getting to, and around, the region by car and by public transport.

For all top sights, a Visitors' Checklist provides the practical information you will need to plan your visit.

3 Sicily's top sights
These are given two or more full pages. Historic buildings are dissected to reveal their interiors. The most interesting towns or city centres are shown in a bird's-eye view, with sights picked out and described.

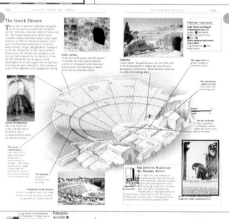

4 Places of Interest
All the important towns and other places to visit are described individually. They are listed in order, following the numbering on the Pictorial Map. Within each town or city, there is detailed information on important buildings and other sights.

INTRODUCING
SICILY

Putting Sicily on the Map

S ICILY IS the largest region in Italy (25,708 sq km, 9,923 sq miles) and the third most highly populated with more than five million inhabitants. The terrain is mostly hilly – the plains and plateaus make up only 14 per cent of the total land area. The most interesting features of the mountain zones are the volcanoes, especially Mount Etna, which is the largest active volcano in Europe. The longest river is the Salso, which is 144 km (89 miles) long. Besides Sicily itself, the Region of Sicily includes other smaller islands: the Aeolian Islands, Ustica, the Egadi Islands, Pantelleria and the Pelagie Islands. Palermo is the Sicilian regional capital, and with its population of almost 700,000 is the fifth largest city in Italy after Rome, Milan, Naples and Turin.

Palermo, Italy's fifth largest city

Ustica

Bay of Carini

Bay of Palermo

Bay of Castellammare

PALERMO

Ba

Lèvanzo

Marèttimo

Erice

A29 dir

A29

A19

Egadi islands

Favignana

Trapani

T

Mediterranean Sea

Marsala

A29

Gibellina

S.Ninfa

Castelvetrano

Mazara del Vallo

Menfi

Lercara Friddi

Sciacca

Porto Empedocle

THE ISLANDS AROUND SICILY

Pantelleria

Linosa

Pelagie Islands

Lampedusa

Aeolian islands

Egadi islands

Palermo

SICILY

Pantelleria

Pelagie islands

0 kilometres	30
0 miles	20

◁ **The carnival at Acireale, one of the most colourful in Sicily**

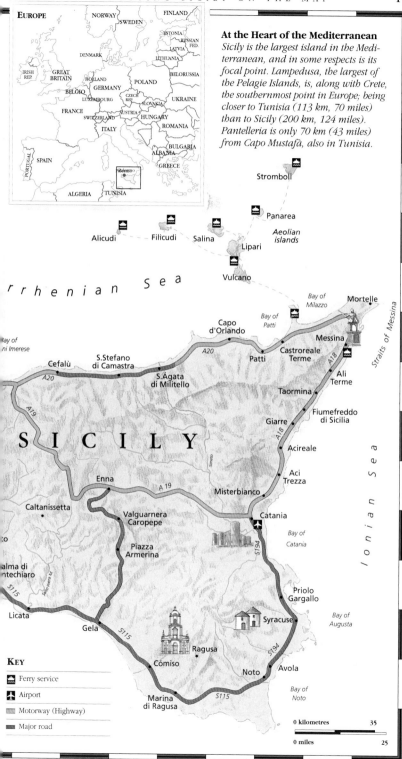

EUROPE

NORWAY
SWEDEN
FINLAND
ESTONIA
RUSSIAN FED.
LITHUANIA
LATVIA
DENMARK
IRISH REP.
GREAT BRITAIN
HOLLAND
GERMANY
POLAND
BELORUSSIA
BELGIQ
LUXEMBOURG
CZECH REP.
SLOVAKIA
UKRAINE
FRANCE
SWITZERLAND
AUSTRIA
HUNGARY
ROMANIA
ITALY
BULGARIA
ALBANIA
GREECE
PORTUGAL
SPAIN
Palermo
ALGERIA
TUNISIA

At the Heart of the Mediterranean

Sicily is the largest island in the Mediterranean, and in some respects is its focal point. Lampedusa, the largest of the Pelagie Islands, is, along with Crete, the southernmost point in Europe; being closer to Tunisia (113 km, 70 miles) than to Sicily (200 km, 124 miles). Pantelleria is only 70 km (43 miles) from Capo Mustafã, also in Tunisia.

Stromboli

Panarea

Aeolian islands

Alicudi   Filicudi   Salina

Lipari

Vulcano

r r h e n i a n   S e a

Bay of Milazzo

Mortelle

Bay of Patti

Capo d'Orlando

Bay of ni Imerese

Cefalù

S.Stefano di Camastra

A20

S.Ágata di Militello

Patti

Castroreale Terme

Messina

Straits of Messina

Ali Terme

A18

Taormina

Fiumefreddo di Sicilia

Giarre

A18

Acireale

Aci Trezza

Simeto

S I C I L Y

Enna

A 19

Misterbianco

Ionian Sea

Caltanissetta

Valguarnera Caropepe

Catania

S194

Bay of Catania

o

Piazza Armerina

alma di ntechiaro

Priolo Gargallo

S115

Licata

Syracuse

Bay of Augusta

Gela

S115

Ragusa

KEY

🚢 Ferry service

✈ Airport

Motorway (Highway)

Major road

Cómiso

Noto

Avola

Bay of Noto

Marina di Ragusa

S115

0 kilometres   35

0 miles   25

A PORTRAIT
OF SICILY

S ICILIAN SHORES are *washed by three different seas, and this is reflected in the island's ancient name for Sicily: "Trinacria", the three-cornered island. Each part of the island has its own history, its own character, creating a varied and complex whole. Yet over the centuries Sicily has acquired a sense of unity and identity.*

Sicily's history can be traced back more than 2,000 years, during which time it has been dominated by many different rulers, from the Greeks to the Romans, Byzantines and Arabs, from the Normans to the Spanish. Each succeeding culture left a mark on the island and may perhaps help to explain aspects of the modern Sicilian character. This diverse inheritance manifests itself in a curious combination of dignified reserve and exuberant hospitality.

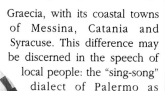

The Easter Week procession in Enna

The western side of the island, which is centred upon Palermo, is historically considered to be of Punic-Arab influence. The eastern side was once the centre of Magna Graecia, with its coastal towns of Messina, Catania and Syracuse. This difference may be discerned in the speech of local people: the "sing-song" dialect of Palermo as opposed to the more clipped accent of Catania and Syracuse. Accent differences are still noticeable, although they have moderated to some degree over the centuries. There are east-west economic and social differences as well as linguistic ones.

However, the island's long, eventful and tortuous history has not been the only factor influencing its life and inhabitants. Few places have been so affected by their climate and topography: in Sicily the

The rural landscape of the Sicilian interior, until recently characterized by its large estates

◁ Messina's Fontana del Nettuno (Fountain of Neptune), a traditional starting point for a tour of the island

Livestock raising, one of the mainstays of the economy in the Sicilian interior

temperature is 30°C (86°F) for six months of the year, and when the sun disappears, destructive torrential rains can take its place. The Sicilian climate is one of extremes and can sometimes even be cruel; it has shaped the island's extraordinary landscape which, as the Sicilian novelist Tomasi di Lampedusa described it, includes the hell of Randazzo and, just a few miles away, the paradise of Taormina. Then there are splendid verdant coasts everywhere, with the arid interior a stone's throw away, marvellous towns overlooking the sea and villages perched on hilltops surrounded by inhospitable, barren uplands. An aerial view of this unique island offers a spectacle that is at once both magnificent and awe-inspiring.

Villagers observing passers-by

ECONOMY AND SOCIETY

The historic, geographic and climatic differences in Sicily have produced a complex and varied society. Yet Sicilians have a strong sense of identity and for centuries made their unique nature a point of honour (in a spirit of independence they used to call the rest of Italy "the continent"). Today this society is at a crossroads between tradition and modernity, much more so than other Mediterranean regions. Sicilian society is attempting to reconcile newer lifestyles and outlooks with deeply rooted age-old customs.

A watermelon seller in Palermo

One of the poorest regions in Italy, Sicily has had to strive for a more streamlined and profitable economy against the resistance of the ancient *latifundia* (feudal estate) system, just as the fervent civic and democratic spirit of the Sicilian people clashes with what remains of Mafia mentality and practice.

The criminal organization known to all as the Mafia is one of Sicily's most notorious creations. Sociologists and criminologists both in Italy and abroad have tried to define the phenomenon without success. Is it a criminal structure that is simply stronger and more efficiently

An outdoor café on the island of Lampedusa

organized than others, partly because of the massive emigration in the early 20th century, which took many Sicilians to the other side of the ocean? Or is it an anti-government movement whose leaders have played on the strong feelings of independence and diversity, which have always characterized Sicily? Is the Mafia the tool of the remaining large estate owners, who once dominated the island and are determined to retain power? Or is it perhaps a combination of all the above factors, which have found fertile soil in the innate scepticism and pessimism of the Sicilians? Whatever the answer may be, eliminating the Mafia is one of Sicily's greatest challenges. After the early 1990s, which saw the deaths of several anti-Mafia figures, there is a new spirit abroad and the tide now seems to be turning in favour of the new Sicily.

ART AND CULTURE

For more than 2,000 years, Sicily has inspired the creation of artistic masterpieces, from the architecture of Magna Graecia to the great medieval cathedrals, from the paintings of Antonello da Messina to the music of Vincenzo Bellini, and from the birth of Italian literature under Frederick II to the poets and novelists of the 19th and 20th centuries. Sadly, this glorious artistic heritage is not always well cared for and appreciated. Noto, near Syracuse, provides one example. This splendid town was built entirely of tufa in the early 1700s and is one of the great achievements of Sicilian Baroque architecture. Today Noto is falling to pieces (the Cathedral collapsed in 1996), and the material used to build the town makes any restoration a difficult task. This mixture of splendour and decay, or as Gesualdo Bufalino, the acute observer of his land, once said, "light and lamentation", is typical of Sicily today. However, the creation of new nature reserves, renewed interest in preserving historic centres, and initiatives such as extended church opening hours, are all causes for cautious optimism in the future.

Renato Guttuso, *View of Bagheria* (1951)

Sicily's Geology, Landscape and Wildlife

TYPICAL SICILIAN landscape consists of coast and sun-baked hills. The irregular and varied coastline is over 1,000 km (620 miles) long, or 1,500 km (931 miles) if the smaller islands are included. The island's geological make-up is also quite varied, with sulphur mines in the centre and volcanic activity in the east. Sicily's many volcanoes, in particular Mount Etna (the largest in Europe), have created a landscape that is unique in the Mediterranean.

SICILIAN FAUNA

Sicily has preserved a variety of habitats in its large nature reserves, the most famous of which is the Mount Etna National Park. These parks are home to a wide range of species, some of which are endangered, including wildcats, martens and porcupines. The birdlife includes the rare golden eagle.

Painted frog

RUGGED COASTS AND STACKS

Vanessa butterfly

The Sicilian coastline is steep and rugged, particularly along the Tyrrhenian sea and the northern stretch of the Ionian, where there are many peninsulas, river mouths, bays and rocky headlands. It is also characterized by stacks, steep-sided pillars of rock separated from the coastal cliffs by erosion.

***The sawwort Serratula cichoriacea** is a perennial found along these coastlines.*

Astroides calycularis *is an alga that thrives in the shaded cliff areas.*

SANDY COASTLINES

Flamingo

Around the Trapani area the Sicilian coast begins to slope down to the Mozia salt marshes, followed by uniform and sandy Mediterranean beaches. This type of coastline continues along the Ionian side of Sicily, where there are marshy areas populated by flamingoes. These birds can be seen nesting as far inland as the Plain of Catania.

***The dwarf palm**, called* scupazzu *in Sicilian dialect, is a typical western Mediterranean plant.*

***The prickly pear** is an example of an imported plant that was initially cultivated in gardens and then ended up crowding out the local flora.*

All kinds of coleoptera, including this shiny-backed carabid beetle, can be found in Sicily. In the Mount Etna area alone, 354 different species have been identified.

The reptile family is represented by numerous species, ranging from various types of snake to smaller creatures such as this green lizard, which is well known for its shiny skin and sinuous body.

Foxes were at one time rare in Sicily, but in recent years they have been spotted near towns foraging for food among household refuse.

Martens love to roam in the woods around Mount Etna. Weasels and ferrets can also be found in Sicily.

THE INTERIOR

Green woodpecker

Sicily's hinterland has not always looked the way it does today. Maquis once carpeted areas that, except for a few stretches far from the towns, are arid steppes today. As a result, apart from grain, which has always been the island's staple, the flora is not native, originating in North Africa or the Italian mainland. Birds like the woodpecker can be seen.

Orchids come in a great number of varieties, but they are sadly becoming more and more rare. They can be seen in uncultivated areas or along screes.

The vegetation in the interior often looks like this: quite low-growing and with brightly coloured flowers.

VOLCANIC AREAS

A falcon, an Etna raptor

Volcanic zones, particularly around Mount Etna, are very fertile and yield rich vegetation: from olive trees growing on mountain slopes to the pines, birch and beech that thrive at 2,000 m (6,560 ft). Higher up grows the milk vetch, forming spiky racemes. Above 3,000 m (9,840 ft) nothing grows. Raptors can often be seen circling.

Moss and lichens cover the walls of houses on the slopes of Mount Etna, which are built using volcanic sand.

Cerastium and Sicilian soapwort flourish on the Mediterranean uplands.

Architecture in Sicily

THREE PERIODS HAVE shaped much of Sicilian architecture. The first was the time of Greek occupation, when monumental works (especially temples and theatres) were built. Aesthetically they were often equal to, and in some cases superior to, those in Greece itself. The medieval period witnessed the fusion of the Byzantine, Arab and Norman styles in such buildings as the Duomo at Monreale near Palermo. Last came the flowering of Baroque architecture in the 17th–18th centuries. The style was so individual that it became known as Sicilian Baroque.

Hygeia, 3rd century BC

LOCATOR MAP

☐ Classical architecture

▨ Medieval architecture

☐ Baroque architecture

STYLES OF CLASSICAL GREEK TEMPLE

The earliest version of the Greek temple consisted of a rectangular chamber housing the statue of a god. Later, columns were added and the wooden elements were replaced by stone. There were three Greek architectural orders: the Doric, Ionic and Corinthian, in chronological order. They are easily distinguished by the column capitals. The temples built in Sicily displayed an experimental, innovative nature compared with those in Greece.

The Doric Temple

The Doric temple stood on a three-stepped base. The columns had no base, were thicker in the middle and tapered upwards, and the capital was a rectangular slab. Other elements were the frieze with its alternating metopes and triglyphs, and the triangular pediment.

The Ionic Temple

The differences between the Ionic and Doric styles lay in the number of columns and in the fact that Ionic columns rest on a base and their capitals have two volutes, giving the appearance of rams' horns.

The Corinthian Temple

The Corinthian temple featured columns that were more slender than in the Ionic temple, and the elaborate capitals were decorated with stylized acanthus leaves.

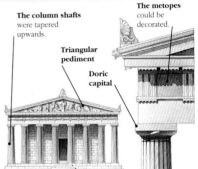

The column shafts were tapered upwards.

Triangular pediment

Doric capital

The metopes could be decorated.

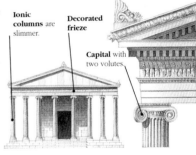

Ionic columns are slimmer.

Decorated frieze

Capital with two volutes.

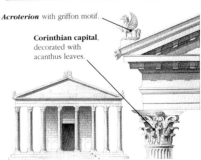

Acroterion with griffon motif.

Corinthian capital, decorated with acanthus leaves.

CLASSICAL ARCHITECTURE

MEDIEVAL CHURCHES

The drawings illustrate two of the greatest achievements of medieval architecture in Sicily. The Duomo of Monreale *(left)* is a masterpiece from the Norman period, with a splendid fusion of Byzantine, Arab and Norman figurative elements in the mosaics in the interior. A similar fusion of styles and cultures can be seen in the exterior architectural features. The Cathedral in Cefalù *(below)* also dates from the Norman period and, like Monreale, has beautiful mosaics. Its austere and stately quality is created by Romanesque elements such as the two lateral towers.

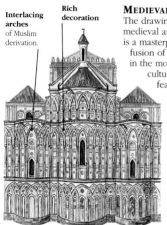

Interlacing arches of Muslim derivation.

Rich decoration

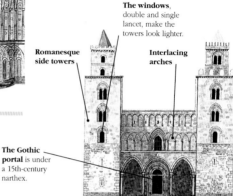

The windows, double and single lancet, make the towers look lighter.

Romanesque side towers

Interlacing arches

The Gothic portal is under a 15th-century narthex.

MEDIEVAL ARCHITECTURE

⑨ Erice *pp96 – 7*
⑩ Monreale *pp74 – 5*
⑪ Palermo *pp40 – 73*
⑫ Cefalù *pp84 – 7*
⑬ Catania *pp158 – 61*
⑭ Syracuse *pp132 – 9*

BAROQUE CHURCHES

After the 1693 earthquake the towns of eastern Sicily were almost totally rebuilt. Spanish-influenced Baroque was combined with Sicilian decorative and structural elements (convex church façades and impressive flights of steps), giving rise to an original, innovative style. Two great examples are shown here: the Cathedral in Syracuse *(left)* and the Basilica di San Giorgio in Ragusa *(below)*. The architect was GB Vaccarini (1702–1769), who also rebuilt Catania.

Curved decorative elements

The columns protrude from the façade.

Decorative elements include statues.

Jutting cornices define the sections of the façade, adding a rhythmic element.

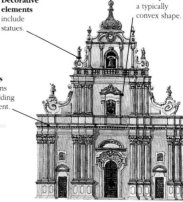

The façade has a typically convex shape.

BAROQUE ARCHITECTURE

⑮ Palermo *pp40 – 73*
⑯ Agrigento *pp110 – 11*
⑰ Caltanissetta *p122*
⑱ Caltagirone *pp150 – 51*
⑲ Ragusa *pp146 – 7*
⑳ Modica *p148*
㉑ Scicli *p145*
㉒ Noto *pp140 – 43*
㉓ Syracuse *pp132 – 9*
㉔ Catania *pp158 – 61*

Sicilian Literature and Art

**Luigi Pirandello, 1934
Nobel Prize winner**

IN THE HISTORY OF Sicilian art and
literature there have been periods
of tremendous creativity and others
when little of note was produced.
In the field of literature, the 13th-
century Sicilian school of lyric
poetry, 19th-century *verismo* or
realism and Luigi Pirandello's
novels and plays scale the heights
of Italian and European literary
production. In the field of art, Sicily
has produced such great artists as
Antonello da Messina, one of the
great figures in 15th-century rationalism and por-
traiture, and the modern painter Renato Guttuso.

WRITERS

**Metope from Temple E in
Selinunte: Artemis and Acteon**

ONLY FRAGMENTS remain of
Greek Sicilian literary
works. Unlike other artistic
fields such as architecture,
Siceliot (ancient Greek-
Sicilian) literature is indistin-
guishable from the local
production, as both were the
expression of the same
religious, cultural and civic
milieu. Apart from Pindar,
who dedicated lyric poems
to Syracuse and Agrigento,
the names of two Siceliot
poets have survived. Stesi-
chorus, who lived in Catania
in the 7th–6th century BC,
"achieved great fame in all
Hellas" according to Cicero,
leaving a few fragments
written in the Homeric style.
Theocritus, a Syracusan who
lived in the 4th–3rd centuries
BC, created the genre of
pastorals, short poems on
bucolic or mythological
subjects. Another important

figure in the Greek context
was the historian Diodorus
Siculus (1st century BC).

The first known figure in
medieval Sicilian literature is
the Arab poet 'Ibn Hamdis,
who was born in Syracuse in
1055 and was forced to leave
the island while still young.
He wrote moving verses
filled with nostalgia for the
land of his youth.

In the 13th century, the
first school of lyric poetry in
Italy developed at the court
of Emperor Frederick II and
his successor Manfred. It
later became known as the
Sicilian School. Among the
key figures were Jacopo da
Lentini, Pier della Vigna,
Stefano Pronotaro, Rinaldo
d'Aquino and Guido delle
Colonne. Their love poetry
took up the themes of
Provençal lyric poetry
but were written in
vernacular Italian
instead of Latin. Their
psychological penetra-
tion and the stylistic
and metric innova-
tions led to the
invention of the
sonnet. After
this period of
splendour,
Sicilian
literature
declined, as
did conditions
generally in
Sicily. This literary "drought"
lasted throughout the
Renaissance and Baroque
periods, and the only

author of note at this time is
Antonio Veneziano (born in
Monreale in 1543), a poet
who wrote in the local
dialect and left a collection
of love poems. The 18th
century was another fallow
period for literary production,
and it wasn't until the mid-
1800s that there was a rebirth
of Sicilian literature. The
writers Giovanni Verga and
Federico De
Roberto became
the mainspring
of the realistic
novel, *verismo*.
This style of
writing was an
extreme and,
to a certain
extent, more
refined version
of French
naturalism, as
embodied in the
work of Emile Zola.
Giovanni Verga was born in
Catania in 1840. After producing work in a late
Romantic vein, in the 1870s
he was drawn to French
naturalism by creating his so-
called "poetic of the defeated", in which he set out to
depict the hardship of
contemporary social reality.
He began with short stories
set in a rural context (the
first was *Nedda*, 1873),
which were followed by his
masterpieces, the novels *I
Malavoglia* (The House
by the Medlar Tree,
1881) and *Mastro
Don Gesualdo*
(1889), which
both depict the
immutable Sicilian
society of the
time. The former –
a truly innovative
work from a stylistic
and linguistic
standpoint – is
the story of a
family of fisher-
men at Aci
Trezza who,
after a short-
lived period
of relative well-
being, plunge into a life
of poverty and suffering.
Mastro Don Gesualdo
narrates the rise on the social

**Guidebook by
Federico De
Roberto**

**Giovanni Verga, author of
I Malavoglia (1881)**

scale and existential drama of a workman (*mastro*) who, thanks to his marriage, becomes a "Don". These two novels were part of Verga's planned *ciclo dei vinti* (cycle of the defeated), which was to have consisted of five novels; but the author left the project unfinished.

In the same vein as Verga were two other Sicilian writers, Luigi Capuana (1839–1915) and, more importantly, Federico De Roberto (1861–1927), who wrote *I Viceré* (The Viceroys, 1894), about a 19th-century aristocratic family in Catania.

The literature of Sicily continued to be at the forefront in the 20th century. The first half was dominated by Luigi Pirandello (1867–1936), who won the Nobel Prize for Literature in 1934. In his novels (such as *The Late Mattia Pascal*, 1904), nearly 300 short stories, plays *(see p23)* and essays he combines wit with a lucid and sometimes ruthless vision of reality.

One of Pirandello's earliest plays

Among the many noteworthy post-war Sicilian writers are the "hermetic" poet Salvatore Quasimodo (1901–68), author of the collection of poems *Ed è subito sera* (And Suddenly it's Evening, 1942). He won the Nobel Prize in 1959. Giuseppe Tomasi di Lampedusa (1896–1957), wrote *Il Gattopardo* (The Leopard, 1958; *see p118*), a vivid portrait of feudal Sicily, later made into a film, and Leonardo Sciascia (1921–89), wrote novels and essays painting a penetrating, lively portrait of post-war Sicily.

Leonardo Sciascia (1921–89)

Renato Guttuso, *Boogie-woogie* (1953 – 4)

ARTISTS

U NTIL THE RENAISSANCE, Sicilian art was basically decorative. During the Greek period probably the best painting was produced in the 7th century BC, when Siceliot vase painters stopped imitating the mainland models and adopted a fresh, eclectic style that combined and elaborated upon the original Greek red-figure ware motifs. The only known artist was Zeuxis, and this only through literature, not his works. The Roman period distinguished itself for some fine wall paintings, in which wax-derived colours were applied, fused into a layer and then fixed onto the wall with heat. The decorative arts in the Middle Ages in Sicily were dominated by mosaics. Among earlier fine works in this medium are the mosaics of the late Roman period at Piazza Armerina and those in the Cappella Palatina in Palermo and Cefalù Cathedral, which are a magnificent combination of Byzantine, Arab and Norman motifs and stylistic elements. Sicilian art reached a peak during the Renaissance, thanks to artists such as Giuffrè (15th century), Quartarano (1484–1501), the unknown author of *Trionfo della morte* (The

Triumph of Death), and, last but by no means least, to the genius of Antonello da Messina (1430–79), one of the greatest Renaissance portraitists and exponents of figurative rationalism, who was active throughout Italy.

Although Sicily was one of the favourite subjects of the great European landscape artists, from the 17th to the 19th century the island produced only one important painter, Pietro Novelli, known as "the man from Monreale" (1603– 47).

In the 20th century, the painter Renato Guttuso (1912–87) took up his artistic heritage in a realistic vein, becoming one of Italy's leading artists.

Antonello da Messina, *St Sebastian* (1476)

Cinema and Theatre in Sicily

ANYONE WHO WITNESSES the colour of Carnival in Sicily, or the bustle of the Vucciria market in Palermo, will appreciate that Sicily is a theatrical place in its own right. The reasons perhaps lie in the turbulent history of the place. One thing is certain: the island has been a source of inspiration for both theatre and cinema, providing subjects from peasant life to the decadent aristocracy and the Mafia, and producing world-famous playwrights, such as the late Luigi Pirandello, and award-winning films.

Burt Lancaster as the Prince of Salina in *Il Gattopardo* (1963)

SICILIAN CINEMA

THE FIRST Sicilian to forge a successful career in the seventh art was probably the playwright Nino Martoglio, who in 1914 directed *Sper-duti nel Buio* (Lost in the Dark), a film set in Naples, and edited with a highly original technique. Shortly afterwards, in 1919, Piran-dello also wrote two screen-plays, *Pantera di Neve* (Snow Panther) and *La Rosa* (The Rose), followed by *Acciaio* (Steel) in 1933. The great playwright and the directors of the films experienced difficulties, however, and the results were not entirely successful. After World War II Sicilian cinema and films set in Sicily reached a peak. In 1948 Luchino Visconti produced *La Terra Trema*, a loose adaptation of Giovanni Verga's *I Malavoglia (see p165)*. The Milanese director returned to the island in 1963 to film *Il Gattopardo* (The Leopard), based on the novel

of the same name by Tomasi di Lampedusa *(see p118)* and starring Burt Lancaster, Alain Delon and Claudia Cardinale. In the same period, the Palermitan director Vittorio De Seta, following some fascinating documentaries on Sicily, directed a feature film set in Sardinia, *Banditi a Orgosolo* (Bandits at Orgo-solo, 1961), and Neapolitan director Francesco Rosi made *Salvatore Giuliano* (1961), the story of the famous Sicilian bandit, acclaimed as "the greatest film on southern Italy". That same year Pietro Germi shot another famous film in Sicily: *Divorzio all'Italiana*, (Divorce – Italian Style), with Marcello Mastroianni and Stefania Sandrelli. Roman director Elio Petri made another important film about the island in the 1960s: *A Ciascuno il Suo* (To Each His Own, 1967), an adaptation of Leonardo Sciascia's novel of the same name *(see p21).* The 1970s and 1980s pro-duced a number of films about the Mafia, while Sicilian filmmaker Giuseppe Tornatore directed *Cinema Paradiso*, set in Palazzo Adriano *(see p117)*, which won an Academy Award as the best foreign film of 1990.

Neon sign of the *Nuovo Cinema Paradiso* in Giuseppe Tornatore's award-winning film

CINEMA AND THE MAFIA

Marlon Brando as Don Corleone in *The Godfather*

Since the end of World War II the Mafia has been a favourite subject for film. (However, there is a distinction between Italian-made and Holly-wood films.) The most distinguished Mafia films made in Italy are Fran-cesco Rosi's *Salvatore Giuliano, Il Giorno della Civetta* (Mafia), adapted from Leonardo Sciascia's novel *(see p21)* directed by Damiano Damiani, who also made *Confes-sione di un Commissario di Polizia al Procuratore della Repubblica* (1971), and Elio Petri's *A Cias-cuno il Suo* (To Each His Own, 1967). Last, the Mafia is also the subject of two films by Giuseppe Ferrara, *Il Sasso in Bocca* (1969) and more recently *Cento Giorni a Palermo* (A Hundred Days in Palermo, 1983), the tragic story of the Carabiniere general Dalla Chiesa, who was killed by the Mafia *(see p34).* Any number of Hollywood movies have been made about the Mafia, though they are almost always set in the US. The most famous is the Academy Award-winning film *The Godfather* (1972), direc-ted by Francis Ford Cop-pola and starring Marlon Brando and Al Pacino.

SICILIAN THEATRE

The original script of *Il Berretto a Sonagli* by Pirandello (1917)

Sicilian theatre is most closely identified with Luigi Pirandello (1867–1936), but there is also a rich tradition of theatre in Sicilian dialect. This theatre form dates from the Middle Ages, but its greatest interpreters were active in the late 19th century. Popular actors included Giuseppe Rizzotto (*I Mafiusi de la Vicaria*, The Mafiosi of the Vicariate, 1863) and Giovanni Grasso, and playwright Nino Martoglio, who in 1903 founded the Grande Compagnia Drammatica Siciliana. Luigi Pirandello also began his theatre career with comedies in dialect such as *Il Berretto a Sonagli* (1917), but he gained international renown in the 1920s with his plays written in Italian. In 1921 he wrote *Six Characters in Search of an Author* and, the following year, *Henry IV*. In these plays, probably his greatest, Pirandello deals with the themes that made him world-famous: the relationship between illusion and reality, existential hypocrisy and the need to find a profound identity.

Sicilian puppets, now sought after by antique dealers

THE OPERA DEI PUPI

Pupi are large Sicilian rod puppets. They date from the 1600s but became a huge success only in the late 1800s. The traditional "puppet opera" stories narrate the adventures of Charlemagne and his paladins, but there are also more modern topics revolving around Garibaldi and King Vittorio Emanuele. Famous puppeteers included Greco, who was based in Palermo, and the Grasso family from Catania, renowned craftsmen in their own right.

CLASSICAL THEATRE IN SICILY

Ancient theatre in Sicily can boast a great genius as its adoptive father, since Aeschylus (525–456 BC), who is regarded as the inventor of Greek tragedy, spent long periods in Sicily and died there. A number of his works were first produced in Syracuse *(see pp134–5).* Sicily was therefore well acquainted with, and assimilated, the subject matter of Greek theatre: freedom versus destiny, the sense of divine power and human suffering, the anguish of the tragedies and excoriating, bitter satire of the comedies. Classical theatre declined with the fall of the western Roman Empire, and it was not until

Sicilian playwright Nino Martoglio (1870–1921)

the 20th century that the great tragedies were again performed in Sicily. In 1913, Count Mario Tommaso Gargallo and his fellow Syracusans, including archaeologist Paolo Orsi *(see pp136–7)* decided to champion the production of Aeschylus' *Agamemnon*. The premiere was held on 16 April 1914 and since then, with the exception of wartime, the Greek Theatre in Syracuse, one of the most beautiful in the world, has remained a venue for ancient theatre – thanks to the efforts of the Istituto Nazionale del Dramma Antico (National Institute of Ancient Drama, *see p135).* Many famous theatre personalities have participated in these productions over the years, including poets Salvatore Quasimodo *(see p21)* and Pier Paolo Pasolini as translators, and the actors Giorgio Albertazzi and Vittorio Gassman.

Programme of the Istituto Nazionale del Dramma Antico, set up in 1925

THE HISTORY OF SICILY

Hercules killing a deer

THE MOST STRIKING aspect of Sicilian history is the enormous influence of all the different peoples who have colonized the island. Even the Sicani, Elymi and Siculi, the first populations to leave traces of their cultures in Sicily, came from other parts of the Mediterranean. They were followed by the Carthaginians and then by the Greeks, under whom Sicily saw its first real period of great splendour. Greek domination ended in 212 BC with the siege of Syracuse, in which the great inventor Archimedes was killed. For the next six centuries, the island became the bread basket of the Roman Empire and during this period acquired a social system that was to be its distinguishing characteristic for centuries. After the fall of the Roman Empire and the barbarian invasions, Sicily was ruled by the Byzantines.

The island was then conquered by the Arabs, under whom it became one of the most prosperous and tolerant lands in the Mediterranean. The next rulers were the Normans, who laid the foundations for the splendid court of Frederick II in Palermo. A long period of decadence coincided with the dwindling of the Middle Ages. The Angevins, Aragonese and Bourbons in turn took power in Sicily, but these dynasties exploited the island and treated it like a colony instead of improving life for the people there. Giuseppe Garibaldi's expedition in 1860 paved the way for the unification of Italy. Despite initial neglect by the central Italian government, Sicilians were finally given control of their own affairs. Yet many long-standing economic and social problems still need to be tackled and resolved, in particular, the continuing presence of the Mafia in Sicily.

Sicily in a 1692 print showing its three provinces: Val di Demona, Val di Noto, Val di Mazara

◁ Pietro Novelli, *St Benedict Offering the Book of the Order*, San Castrense Monreale (16th century)

The Conquerors of Sicily

BECAUSE OF ITS STRATEGIC position in the middle of the Mediterranean, Sicily has always been fought over by leading powers. Its history is therefore one of successive waves of foreign domination: Greek tyrants, Roman proconsuls and barbarian chieftains, then the Byzantines, Arabs and Normans, the Hohenstaufen monarchs, the Angevin and Aragonese dynasties, the Spanish viceroys and then the Bourbons, the last foreign rulers in Sicily before Italy was unified.

Justinian I, the Byzantine emperor, annexes Sicily in AD 535

5th century BC
Battles for supremacy in Sicily between the Greek and Punic colonies

Cleandros initiates the period of tyrannical rule in Gela

Hippocrates succeeds Cleandros and extends Gela's dominion

Agathocles, king of Syracuse (317–289 BC)

King Pyrrhus at Syracuse (280–275 BC)

Hieron II (265–215 BC)

Genseric, chief of the Vandals, conquers Sicily in AD 440

Verres becomes the Roman governor in 73–71 BC and is notorious for his corrupt rule

600 BC	400	200	AD 1	200	400	600
GREEKS		ROMANS			BARBARIANS AND B
600 BC	400	200	AD 1	200	400	600

Gelon conquers Syracuse in 490 BC

Theron tyrant in Agrigento in 488 BC

Ducetius, last king of the Siculi, dies in 440 BC

The Peloponnesian War (431–404 BC), brings an attack on Syracuse by the Athenian army, who are later defeated

Timoleon restores democracy in Syracuse in 339 BC

The Romans conquer Sicily definitively in 212 BC

Dionysius the Younger succeeds his father in 368 BC

Dionysius the Elder becomes tyrant of Syracuse in 405 BC and rules for 38 years

Odoacer and the Ostrogoths conquer Sicily in AD 491. He is succeeded by **Theodoric**

ARTISTS AND SCIENTISTS

In at least two significant periods, artists and scientists played a leading role in the long and eventful history of Sicily. The outstanding figure was Archimedes, born in Syracuse in 287 BC and on intimate terms with the ruler Hieron II. Thanks to the ingenious machines of war he invented, the city was able to resist Roman siege for three years (215–212 BC). Another great moment in Sicilian history came when the court of Frederick II in Palermo became known for its artists, poets and architects in the 1300s. Palermo became a leading centre for intellectuals.

Archimedes, the great Syracusan scientist

Diocletian divides the Roman Empire in AD 285. Sicily remains part of the Western Empire

Charles I of Anjou wrests the throne of Sicily from Manfred. He dies in 1285.

Charles II succeeds his father Charles I but in 1288 is forced to cede Sicily to **Peter III of Aragón**, who had occupied the island in 1282

Ferdinand II (1830–59) is the last Bourbon ruler in Sicily

Frederick II, emperor from 1216, is King of Sicily from 1197 to 1250, the year of his death. He moved his court to Palermo

James II of Aragón (1286–96)

The viceroys (above, Severino Filangieri) govern Sicily for the Spanish sovereigns until 1713

Tancred (1190–94)

Frederick II of Aragón (1296–1337)

William I (1154–66)

Peter II of Aragón (1337–41)

Ferdinand (1759–1825) unifies the kingdoms of Naples and Sicily in 1816

Roger I, the Norman lord, conquers Sicily in 1091 after a war lasting 30 years

Louis of Aragón (1341–55)

800	1000	1200	1400	1600	1800	
TINES	ARABS	NORMANS	ANGEVINS AND ARAGONESE		BOURBONS	SAVOY
800	1000	1200	1400	1600	1800	

Roger II (1105–1154)

Manfred, the natural son of Frederick II, rules Sicily until 1266

Duke John of Pegnafiel, son of Ferdinand of Castille, begins the viceroyalty period in 1412. This system of rule lasts for three centuries

Vittorio Amedeo II of Savoy acquires Sicily in 1713 through the Peace of Utrecht, ceding it to the **Hapsburgs of Austria** in 1718

Vittorio Emanuele II of Savoy becomes the first king of a unified Italy. Sicily forms a part of the new kingdom, having voted for annexation following Garibaldi's conquest of the island in 1860

Henry VI, emperor and son of Barbarossa, conquers Sicily in 1194. He dies in 1197

Frederick III of Aragón (1355–77), whose death triggers a period of struggle and strife that brings about the end of the Kingdom of Sicily

William II (1166–89)

The Arabs begin their invasion of Sicily in 827 and conquer the island in 902

Charles III of Spain acquires Sicily from Austria in 1735 and governs until 1759

Prehistoric and Ancient Sicily

Female bust (470 – 460 BC)

WHEN GREEK colonists arrived in Sicily in the 8th century BC, in the east they found the Siculi – a Mediterranean population that had been there since 2,000 BC – and the Phoenicians to the west. The former were soon assimilated, while the latter were ousted after the Battle of Himera (480 BC). This marked the beginning of Greek supremacy and the height of the Magna Graecia civilization, which ended in 212 BC with the Roman conquest of Syracuse. Roman Sicily saw the rise of large feudal estates and the imposition of taxes. Christianity began to spread in the 3rd–4th centuries AD.

GREEK COLONIZATION

MYTHS AND GODS

Magna Graecia adopted the religion of the mother country while adding local myths and legends. Mount Etna was seen as the home of Hephaestus, the god of fire, whom the Romans identified with Vulcan. Homer chose the island of Vulcano, in the Aeolians, as the workplace of this fiery god of blacksmiths. At Aci Trezza on the Ionian Sea, a group of stacks is known as "the islands of the Cyclops", since it was believed that they were the boulders Polyphemus hurled against Ulysses in the famous episode in Homer's *Odyssey.*

Zeus, the supreme Greek deity

VOYAGE TO SICILY

The ships the Greeks used for the dangerous trip to Sicily were called triremes. These galleys were about 35 m (115 ft) long, were faster and more agile than the Phoenician vessels and travelled about 100 km (62 miles) per day. They were manned by a crew of 200 and were equipped for transport and battle.

The double oar on the stern was used as a rudder.

Stern

Mother Goddess
This intense limestone statue, an archetype of femininity, dates from the middle of the 6th century BC and is in the Museo Archeologico of Syracuse (see pp136–7).

TIMELINE

1600 BC	1300 BC	1000 BC	800 BC	600 BC	4

1500 BC Contacts between Aeolian and Cretan and Minoan cultures

1000–850 BC Second period of Siculan civilization

730–650 BC Fourth period of Siculan civilization

733 BC Dorians from Corinth found Syracuse

628 BC Selinunte founded

413 BC Athenian invasion led by Nicias and Alcibiades a total failure

1270–1000 BC First period of Siculan civilization

850–730 BC Third period of Siculan civilization

8th century BC Greeks colonize east, Phoenicians west. *Panormos* (Palermo) founded

729 BC *Katane* (Catania) founded

480 BC Battle of Himera: Greeks defeat Carthaginians

The goddess Athena

The Roman Villas

Roman dominion in Sicily brought about the spread of latifundia (large feudal estates) and landowners' villas such as the Villa del Casale (see pp126–7), whose mosaics were preserved thanks to a flood that buried them for centuries.

A trireme drew only about 60 cm (24 in).

The spur was used to destroy the oars on enemy vessels.

The third rank of oars (hence "trireme" or three oars), was on an external deck jutting out from the hull. Everything was carefully calculated so that the 170 oar movements were synchronized.

Prehistoric village

Remains of settlements dating from the beginning of the first millennium BC lie all over Sicily. However, the first populations who left traces in Sicily (Sicani, Elymi and Siculi) were not native people.

Aeschylus, the great Greek tragedian who was also active in Syracuse

AD 293 The emperor Diocletian makes Sicily *regio suburbicaria*, or directly dependent on Rome

AD 325 Christianization of the Syracuse area

AD 535 Sicily becomes part of Justinian's Eastern Roman Empire

200	AD 1	AD 200	400	600

212 BC Syracuse conquered by Romans. Sicily loses its autonomy

Female clay bust

AD 440 During the barbarian invasions of Italy the Vandals led by Genseric conquer Sicily

AD 600 Christianization of all of Sicily

AD 491 The Ostrogoths under Odoacer take Sicily from the Vandals

Medieval Sicily

Coin with imperial coat of arms

T HE FREQUENT ARAB raids became in 827 a real campaign to conquer Sicily, which ended successfully in 902. Arab dominion coincided with the rebirth of the island after the decadence of the final years of Byzantine rule. In 1061 the Christian crusade began, the Normans conquering Sicily 30 years later. The Kingdom of Sicily was established in 1130 and reached its zenith with the splendour of Frederick II's court. In 1266 the Angevin dynasty took power, followed by the Aragonese, initiating a long period of decline in which powerful feudal landowners ruled the island.

THE ARAB REGIONS OF SICILY

☐ *Val Demone*

☐ *Val di Noto*

☐ *Val di Mazara*

Tancred

The natural son of Roger II, Tancred was appointed king of Sicily by the feudal barons in 1190. He was the last Norman to rule Sicily. When he died, the emperor Henry VI, son of Barbarossa and father of Federico II, ascended the throne.

Sicily under Arab rule
During the century of Arab dominion Sicily was the richest and most tolerant land in the Mediterranean. The governing administration was reorganized and the arts and culture flourished to an exceptional degree, as can be seen in this decorated coffer.

The poor and ill are spared.

The dog leads the man in the night of death.

TIMELINE

725 Worship of sacred images is prohibited. The possessions of the Sicilian church confiscated by the patriarchate in Constantinople

831 Palermo becomes capital of the Arab emirate

902 Taormina surrenders, Arab conquest completed

1091 After 30 years of warfare, Sicily is once again Christian land thanks to the Norman Roger

700	800	900	1000

The Virgin of Odigitria, Lentini

827 Arab conquest of Sicily begins

1038–1043 Eastern Sicily is temporarily reconquered by Byzantium

Coin with Arab inscriptions

MEDIEVAL CASTLES

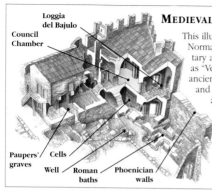

Loggia
del Bajulo
Council
Chamber

Paupers'/ Cells
graves
Well   Roman   Phoenician
baths   walls

This illustration shows the 12th–13th-century Norman castle at Erice, an example of the military architecture of the time. It is also known as "Venus' Castle" because it was built near an ancient temple and incorporated Phoenician and Roman architectural elements. There are many other medieval fortifications in Sicily. The main ones are those at Sperlinga (see p89), Caccamo (see pp90–91), Mussomeli and Naro (see p117), Montechiaro and Falconara (see pp118–9), Enna (see p123), Syracuse (see p139), Catania (see p161), Aci Castello (p164) and Milazzo (see p183).

Death
strikes with bow and arrows, like a horseman of the Apocalypse.

A lady
maintains her proud attitude.

Representation of the World

After the conquest of Sicily, the Normans and Hohenstaufens assimilated the culture of the Arabs, as can be seen in this representation of the world, executed in the Norman period by an Arab artist.

THE TRIUMPH OF DEATH

This mid 15th-century fresco, painted and kept in Palermo (see pp50–51), drew inspiration from the Apocalypse: Death is a horseman armed with bows and arrows who kills the rich and spares the poor. These symbolic "triumphs" were common in medieval iconography.

The rich and powerful are killed with arrows.

WHERE TO SEE MEDIEVAL SICILY

Besides the castles (see above), don't miss the Cappella Palatina in Palermo (see pp60–61), Monreale Cathedral (see pp74–5), and the towns of Cefalù (see pp84–7) and Erice (see pp96–7), including their cathedrals. Despite some rebuilding, the many villages that have preserved their Arab town planning layout are also interesting sites.

1194 Henry VI conquers Sicily and makes it part of his empire

The tiara of Constance of Aragón, Frederick II's wife

1282 The Sicilian Vespers revolt overthrows the Angevin rulers and Peter of Aragón becomes the new king

1415 Ferdinand of Castile sends his first viceroy, Giovanni di Pegnafiel, to Sicily

1100	1200	1300	1400

1130 Roger II is crowned King of Sicily. Palermo is the capital

1250 The death of the emperor Frederick II marks the end of Sicily's most glorious period

1302 The Peace of Caltabellotta sanctions the independence of the Kingdom of Sicily

1265 Charles of Anjou crowned King of Sicily by the Pope

1377 Under Maria of Aragón war breaks out among the feudal landowners, which leads to the union of the Kingdom of Sicily and the Kingdom of Aragón

From Spanish Rule to Unified Italy

Painter Pietro Novelli (1603–47)

IN 1415 SICILY became an Aragonese province ruled by a viceroy. The island's economic and cultural decadence continued, partly because the Jews were driven away. A series of revolts was subdued with the help of the Pope's Holy Office. There was a slight recovery after the devastating earthquake of 1693, which destroyed eastern Sicily. After brief periods of Savoyard and Austrian dominion, in 1735 Sicily passed to the Bourbons, in constant battles with the land barons. In 1814 the island became a province of the Kingdom of Naples; popular unrest led to Garibaldi's 1860 expedition and union with the burgeoning Kingdom of Italy. The late 1800s were marked by banditry and poverty in the rural areas.

THE STATES OF ITALY

- ☐ *Kingdom of Two Sicilies*
- ☐ *Papal States*
- ☐ *Grand Duchy of Tuscany*
- ☐ *Hapsburg Empire*
- ☐ *Kingdom of Sardinia*
- ☐ *Duchy of Modena*
- ☐ *Duchy of Parma-Piacenza*

The 1693 Earthquake
On the night of 9 January 1693, Mount Etna burst into life. Two days later, "the Earth was rent from its bowels", as the historian Di Blasi said. The earthquake, seen above in a print of the time, levelled 23 towns, including Catania, Noto and Lentini.

Nino Bixio was immortalized in Giovanni Verga's short story *Libertà (see p170)*

Many volunteers joined Garibaldi's 1,000 Red Shirts

Giuseppe Garibaldi, a socialist, set off for Sicily despite Cavour's initial opposition

TIMELINE

1415 First year of the Viceroyalty, which ends in 1712

1458 Alfonso V dies and Sicily is again ruled by Spain

1571 The harbour in Messina houses the Christian fleet that later wins the Battle of Lepanto against the Ottomans

1649 Palermo revo

| 1450 | 1500 | 1550 | 1600 |

1442 Alfonso V unites the crowns of Sicily and Naples, thus founding the Kingdom of Two Sicilies

1535 Emperor Charles V visits Sicily

The Battle of Lepanto

The Revolt of Messina
This print depicts the 1848 insurrection at Messina. The city was bombarded by Ferdinand, afterwards known as "re Bomba", or "king Bomb".

The Sulphur Mines
After the unification of Italy, sulphur mining began in the Sicilian interior. Children were employed for their small size and agility.

The Baroque Period
This stucco work (c. 1690) in Palermo (see pp54–5) by Giacomo Serpotta represents The Battle of Lepanto *and is a marvellous example of the style that became known as "Sicilian Baroque".*

GARIBALDI INVADES SICILY

On 11 May 1860, a thousand volunteers led by Giuseppe Garibaldi (1807–1882) landed in Marsala to conquer the Kingdom of the Two Sicilies. They succeeded in this incredible feat, taking Palermo, then Messina and lastly Naples by storm.

Composers and authors
In the 19th century, cultural life flourished in Sicily. The leading figures at this time were writer Giovanni Verga (1840–1922) and composer Vincenzo Bellini (1801–35), seen in this portrait.

The Sicilian Parliament

1674 Revolt in Messina

1759 Sicily taken over by the Kingdom of Naples

1812 The Sicilian Parliament sanctions an English-type constitution

1860 Garibaldi's Red Shirts invade island in May. In October the people vote to merge with Kingdom of Italy

50	1700	1750	1800	1850

1693 A disastrous earthquake destroys most of eastern Sicily

1735 The Spanish Bourbons become new rulers of Sicily

1713 With the Peace of Utrecht, Sicily is ceded first to Vittorio Amedeo II of Savoy and then (1720) to the Hapsburgs

1820 First uprisings

1848 The entire island hit by revolts, especially Messina

Giovanni Verga

Sicily in the 20th Century

THE NEW CENTURY began with the catastrophic 1908 quake in Messina. For the most part excluded from the process of modernization, Sicily was a living contradiction: its splendid cultural life as opposed to poverty, backwardness and the spread of the Mafia which, despite all attempts to curb its activities, had become a veritable state within a state. However, thanks to the perseverance and courage of public servants and growing public awareness of the problem, the Mafia seems to be less powerful than before.

1943 After heavy bombardments, the Allies land in Sicily on 10 July and take it in 38 days

1941 Syracusan novelist Elio Vittorini publishes *Conversation in Sicily*

1937 Popular Catanian actor Angelo Musco dies

1908 The night of 28 December marks the greatest disaster in 20th-century Sicily: a quake totally destroys Messina and kills 100,000 persons

1920 The farmers rebel against the landowners. At Ribera the Duke of di Bovina is kidnapped

1936 Luigi Pirandello dies in Rome

1901 Many people wounded during clashes between police and workmen

1900	1910	1920	1930	1940

1900	1910	1920	1930	1940

1902 Heavy autumn rainfall triggers a tragic flood in southern Sicily, especially in Modica, in which 300 people lose their lives

1923 Mount Etna eruption in June destroys towns of Catena and Cerro, barely missing Linguaglossa and Castiglione. The king and Mussolini inspect the damage

1945 The founder of the the Sicilian Separatist Movement, Finocchiaro, is arrested

1934 Pirandello wins Nobel Prize for Literature

1947 Salvatore Giuliano's bandits shoot demonstrators: 11 dead, 56 wounded

1922 Giovanni Verga dies in Catania

1930 Mussolini sends prefect Cesare Mori to try to suppress the Mafia

1919 Don Luigi Sturzo, from Caltagirone, founds the Partito Popolare and becomes its leader. After World War II the party is renamed Democrazia Cristiana

1921 At Rome, Luigi Pirandello directs the première of his famous play *Six Characters in Search of an Author*

1901 Famous statesman from Agrigento, Francesco Crispi, dies

1987 In a trial in Palermo hundreds of Mafiosi are condemned to a total of 2,600 years in prison. The verdict is based on the confessions of Tommaso Buscetta

1950 The bandit Giuliano is betrayed by his cousin Gaspare Pisciotta and killed

1982 Communist deputy Pio La Torre is killed by the Mafia

1983 Thanks to a sophisticated system of controlled explosions, a lava flow from Mount Etna is deviated for the first time

1966 A landslide at Agrigento, perhaps caused by illegal building construction, leaves 10,000 people homeless

1979 Tragic eruption of Mount Etna kills ten tourists

1957 Rebellion in Ucciardone prison in Palermo

1984 The former mayor of Palermo, Vito Ciancimino, is arrested

1995 After years in hiding, top Mafia boss Totò Riina is arrested

1968 A huge quake in northwestern Sicily claims over 400 victims

50	1960	1970	1980	1990

50	1960	1970	1980	1990

1958 Giuseppe Tomasi di Lampedusa's novel *Il Gattopardo*, published posthumously, is a great success

1959 Poet Salvatore Quasimodo, born in Modica, wins Nobel Prize for Literature, the second Sicilian to do so in less than twenty years' time

1972 In May a plane crashes near Punta Raisi, the Palermo airport, and 115 persons are killed. In December, Mafia boss Tommaso Buscetta is arrested; he is the first Mafioso to cooperate with Italian justice

July 1992 Paolo Borsellino, the magistrate who worked with Falcone, is assassinated in Palermo

1968 Clashes between farm labourers and police at Avola cause 2 deaths

1982 Carabiniere general Carlo Alberto Dalla Chiesa, new prefect of Palermo, is assassinated

1980 A DC9 crashes near Ustica, with 81 victims. The cause of the accident has never been explained

May 1992 Judge Giovanni Falcone, for years a huge thorn in the side of the Mafia, is killed in an ambush near Capaci

1971 Another eruption of Mount Etna. In Palermo, the Mafia kills Public Prosecutor Pietro Scaglione

SICILY THROUGH THE YEAR

SICILIANS SAY that Sicily has the most beautiful sky in the world, and certainly the island enjoys more than 2,000 hours of sunshine per year, more than any other part of Europe. The climate is generally mild, but it can get hot in high summer. In 1885 the temperature rose to 49.6° C

The Trinacria, ancient symbol of Sicily

(121.3° F), the highest ever recorded in Italy. However, winters can be cold and snowy, especially inland, and Mount Etna remains snow-capped into the spring. A land of ancient customs and deep-rooted beliefs, Sicily has preserved most of its traditional celebrations, almost all of them religious in nature.

SPRING

SPRING GENERALLY begins early in Sicily, although the weather can be quite unpredictable and patterns vary from year to year. In areas with orchards the air is filled with the scent of spring blossoms, and early flowers make this a particularly lovely time for visiting ancient sites. This is also the season with the greatest number of feast-days, processions and festivals *(sagre)*. Almost all these events are linked with the celebration of Easter.

Festa della Crocifissione (Feast of the Crucifix) procession, Calatafimi

The Sfilata dei Misteri, which takes place on Good Friday in Trapani

MARCH

Sagra del Carciofo (artichokes), Cerda, Palermo.
Sagra della Ricotta, Sicilian cheese, celebrated at Mussomeli near Caltanissetta.

APRIL

Sagra della Ricotta e del Formaggio (cheeses), Vizzini.

EASTER WEEK

Celebrazione dei Misteri *(all week)*, Enna. The Stations of the Cross celebrations and processions all week long.
Festa del Pane (bread) *(all week)*, San Biagio dei Platani and Agrigento. Bread sculpture and decoration.
Giorni della Pena *(Wed, Thu, Fri)*, Caltanissetta. "Days of suffering and grief", with impressive processions.
Maundy Thursday Procession, Marsala. A kilometre of masked figures.
Festa della Crocifissione *(Fri)*, Calatafimi, Trapani.
Il Cristo Morto *(Fri)*, Partanna, Trapani. The Crucifixion is re-enacted.
Processione dei Misteri *(Fri)*, Trapani. Groups of statues and hooded men commemorate Christ's sacrifice in the Procession of Mysteries, which lasts for 20 hours.
Ballo dei Diavoli *(Sun)*, Prizzi, Palermo. Masked men perform the "devils' dance", which symbolizes the struggle between good and evil.

MAY

International Windsurfing Championship, Mondello and Palermo.
Classic Theatre, alternate years at Syracuse and Segesta.
Settimana delle Egadi, island of Favignana. The traditional *mattanza* tuna fishing method is celebrated.
L'Infiorata, Noto. The streets are filled with images and words created with flowers.

Christ's crucifixion re-enacted at Partanna, Trapani

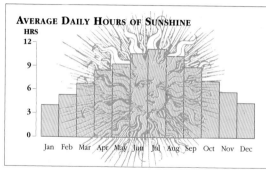

AVERAGE DAILY HOURS OF SUNSHINE

HRS

12
9
6
3
0

Jan Feb Mar Apr May Jun Jul Aug Sep Oct Nov Dec

Sunshine
Sicily has the highest average hours of sunshine in the whole of Europe. As the chart shows, the sunniest time is from May to September. In the autumn and winter months it may be cold and rainy.

The Pepper Festival at Sutera

SUMMER

SPORTS, summer vacations, many important musical events, folk celebrations and food festivals characterize the long summer in Sicily.

The weather does, however, get extremely hot in certain places on the island, particularly inland but occasionally even in coastal areas.

JUNE

Fiera Campionaria *(first two weeks)*, Palermo. A samples fair for the Mediterranean countries, with exhibitions and meetings.
International Tennis Tournament, Palermo.
Sagra della Ricotta (cheese), Prizzi, Palermo.
Rappresentazioni Pirandelliane *(Jun–Aug)*, Agrigento. Luigi Pirandello's home town is the venue for theatre events.
Efebo d'Oro International Prize, Agrigento. A prize is awarded to the best film adaptation of a novel.
Sagra delle Fragole e dei Frutti di Bosco (fruits), Maletto sull'Etna, Catania.
Taormina Arte *(Jun–Aug)*. Cultural events at the Greek Theatre, with leading figures from the entertainment world.

JULY

Festa di Santa Rosalia *(9–14 Jul)*, Palermo. Six days of festivities in honour of the city's patron saint, who, according to legend, saved Palermo from the terrible plague of 1624.
Sagra del Peperone (peppers), Sutera, Caltanissetta.
International Medieval and Renaissance Music Week *(Jul–Aug)*, Erice. A celebration of ancient music.
Festa di San Giuseppe *(last week)*. Terrasini, Palermo. St Joseph is honoured with a procession of fishing boats bearing the saint's statue. Fried fish for everybody in the main square.
Festa di San Giacomo *(24 and 25 July)*, Caltagirone. The town's long ceramic stairway is decorated with lighted candles representing assorted figures and scenes.
International Cinema, Music, Theatre and Dance Festival *(Jul–Aug)*, Taormina. An important international festival that forms part of the Taormina Arte series of events.

AUGUST

Festa della Spiga *(1–10 Aug)*, Gangi, Palermo. An entire week of games, parades and spectacles.
Festa della Castellana *(first Sun)*, Caccamo. An all-women feast that re-enacts the period when the lords – and grand ladies – of the castle ran the town.
Palio dei Normanni *(13–14 Aug)*, Piazza Armerina. Historical re-enactment in period costume of various tests of courage on horseback, in honour of the great Norman king, Roger I.
Processione della Vara and Cavalcata dei Giganti *(15 Aug)*, Messina. Gigantic statues of the founders of Messina, Mata and Grifone, are paraded through the streets, followed by a float bearing a huge, elaborate triumphal cart and tableau called the "Vara".
Sagra del Pomodoro "Seccagno" (tomatoes), Villalba, Caltanissetta. Celebration of one of the island's most commonly and successfully grown products.

The statues of Mata and Grifone at Messina

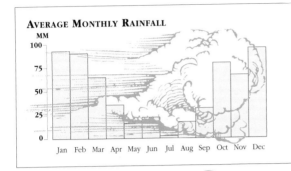

AVERAGE MONTHLY RAINFALL

Rainfall
As the chart shows, in the six months from April to September there is very little rain. In autumn, by contrast, violent storms are common throughout the island, raising the average rainfall.

AUTUMN

THIS SEASON begins late in Sicily, as September and often October continue sunny and warm. In autumn you can see many of the characteristic festivals celebrating local produce, such as grapes, and the theatre, classical music, opera and the football (soccer) season all resume their annual cycle.

SEPTEMBER

Sagra del Miele (honey; *Sep–Oct*), Sortino, Syracuse.
Sagra del Pane (bread), Monterosso Almo, Ragusa.
Sagra della Salsiccia (sausages), Milena, Caltanissetta.
Sagra della Mostarda Regalbuto, Enna.
Sagra dell'Uva (grapes), Vallelunga, Caltanissetta; Roccazzo and Chiaramonte Gulfi, Ragusa.
Coppa degli Assi, Palermo. Grand Prix of horsemanship at the Parco della Favorita.
Festa della Madonna della Luce (*8–11 Sep*), Mistretta, Messina. The symbolic dance

Statue for the Festa di San Vincenzo, at Aragona

of two armed giants and (on the third day) the Madonna della Luce procession.
Festa di San Vincenzo Aragona, Agrigento. Masked revellers go in procession through the town.
Bellini Festival, Catania. Organized by the city opera company.
Vini dell'Etna, Milo sull'Etna, Catania. Exhibition and sale of the wines made from grapes grown on the slopes of Mount Etna.

OCTOBER

Sagra del Pesco (peaches), Leonforte, Enna.
Extempora, Palermo. An important and fascinating antiques fair.
Festival sul Novecento, Palermo. First held in 1997, the 20th Century Festival attracts media people, leading artists, writers and film directors.
Ottobrata, Zafferana Etnea, Catania. Every Sunday in October, in this village close to Mount Etna, the main square is filled with stalls selling produce and articles made by local craftsmen.

NOVEMBER

Medilibro (*mid-Nov*), Palermo. Mediterranean book fair with the participation of all the leading publishers in the area.
Religious Music Week, Monreale. Another great musical event, after the one held at Erice (July), which takes place in Monreale's splendid medieval abbey.

PUBLIC HOLIDAYS IN SICILY

New Year's Day (1 Jan)
Epiphany (6 Jan)
Easter Sunday and Monday
Liberation Day (25 Apr)
Labour Day (1 May)
Ferragosto (15 Aug)
All Saints' Day (1 Nov)
Immaculate Conception (8 Dec)
Christmas (25 Dec)
Santo Stefano (26 Dec)

Ballet performances, staged at the theatres in Catania and Palermo

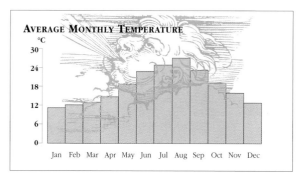

AVERAGE MONTHLY TEMPERATURE
°C

Temperature
From May to September the average temperature is rarely below 20° C (68° F), and, except for very unusual weather, it is seldom below 10° C (50° F) any other month. July and August may see peaks of more than 40° C (104° F).

WINTER

WINTER IN SICILY is usually cool and often rainy, and may not be the ideal season to visit the interior and the larger towns. In February you might see one of the many Carnival festivities held throughout the island, which are famous for their originality and the enthusiastic participation of the local people.

DECEMBER

Handicrafts Fair, Palermo. In Piazza Politeama, an exhibition of handicrafts from all over the island.
Rassegna di Studi Pirandelliani, Agrigento. This workshop is important for all Pirandello scholars.

The Madonna del Soccorso, celebrated at Sciacca in February

It includes lectures and productions of his plays.
Festa di Santa Lucia *(13 Dec)*, Syracuse. On the saint's feast day, her statue is taken out in a public procession and is then placed on public exhibition for eight days for people to worship.
Natale a Taormina *(Dec–Jan)*. Christmas fair with street theatre and gospel music.

JANUARY

Festival di Morgana *(Jan–Feb)*, Palermo. An international marionette workshop of the Opera dei Pupi, held at the Museo Internazionale delle Marionette, with plays and exhibits.
Festa di San Sebastiano Acireale, Catania. On 20 Jan

The Festa del Mandorlo in Fiore, Valle dei Templi at Agrigento

the saint's statue is taken from his church on an elaborately decorated wooden float and borne in a procession in front of a huge crowd.

FEBRUARY

Festa della Madonna del Soccorso, Sciacca.
Festa del Mandorlo in Fiore (Festival of the Almond Tree in Bloom), Agrigento. The arrival of spring is celebrated in the Valley of Temples. At the same time there is the **Folklore Festival**, which for more than 50 years has featured folk music and dance from all over the world.
Festa di Sant'Agata *(3–5 Feb)*, Catania. The city is filled with "strangers" who invoke the saint's protection, while Catanians, dressed only in "sackcloth", bear her statue in an impressive procession.
Carnival, Acireale. Allegorical floats, a colourful atmosphere and huge crowds.
Carnival, Sciacca. Together with Acireale, the most famous carnival in Sicily.
Sagra della Salsiccia, del Dolce e della Trota (sausage, pastries and trout), Palazzolo Acreide, Syracuse.

The carnival at Acireale, considered one of the most colourful in Sicily

PALERMO
AREA BY AREA

Palermo at a Glance

T HE CAPITAL of Sicily is built along the bay at
the foot of Monte Pellegrino. Palermo owes
its name to the sea: it was originally called
Panormos, or "port", in Phoenician times. The
town prospered under the Romans, but its
golden age was under Arab domination, when
it rivalled Cordoba and Cairo in beauty. Later,
Palermo became the capital of the Norman
kingdom. Today very little remains of the
fabulous city of bygone times, but the Middle
Eastern influence can still be seen in the architecture of the churches, the many alleys in the
old town and the markets. The other age of
splendour, which left a lasting mark on the
city's civic and religious buildings, was the
Baroque period (17th–18th centuries). Palermo
suffered badly in the massive bombardments
of 1943 and was then rebuilt chaotically, the
result of political corruption and the Mafia.
Recently things have taken a turn for the better.

*The Oratorio del Rosario di
Santa Cita (or Santa Zita), with
its stuccoes by Giacomo Serpotta,
is a splendid example of Baroque
ornamentation (see pp54–5).*

*The Palazzo dei Normanni, of Arab
origin, has superb mosaic and fresco
decoration. It became the royal palace
under the Normans (see p62).*

SOUTH PALERMO
(see pp56–67)

*The Cappella Palatina,
a masterpiece of Norman
art, is covered with
Byzantine-influenced
mosaics
representing
scenes from
the Bible (see
pp60–61).*

| 0 metres | 350 |
| 0 yards | 350 |

◁ **The cloister of San Giovanni degli Eremiti** *(pp62–3)*

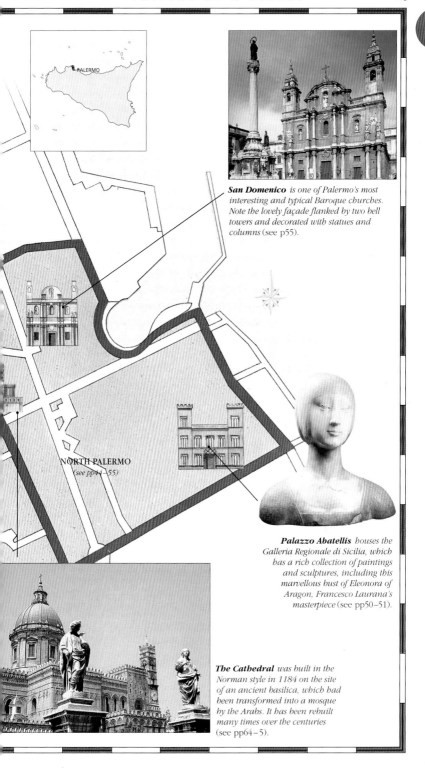

San Domenico is one of Palermo's most interesting and typical Baroque churches. Note the lovely façade flanked by two bell towers and decorated with statues and columns (see p55).

NORTH PALERMO
(see pp44–55)

Palazzo Abatellis houses the Galleria Regionale di Sicilia, which has a rich collection of paintings and sculptures, including this marvellous bust of Eleonora of Aragon, Francesco Laurana's masterpiece (see pp50–51).

The Cathedral was built in the Norman style in 1184 on the site of an ancient basilica, which had been transformed into a mosque by the Arabs. It has been rebuilt many times over the centuries (see pp64–5).

NORTH PALERMO

BETWEEN VIA MAQUEDA and the sea lie the old Arab quarters of Palermo, with their maze of narrow streets and blind alleys. This area includes the Kalsa quarter (from the Arabic *al-Halisah,* or the Chosen), which was built by the Arabs in the first half of the 10th century as the seat of the Emirate, the government and the army. During the Norman era it became the sailors' and fishermen's quarter. It was badly damaged in World War II, and many parts are still being restored. Most of the Aragonese

Statue of the Fontana Pretoria

monuments, dating from the late Middle Ages and the Renaissance, are in the Kalsa. The focal point is Piazza Marina, for a long time the heart of city life and seat of the Aragonese court and the Inquisition courtroom. Via Maqueda opens onto Piazza Pretoria, the civic heart of Palermo, with Palazzo delle Aquile, Santa Caterina and San Giuseppe dei Teatini. West of Corso Vittorio Emanuele is Castellammare, with the Vucciria market and the Loggia quarter near the port, where Catalan, Pisan and Genoese communities once lived.

SIGHTS AT A GLANCE

Museums and Galleries
Museo Archeologico
  Regionale ⑭
Museo Internazionale
  delle Marionette ④
Palazzo Abatellis pp50–51 ②

Historic Buildings
Palazzo delle Aquile ⑧
Palazzo Mirto ⑤

Streets and Squares
Piazza Marina ①

Churches
La Gancia ③
La Magione ⑫
La Martorana ⑩
Oratorio del Rosario
  di San Domenico ⑱
Oratorio del Rosario
  di Santa Cita ⑯
San Cataldo ⑪
San Domenico ⑰
San Francesco d'Assisi ⑥

Santa Caterina ⑨
Santa Maria dello Spasimo ⑬

Markets
Mercato della Vucciria ⑮

Monuments
Fontana Pretoria ⑦

KEY

Street-by-Street map
See pp46–7

Main bus stop

Taxi rank (stand)

Public telephone

Post Office

Tourist information

Parking

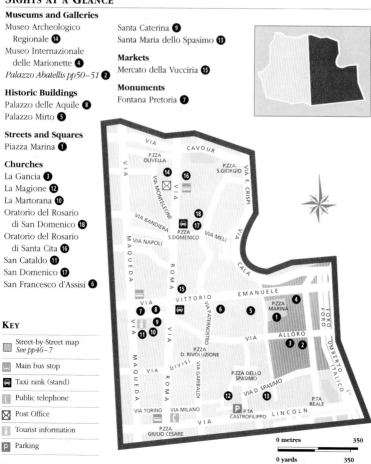

◁ **Christ Pantocrator in the mosaic decoration on the cupola of La Martorana (12th century)**

Street-by-Street: around Piazza Marina

Poster for the Museo delle Marionette

THE MAIN SQUARE in Old Palermo lies at the edge of the Kalsa quarter. From the Middle Ages onwards it was used for knights' tournaments, theatre performances, markets and public executions. On the occasion of royal weddings, such as the marriage of Charles II and Marie Louise in 1679, impressive shows were put on in specially built wooden theatres. The square's irregular four sides are flanked by such monuments as Palazzo Steri-Chiaramonte, Palazzo del Castillo, Palazzo della Zecca, San Giovanni dei Napoletani, Palazzo della Gran Guardia, Santa Maria della Catena, Palazzo Galletti and Palazzo Villafiorita. In the middle is the Giardino Garibaldi, shaded by enormous fig trees.

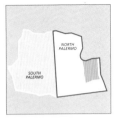

LOCATOR MAP

Santa Maria della Catena (early 16th century) owes its name to the chain (*catena*) across the mouth of the city harbour. A broad stairway leads to the beautiful three-arched porch of this Catalan Gothic church.

0 metres   60

0 yards   60

CORSO VITTORIO EMANUELE

PIAZZA MARINA

Santa Maria dei Miracoli

Piazza Marina

This is one of the largest squares in Palermo. Once part of the harbour, but long since silted up and reclaimed, its central garden is home to massive ficus magnolioides *trees, with strange, exposed roots* ❶

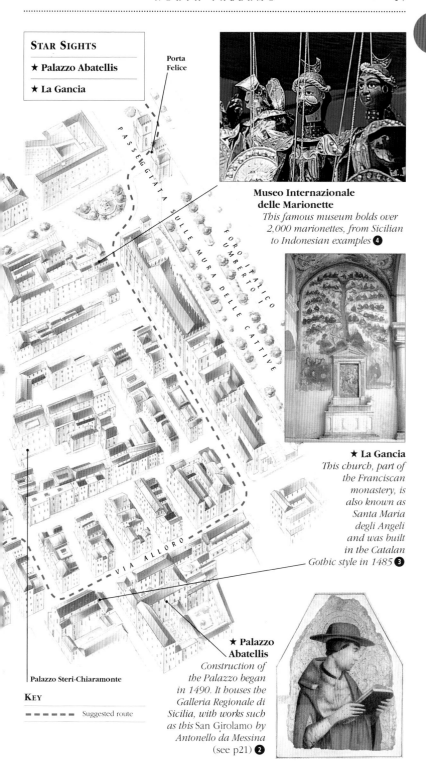

STAR SIGHTS

★ **Palazzo Abatellis**

★ **La Gancia**

Porta
Felice

PASSEGGIATA SULLE MURA DELLE CATTIVE

FORO ITALICO UMBERTO I

**Museo Internazionale
delle Marionette**
*This famous museum holds over
2,000 marionettes, from Sicilian
to Indonesian examples* ④

★ **La Gancia**
*This church, part of
the Franciscan
monastery, is
also known as
Santa Maria
degli Angeli
and was built
in the Catalan
Gothic style in 1485* ③

VIA ALLORO

Palazzo Steri-Chiaramonte

KEY

━ ━ ━ ━ Suggested route

★ **Palazzo
Abatellis**
*Construction of
the Palazzo began
in 1490. It houses the
Galleria Regionale di
Sicilia, with works such
as this* San Girolamo *by
Antonello da Messina*
(see p21) ②

The Giardino Garibaldi, in the middle of Piazza Marina

Piazza Marina ❶

THIS square is one of the largest in Palermo. It lies on what was once the southern side of the natural harbour. In the middle of the square is the **Giardino Garibaldi**, designed in 1863 by GB Basile and planted with *Ficus magnolioides*, a species of fig tree, which are now enormous. The garden is surrounded by a cast-iron fence decorated with bows and arrows, rabbits and birds. Inside are a fountain and busts of Risorgimento figures, including Benedetto De Lisi's monument to the Italian leader Garibaldi.

The most important building in Piazza Marina is **Palazzo Steri-Chiaramonte**, built in 1307 by Manfredo Chiaramonte, a member of one of Sicily's most powerful families. In the Middle Ages the family controlled most of the island. The name "Steri" comes from *Hosterium*, or fortified building, as most patrician mansions were just that during the turbulent period of Norman and Hohenstaufen rule. Built in the Gothic style with Arab and Norman influences, the palazzo has an austere façade. The portal is decorated with a double arched lintel of ashlars and a series of double and triple Gothic lancet windows with multi-coloured inlay. When the new Aragonese rulers arrived in 1392, Andrea Chiaramonte was beheaded right in front of Palazzo Steri. It later became the palace of the Aragonese kings and then of the viceroys. In the 17th century it housed the Inquisition courtroom, or Holy Office, and later the city court of law. Across the square is the Renaissance **Santa Maria dei Miracoli** (1547). On the corner of Via Vittorio Emanuele is the Baroque **Fontana del Garraffo** designed by Paolo Amato, a fountain with three shell-shaped basins supported by dolphins' heads. At the northeastern corner is the church of **San Giovanni dei Napoletani** (1526–1617), with a trapezoidal portico.

Palazzo Abatellis ❷

See pp50–51.

La Gancia ❸

Via Alloro. **[** 091-616 52 21. **[** 9am–noon, 3:30–6pm. **[** Sun pm.

The Gothic portal of La Gancia, with bas-relief on the arch

THIS CHURCH was built in 1485 and dedicated to Santa Maria degli Angeli. The façade is decorated with Spanish-Gothic portals. The aisleless nave in the interior has 16 side chapels, a multi-coloured marble floor and a wooden patterned ceiling. In the Baroque period, stucco decoration was added by the sculptor Giacomo Serpotta. The choir, in a separate room near the church's entrance, has a fine late 16th-century organ. The panels dating from 1697 show Franciscan saints painted by Antonio Grano.

Museo Internazionale delle Marionette ❹

Via Butera 1. **[** 091-328 060. **[** 9am–1pm, 4–7pm. **[** Sat pm, Sun. **[**

Palermitan marionette from the theatre of Francesco Sclafani

THIS ORIGINAL museum boasts one of the most important collections of puppets, marionettes and shadow puppets in the world. The first room features the great schools of marionettes, from the Catania style to those of Liège, Naples and Brussels. The second room has a varied collection of Palermitan puppets belonging to puppeteers from Palermo, Alcamo, Partinico and Castellammare del Golfo. Among the historic stage scenery here is *Charlemagne's Council* and *Alcina's Garden*. The international section of the museum includes Chinese shadow theatre puppets and

Stage backdrop in the Museo delle Marionette depicting knights errant

hand puppets, Thai *hun krabok* and Vietnamese aquatic marionettes, Burmese and Rajastan marionettes, and Javanese *wayang* figures. The animated figures from Oceania and Africa are a delightful surprise. Lastly, there is the theatre of puppeteer Gaspare Canino di Alcamo, with backcloths showing the feats of Orlando; most of the productions of the famous Opera dei Pupi (puppet opera), featured the daring exploits of Charlemagne's knights errant.

Coat of arms of Palazzo Mirto

The museum is also responsible for the annual Festival di Morgana, which usually takes place in October. The festival features puppet operas from around the world, all of which are performed in Italian.

Palazzo Mirto ❺

Via Merlo 2. ☎ 091-616 47 51.
⏰ 9am–1pm, 3–6:30pm Mon–Sat, 9am–12:30pm Sun.

THIS IS A SPLENDID example of a centuries-old nobleman's mansion that has miraculously preserved its original furnishings. Palazzo Mirto was built in the 18th century onto pre-existing 15th- and 16th-century architectural structures. The palazzo passed from the aristocratic Des Puches family to the equally noble Filangeri, who lived here until 1980, when the last heir donated it to the Region of Sicily.

An 18th-century portal with the coat of arms of the Filangeri family leads to the courtyard, where a majestic marble stairway takes you to the piano nobile. Here there is a series of elegantly furnished drawing rooms. The first of these is the Sala degli Arazzi (Tapestry Hall), with mythological scenes painted by Giuseppe Velasco in 1804, then there is the "Chinese" room, and lastly the so-called Baldachin Salon with late 18th-century allegorical frescoes. The furniture and other furnishings date from the 18th and 19th centuries. Some rooms overlook a courtyard garden dominated by a theatrical Rococo fountain flanked by two aviaries.

San Francesco d'Assisi ❻

Piazza San Francesco d'Assisi. ☎ 091-616 28 19. ⏰ 7am–noon Mon–Sat, 7am–1pm, 4–6pm Sun & hols.

THIS 13TH-CENTURY CHURCH has retained its medieval aspect despite the numerous alterations it has undergone. Built in the early 13th century together with the Franciscan monastery, it was destroyed by Frederick II soon afterwards when he was excommunicated by the Pope. In 1255, work on the new church began, reaching completion only in 1277. The 15th and particularly the 16th centuries witnessed additions and alterations; for example, the wooden roof was replaced and the presbytery was enlarged.

After the 1943 bombardments the church was restored to its original state. The austere façade has a large rose window and Gothic portal, while the interior boasts many noteworthy works of art, including sculptures by Giacomo Serpotta (*see p33*) and Antonello Gagini. The side chapels house funerary stelae and sarcophagi.

The fourth chapel in the left-hand aisle is the Cappella Mastrantonio, with one of the first Renaissance works in Sicily, the portal by Francesco Laurana. Behind the high altar is a wooden choir built in 1520, as well as 17th-century paintings of the *Resurrection, Ascension* and *Mission*.

The drawing rooms in Palazzo Mirto, still with their original furniture

Palazzo Abatellis ❷

THIS CATALAN GOTHIC building has an austere air. The elegant doorway leads to the large courtyard, which has a portico on the right side and a stairway to the upper floors. The building now houses the 16 rooms of the Galleria Regionale della Sicilia. On the ground floor is one of its most famous works, the *Triumph of Death* fresco (located in the former chapel) as well as a fine collection of statues by Antonello Gagini and Francesco Laurana. The first floor has noteworthy late medieval crucifixes including one by Pietro Ruzzolone (16th century), and paintings by Antonello da Messina. The most interesting work by a foreign artist is the *Malvagna Triptych* by Jan Gossaert (known as Mabuse).

★ Annunciation
This is perhaps the best-known work by the great Antonello da Messina (1430–79). It is a masterful and exquisite example of 15th-century figurative rationalism and the artist's fusion of Northern and Italian painting.

The "Laurana Room"
houses the great sculptor's famous Bust of Eleonora of Aragon *(see p43).*

Ground floor

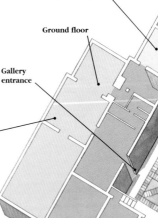

Gallery entrance

★ The Triumph of Death
This fine medieval fresco by an unknown artist was executed around the mid-15th century. It portrays Death in the guise of a knight shooting his bow (see pp30–31).

Foyer

Virgin and Child
This sculpture group, attributed to Domenico Gagini (ca. 1420–1492) comes from the Basilica di San Francesco d'Assisi in Palermo (see p49). Note the delicate treatment of the Virgin's features.

Main entrance

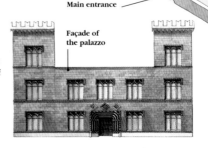

Façade of the palazzo

The Malvagna Triptych
This work by the Flemish artist Mabuse (1478– 1532) portrays the Virgin and Child among angels and saints.

VISITORS' CHECKLIST

Via Alloro 4. ☎ 091-623 00 11.
🕐 9am–1:30pm Mon, Wed, Fri & Sat, 3–7:30pm Tue & Thu, 9am– 12:30pm Sun. 🚫

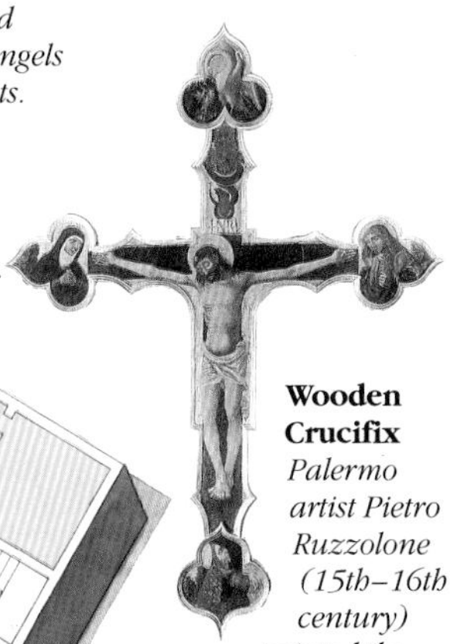

Wooden Crucifix
Palermo artist Pietro Ruzzolone (15th–16th century) painted the Crucifixion (seen above) on the front and the risen Christ on the reverse.

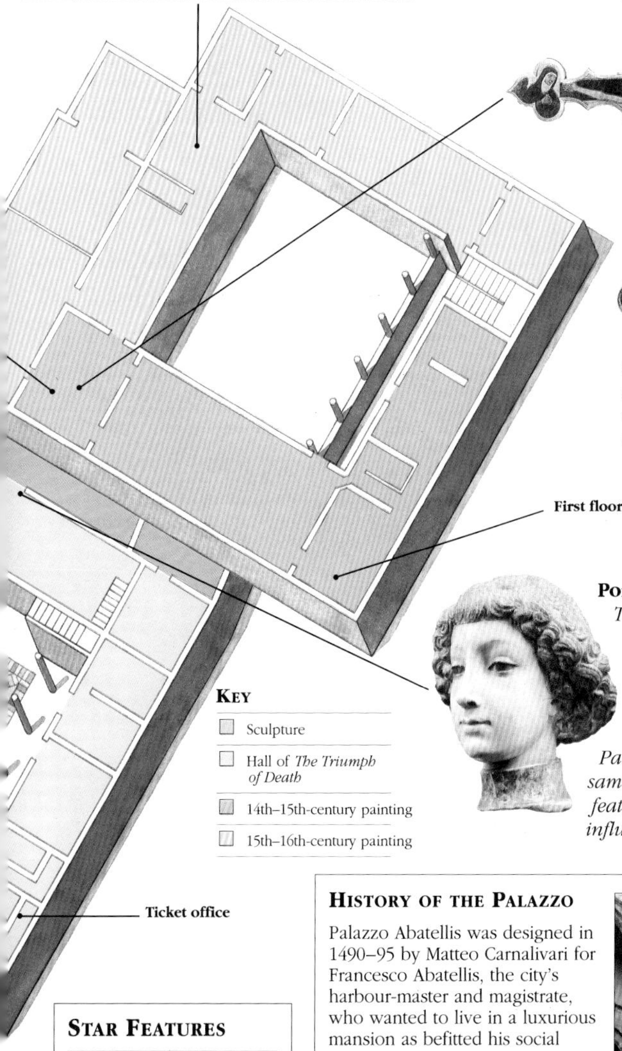

First floor

Portrait of a Youth
This work is attributed to Antonello Gagini (1478–1536), son of Domenico, and was once part of a statue of San Vito in the Palermo church of the same name. The facial features reveal the influence of Laurana.

KEY

- ☐ Sculpture
- ☐ Hall of *The Triumph of Death*
- ☐ 14th–15th-century painting
- ☐ 15th–16th-century painting

Ticket office

STAR FEATURES

★ **The Triumph of Death**

★ **Annunciation by Antonello da Messina**

HISTORY OF THE PALAZZO

Palazzo Abatellis was designed in 1490–95 by Matteo Carnalivari for Francesco Abatellis, the city's harbour-master and magistrate, who wanted to live in a luxurious mansion as befitted his social status. He died without leaving an heir, and the mansion was taken over by the Benedictine order and then by the Region of Sicily. It was damaged in the 1943 bombings and then restored by architect Carlo Scarpa.

The loggia

The Fontana Pretoria, once called "the fountain of shame" because of its statues of nude figures

Fontana Pretoria ❼

Piazza Pretoria.

LOCATED IN THE MIDDLE of Palermo's most intriguing square, this fountain is on a slightly higher level than Via Maqueda. It was designed in 1552–55 by Tuscan sculptor Francesco Camilliani for the garden of a Florentine villa and was later installed in Piazza Pretoria. The concentric basins are arranged on three levels, with statues of mythological creatures, monsters, tritons, sirens and the four rivers of Palermo (Oreto, Papireto, Gabriele, Maredolce). Because of the nude statues it was known as "the fountain of shame".

A statue on the Fontana Pretoria

Palazzo delle Aquile ❽

Piazza Pretoria. 📞 091-740 11 11. ⏰ 8am–8pm Mon–Fri, 8am–2pm Sat.

ITS PROPER NAME is Palazzo Senatorio, or Palazzo del Municipio, but it is commonly called "delle Aquile" because

of the four eagles (*aquile*) decorating the exterior and the portal. Now the town hall, it is Palermo's major civic monument, although its original 16th-century structure was radically altered by 19th-century restoration. However, a statue of Santa Rosalia by Carlo Aprile (1661) still lies in a niche on the top of the façade. At the entrance, a grand staircase with a coffered ceiling takes you to the first floor, where there are various public rooms: the Sala delle Lapidi, Sala dei Gonfaloni and Sala Rossa, which is also known as the Mayor's Hall.

Santa Caterina ❾

Piazza Bellini. ⏰ Easter and Christmas services.

THE CHURCH of the Dominican monastery of Santa Caterina is a splendid example of Sicilian Baroque art, despite the fact that both buildings originated in the 14th century.
The main features of the late Renaissance façade (the present church was built in 1580–96) are its double stairway and the statue of St Catherine (Caterina) in the middle of the portal. The large cupola was built in the mid-18th century. The interior is a blaze of decoration, with marble inlay, sculpture pieces, stuccoes and frescoes. In the chapel to the right of the transept is a fine statue of Santa Caterina, sculpted by Antonello Gagini in 1534.

La Martorana ❿

Piazza Bellini 3. 📞 091-616 16 92. ⏰ 9:30am–1pm, 3:30–5:30pm.

SANTA MARIA dell'Ammiraglio is called La Martorana in memory of Eloisa della Martorana, who founded the nearby Benedictine convent. It was built in 1143 by King Roger II's admiral (*ammiraglio*, hence the name) on a Greek cross plan and was partly altered and enlarged in the Baroque period. The 16th-century façade is also Baroque. This church is a unique work of art, combining Norman features and decoration with those of later styles. You enter the church by the

The portal on the Baroque façade of La Martorana

bell tower, whose dome was destroyed in the 1726 earthquake and never replaced. The Baroque interior is decorated with stuccoes and enamel-work. The bay vaulting has striking frescoes, in particular Olivio Sozzi's *Glory of the Virgin Mary* (1744). The original church was decorated with 12th-century mosaics, perhaps made by the same craftsmen who worked in the Cappella Palatina. On the cupola is *Christ Pantocrator Surrounded by Angels (see p44)*, on the tambour *The Prophets* and *The Four Evangelists*; figures of saints are on the arches, and on the walls are *The Nativity*, *The Presentation at the Temple* and an *Annunciation*. The inlaid pavement, the marble and mosaic choir partition and lapis lazuli tabernacle are also of note.

San Cataldo ⓫

Piazza Bellini 3.
◻ 9:30am–1pm, 3:30–5:30pm (ask for custodian at La Martorana).

S AN CATALDO was the chapel of a palazzo built by Maio of Bari, William I's admiral, in the 12th century. It now belongs to the Order of Knights of the Holy Sepulchre. It has preserved the linear Arab-

Norman style, with three red domes raised above the wall, the windows with pointed arches and the battlement decoration. Inscriptions with quotations from the Koran can still be seen. The interior has no decoration except for the mosaic patterned floor. In the middle of the nave is a series of Arab arches supported by ancient columns, above which are three domes with conical vaults.

La Magione ⓬

Via Magione 44. ◧ 091-617 05 96.
◻ 8am–noon, 4–6:30pm Mon–Sat, 8am–1pm, 5–8pm Sun.

F OUNDED BY Matteo d'Aiello together with the Cistercian monastery in the mid-12th century, La Magione became the mansion of the Teutonic Knights from 1197 to 1492. The church was frequently rebuilt and was then badly damaged in the bombings of 1943. Careful restoration has revived its original Norman features. A Baroque portico, with marble columns and statues, affords access to a lovely garden. The Teutonic Knights' coat of arms can be seen on the tympanum. The austere façade has three doorways with double arched lintels and convex rustication,

a series of blind arches and windows. Pointed arches run along the length of the nave. A double row of columns lead to the apses, which are decorated with interlaced arches.

Santa Maria dello Spasimo ⓭

Via dello Spasimo. ◧ 091-616 14 86. ◻ 6am–12:45pm daily.

The roofless interior of Santa Maria dello Spasimo

S ANTA MARIA dello Spasimo lies in the heart of the Kalsa quarter. It was founded in 1506 by the monks of Santa Maria di Monte Oliveto and was dedicated to the Virgin Mary grieving before Christ on the Cross, subject of a painting by Raphael in 1516, which is now in the Prado Museum in Madrid. Santa Maria was the last example of Spanish Gothic architecture in the city. The cells and courtyards of the monastery were built around the church and in 1536 the complex, at that time outside the city walls, was incorporated into a rampart, so that it now looks like a watchtower.

The church was bought by the city and became, in turn, a theatre, warehouse, hospice and hospital, while all the time falling into a state of neglect. A few years ago, the Spasimo area was redeveloped and transformed into a cultural centre for exhibitions and concerts. Performances are held inside the church, part of which no longer has a roof.

San Cataldo, with its characteristic Arab architectural elements

One of the rooms in the Museo Archeologico Regionale

Museo Archeo-logico Regionale ⑭

Piazza Olivella. 🄲 091-611 68 07.
🄾 9am–1:30pm, 3–7:45pm Mon–Fri,
9am–1:15pm Sat & Sun. 🄰

THE ARCHAEOLOGICAL Museum is housed in a 17th-century monastery and holds treasures from excavations across the island. The entrance leads to a small cloister with a fountain bearing a statue of Triton. The former cells contain finds such as the large Phoenician sarcophagi in the shape of human beings (6th–5th centuries BC) and the *Pietra di Palermo*, a slab with a hieroglyphic inscription (2900 BC). On the first floor there is a display of Punic inscriptions and objects, as well as terracotta and bronze sculpture, including a fine 3rd-century BC ram's head. On the second floor is the Sala dei Mosaici, with mosaics and frescoes from digs at Palermo, Solunto and Marsala. The large cloister houses Roman statues, slabs and tombstones. At the end of the cloister are three rooms with the marvel-lous pieces taken from the temples at Selinunte; these include a lovely leonine head from the Temple of Victory and the valuable metopes from other temples. Those from Temple C represent

Roman bust, Museo Archeologico

Helios's Chariot, Perseus Helped by Athena while Killing the Gorgon and *Heracles Punishing the Cercopes*; the metopes from Temple E are *Heracles Fighting the Amazons, Hera and Zeus on Mount Ida, Actaeon Attacked by Dogs in the Presence of Artemis* (see p20) and *Athena Slaying the Giant Enceladus*.

Mercato della Vucciria ⑮

Piazza Caracciolo and adjacent streets.

THIS IS PALERMO'S most famous market, immortalized by Renato Guttuso in his painting *La Vucciria (see p210)*. The name derives from *Bocceria nuova*, the "new market" built for the sale of vegetables, to dis-tinguish it from *Bocceria veccia*, which was in Piazza

Sant'Onofrio and sold meat. Today, this outdoor market-place trades not only in vegetables, dried fruit and preserves, but also sells other foods such as cheese, fish and meat, amid a tumult of colours, sounds and smells reminiscent of the souks in North Africa. The Vucciria is especially impressive at sunset, when the atmosphere is heightened by a thousand lights. There are stalls that prepare octopus or will do skewered giblets for you on the spot. Another speciality is boiled spleen, also used for making *ca' meusa* bread, the locals' favourite snack. To get to the market, from Piazza San Domenico take Via Maccheronai, once the colourful pasta-producing area, where freshly made pasta was hung out to dry.

Oratorio del Rosario di Santa Cita ⑯

Via Valverde 3. 🄲 091-336 432,
332 779. 🄾 4–5:30pm (ring at Via
Valverde 3 for morrning admittance).

FOUNDED IN 1590 by the Society of the Rosary, this was one of the city's richest oratories. A marble staircase opens onto a cloister and then goes up to the upper loggia, which is decorated with marble busts, and the vestibule, with portraits of the Superiors of the Society. The Oratory is an example of Giacomo Serpotta's best work *(see p33)*, a lavish display of

The Mercato della Vucciria, Palermo's colourful open-air market

The Baroque façade of San Domenico

decorated walls. The altar in the transept is adorned with lateral volutes and bronze friezes, while the 18th-century high altar is made of marble and decorated with semi-precious stones.

Oratorio del Rosario di San Domenico ⑱

Via dei Bambinai. **(** *091-320 559.* ☐ *For admittance, ask custodian at No 16 Via dei Bambinai.*

BEHIND SAN LORENZO, in the Vucciria market area, is the Oratory of San Domenico, founded at the end of the 16th century by the Society of the Holy Rosary. Two Society members were painter Pietro Novelli and sculptor Giacomo Serpotta, who left the marks of their genius on this elegant monument.

The black and white majolica floors fit in well with the tumult of figures of great ladies, knights and playful putti. These form a kind of frame for the statues of Christian virtues by Giacomo Serpotta and the paintings representing the mysteries of the Rosary. The latter were executed by Pietro Novelli and Flemish artists, while the altarpiece, *Madonna of the Rosary with St Dominic and the Patronesses of Palermo,* was painted by Anthony Van Dyck in 1628. In the middle of the vault is Novelli's *Coronation of the Virgin.*

Baroque decoration, its fusion of putti volutes, statues, festoons and floral elements creating an amazing theatrical atmosphere. The *Battle of Lepanto* sculpture group *(see p33)* is simply spectacular. On the sides of the tribune are statues of Esther and Judith, while the altarpiece is Carlo Maratta's *Madonna of the Rosary,* executed in 1695. Along the walls there are seats with mother of pearl inlay, and the floor is made of red, white and black marble.

Detail of stucco-work, Santa Cita

San Domenico ⑰

Piazza San Domenico. **(** *091-584 872.* ☐ *7:30am–noon daily; 7:30am–6:30pm Sat–Sun. Closed for restoration.*

THIS CHURCH, which belongs to the Dominican monastery, has been rebuilt many times over the past six centuries. The most drastic

alteration was in 1640, when Andrea Cirincione tore down part of the cloister to enlarge the church. In 1724, when Piazza San Domenico was remodelled, the façade was rebuilt and is now animated by the fusion of curves on the one hand, and jutting columns and statues, niches and twin bell towers on the other. The interior has a typical Latin cross plan with two aisles and a deep semicircular dome. The total lack of decoration serves to heighten the elegance of the architecture. In contrast, the chapels, used since the 19th century as the burial place for the city's most illustrious personages, are quite richly decorated. The third chapel is the tomb of the Oneto di Sperlinga family and has multicoloured marble funerary monuments, a statue of St Joseph by Antonello Gagini, and stucco- and putti-

Van Dyck's fine canvas stands behind the Oratorio altar

SOUTH PALERMO

THE QUARTERS south of Via Roma lie on the slopes occupied by the city's original Phoenician settlement, which was enlarged during the Roman era. In the 11th century the Arabs built a castle on the site where the Palazzo dei Normanni now stands. The Arab word *Al Qasar* (the castle) was used as the name of the quarter and the street that led to the castle, the present-day Corso Vittorio Emanuele, known as "Cassaro" to the people of Palermo. The area contains many impressive buildings and churches, including Palermo's

One of the statues on the Cathedral

Cathedral, as well as good shops and hotels. Between the Palazzo dei Normanni and Via Maqueda is the Albergheria quarter, the home of merchants and craftsmen in the Middle Ages. It is still enlivened by the daily market, the Mercato Ballarò, which is less famous but more authentic than the Vucciria market. The many oratories of the medieval brotherhoods demonstrate the wealth and industry of the inhabitants. In the first half of the 20th century parts were demolished, and the 1943 air raids dealt an additional blow to the area.

SIGHTS AT A GLANCE

Streets and Squares

KEY

- ▨ Street-by-Street map *pp58–9*
- Main bus stop
- 🚕 Taxi rank (Stand)
- Police headquarters
- Casualty (Emergency room)
- 🅿 Parking

0 metres   350
0 yards   350

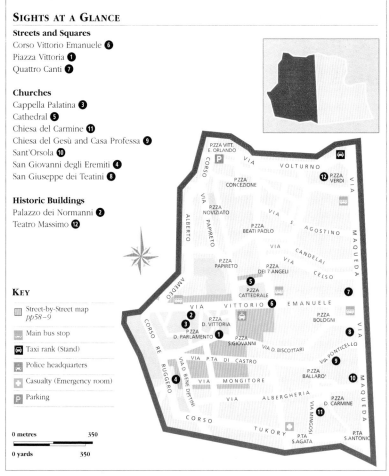

◁ **The Atlantes at Porta Nuova, the city gate built in 1583 in honour of Emperor Charles V**

Street-by-Street: Around Piazza della Vittoria

Mosaic lunette in the Stanza di Ruggero, Palazzo dei Normanni

PIAZZA DELLA VITTORIA, opposite the Palazzo dei Normanni, is one of the city's major squares. Since the time of the Roman *castrum superius,* the Arab Alcazar and the Norman Palace, this area has been the military, political and administrative heart of Sicily, and religious prestige was added in the 12th century when the Cathedral was built nearby. In the 17th and 18th centuries the square was the venue for public festivities. It became a public garden in the early 20th century, surrounded by important monuments such as Porta Nuova, Palazzo Sclafani and Palazzo Arcivescovile.

The monument to Philip V, in the middle of Piazza della Vittoria, was built of marble in 1662.

The former hospital of San Giacomo

Porta Nuova was built in 1583 to commemorate Charles V's arrival in Palermo in 1535.

Palazzo dei Normanni
This has always been the palace of the city's rulers. Traces of the original Arab-Norman architecture can still be seen on the exterior ❷

★ Cappella Palatina
Founded in 1130 by the Norman king Roger II, the chapel boasts an extraordinary cycle of mosaics ❸

★ San Giovanni degli Eremiti
This church, surrounded by a luxuriant garden, is one of the most important monuments in Palermo, partly because of its Arab architecture ❹

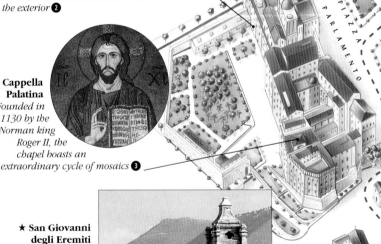

CORSO VITTORIO

PIAZZA DEL PARLAMENTO

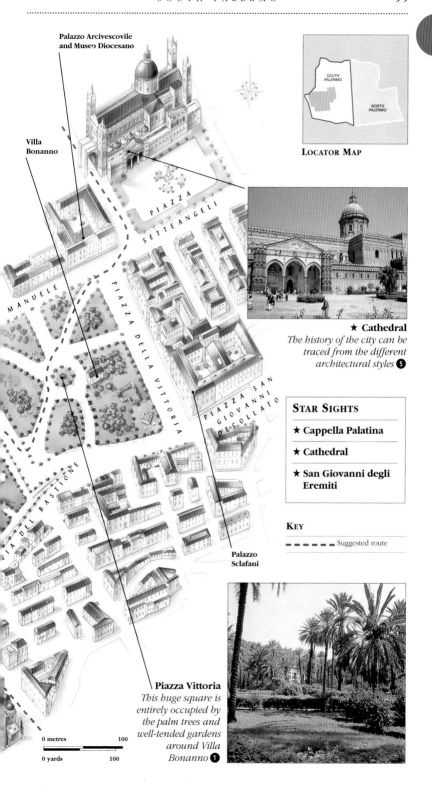

Palazzo Arcivescovile
and Museo Diocesano

Villa
Bonanno

PIAZZA
SETTEANGELI

MANUELE

PIAZZA DELLA VITTORIA

PIAZZA SAN
GIOVANNI
DECOLLATO

VIA DEL BASTIONE

Palazzo
Sclafani

LOCATOR MAP

★ **Cathedral**
*The history of the city can be
traced from the different
architectural styles* ❺

STAR SIGHTS

★ **Cappella Palatina**

★ **Cathedral**

★ **San Giovanni degli
Eremiti**

KEY

▬ ▬ ▬ Suggested route

Piazza Vittoria
*This huge square is
entirely occupied by
the palm trees and
well-tended gardens
around Villa
Bonanno* ❶

0 metres   100

0 yards   100

Cappella Palatina ❸

Detail of a mosaic in the interior

FOUNDED IN 1132 by Roger II *(see pp26–7)*, the Cappella Palatina with its splendid mosaics is a jewel of Arab-Norman art. The basilica has two side aisles and three apses, granite columns dividing the nave. The walls are decorated with Biblical scenes. On the cupola is the image of Christ Pantocrator surrounded by angels, while the niches house the Four Evangelists. Old Testament kings and prophets are on the arches, Christ blessing the faithful dominates the middle apse, and the transept walls bear scenes from the Gospel. Other important features are the wooden ceiling, a masterpiece of Muslim art, and the marble pulpit and candelabrum. The overall harmony of the design, and the perfection of the details, make this a unique monument.

★ **The Central Apse**
In the middle is Christ blessing the faithful; below him are archangels.

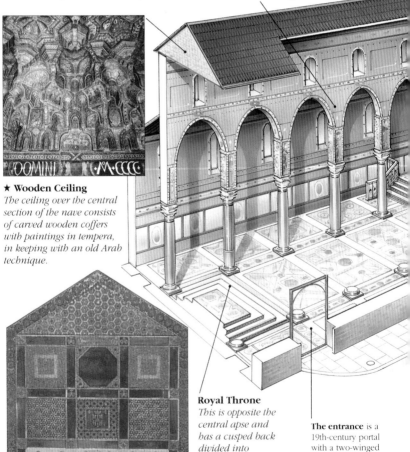

★ **Wooden Ceiling**
The ceiling over the central section of the nave consists of carved wooden coffers with paintings in tempera, in keeping with an old Arab technique.

Royal Throne
This is opposite the central apse and has a cusped back divided into squares bearing the Aragonese coat of arms.

The entrance is a 19th-century portal with a two-winged wooden door.

★ **Christ Pantocrator**
*In the middle of the cupola
is this glory of mosaic
decoration, the figure of
Christ Pantocrator,
holding a closed book.
Around him is the
Greek text from the
Book of Isaiah.*

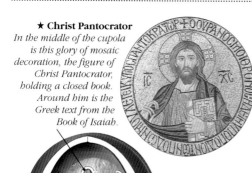

Candelabrum
*Made entirely of
white marble, this
beautiful candela-
brum is the oldest
Romanesque work
of art in Sicily. Four
lions devouring
animals decorate
the base, while
there are interlaced
floral and human
motifs along the
shaft. On the top
are three slender
figures supporting
the disc that held
the Easter candle.*

The side apse is
decorated with
images of
St Paul and the
Virgin Mary.

The Crypt
*This lies under the
presbytery. It is built on
a square plan and was
probably King Roger's
original chapel.
Sacred objects and
works of art such as this
Byzantine school
Madonna and Child
are now kept here.*

STAR FEATURES

★ **The Central Apse**

★ **Wooden Ceiling**

★ **Christ Pantocrator**

Piazza della Vittoria, with Palazzo dei Normanni in the background

Piazza Vittoria ❶

THIS SQUARE is completely occupied by the **Villa Bonanno** garden. In the middle is the **Teatro Marmoreo** fountain, built in honour of Philip V, with statues of the continents partly under this ruler's dominion (Europe, America, Asia and Africa). Archaeological digs have unearthed Roman villas and mosaics; the finds are in the Museo Archeologico Regionale *(see p54)* and the Sala dell'Orfeo pavilion. Among the palazzi and churches facing the square are the Baroque **Cappella della Soledad**, with multi-coloured marble and stucco decoration, and the former hospital of **San Giacomo** (now the Bonsignore barracks), with the lovely Norman **Santa Maria Maddalena** in the interior.

Palazzo dei Normanni ❷

Piazza Indipendenza. ☎ 091-705 11 11. ◷ 9am–noon Mon, Fri, Sat.

THE ARABS BUILT this palace over the ruins of a Roman fort in the 11th century. The following century it was enlarged and became the royal palace of the Norman king Roger II, with Arab architects and craftsmen building towers and pavilions for the king and his retinue. Not much is left of the Norman age, partly because

the palace was abandoned when Frederick II left his Palermo court. The Spanish viceroys preferred to use the more modern Palazzo Steri. The present-day appearance of the palace, now the seat of the Sicilian Regional Assembly, dates back to alterations made in the 16th and 17th centuries. The entrance is in Piazza Indipendenza. After a short walk uphill, you enter the Maqueda courtyard, built in 1600 with three rows of arcades and a large staircase leading to the first floor and the Cappella Palatina *(see pp60–61)*, one of the few remaining parts from the Norman period. The royal apartments, which now house

the Sicilian Parliament, are on the second floor. To visit them you must be accompanied by a guard. The most interesting room is the Sala di Re Ruggero, the walls and arches of which are covered with 12th-century mosaics with animal and plant motifs in a naturalistic vein that probably reveals a Persian influence: centaurs, leopards, lions, deer and peacocks. The vault has geometric motifs and medallions with owls, deer, centaurs and lions. The tour ends with the Chinese Room, frescoed by Giovanni and Salvatore Patricolo, and the Sala Gialla, with tempera decoration on the vaults.

Cappella Palatina ❸

See pp60–61.

San Giovanni degli Eremiti ❹

Via dei Benedettini 18. ☎ 091-651 50 19. ◷ 9am–1pm Mon; 9am–1pm, 3–6pm Thu; 9am–12:30pm Sun.

BUILT IN 1132 for Roger II *(see pp26–7)* over the foundation of a Benedictine monastery that had been constructed in 581 for Pope Gregory the Great, San Giovanni degli Eremiti displays a

King Roger's Hall in Palazzo dei Normanni, showing the mosaics

The three typically Arab domes on San Giovanni degli Eremiti

clearly Oriental influence. It was built by Arab-Norman craftsmen and labourers, and their work is at its most striking in the red domes and cubic forms.

The delightful garden of citrus trees, pomegranate, roses and jasmine leads to the ruins of the monastery, a small cloister with twin columns and pointed arches *(see pp40–41)*.

The cross-plan interior has an aisleless nave ending in the presbytery with three apses. The right-hand apse is covered by one of the red domes, while above the left-hand one is a fine bell tower with pointed windows and a smaller red dome on top.

Cathedral ❺

See pp64–5.

Corso Vittorio Emanuele ❻

T HIS IS THE MAIN street in the heart of Palermo, which lies on the Phoenician road that connected the ancient city and the seaside. The locals call it "Cassaro", from the Arab *el Qasar* or castle, to which the road led. In the Middle Ages it was the most important artery in the city, but in the 1500s it became an elegant street. In that period the street was extended to the sea, and two city gates were built: **Porta Felice** to the north and **Porta Nuova** to the south, next to Palazzo dei

Normanni. It was called Via Toledo during the Spanish period. The stretch between Porta Nuova and the Quattro Canti boasts several patrician mansions. On the western side is the former hospital of San Giacomo, now the Bonsignore barracks; the Baroque **Collegio Massimo dei Gesuiti**, the present Regional Library; **Palazzo Geraci**, a Baroque residence rebuilt in the Rococo style; the 18th-century **Palazzo Tarallo della Miraglia**, restored as the Hotel Centrale. On the eastern side are the **San Salvatore**, a

lovely Baroque church with an elliptical plan and lavish decoration, and **San Giuseppe dei Teatini**. Just beyond Vicolo Castelbuono is **Piazza Bologna**, which has several Baroque buildings.

Quattro Canti ❼

Piazza Vigliena.

T HE INTERSECTION of Corso Vittorio Emanuele and Via Maqueda is Palermo's most fashionable square. Quattro Canti dates from 1600, when the new town plan was put into effect and the city was divided into four parts, called *Mandamenti*: the north-eastern *Kalsa* section, the southeastern one of Albergheria, Capo to the southwest and Castellammare or Loggia in the southeast. The piazza is rounded, shaped by the concave façades of the four corner buildings (hence the name) with superimposed architectural orders – Doric, Corinthian and Ionic. Each façade is decorated with a fountain and statues of the *Mandamenti* patron saints, of the seasons and of the Spanish kings.

One of the façades making up the corners of the Quattro Canti

Cathedral ❺

One of the statues that decorate the Cathedral

Dᴇᴅɪᴄᴀᴛᴇᴅ ᴛᴏ Our Lady of the Assump-tion, the Cathedral stands on the site of an Early Christian basilica, later a mosque. It was built in 1179–85 but, because of frequent rebuilding and alterations, very little of the original structure remains. The most drastic changes occurred in the late 1700s, when the nave was widened and the central cupola was added. The original Norman structure can be seen under the small cupolas with majolica tiles, with the typical arched crenellation decoration on the wall tops. The exterior of the apses has maintained its original character with its interlaced arches and small columns. As a result of the mixture of styles, the right-hand side forms a kind of "carved history" of the city. Opposite the façade, on the other side of the street, is the medieval campanile.

Cupolas with majolica tiles
The small cupolas were built in 1781 over the side chapels, the addition of which drastically changed the Cathedral's original plan.

Arab inscription
Various parts of the former mosque were retained in the Cathedral, such as this passage from the Koran inscribed on the left-hand column of the southern portico.

★ Catalan Gothic portico
The work of Antonio Gambara (1430), the portico has three pointed arches and a Gothic tympanum with Biblical scenes and the city coat of arms in bas-relief.

The portal was built in the 1400s and is decorated with a two-winged wooden door with a mosaic of the Virgin Mary above.

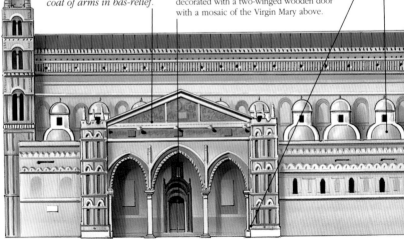

The Cappella di Santa Rosalia, patron saint of Palermo

Middle section of the nave, with statues by Antonello Gagini

THE INTERIOR OF THE CATHEDRAL

Alterations carried out in the 18th century gave the interior a Neo-Classical look. Of the many chapels, the most important are the first two on the right-hand side of the nave with the imperial tombs, and the chapel of Santa Rosalia, where the saint's remains are in a silver coffer on the altar.

VISITORS' CHECKLIST

Corso Vittorio Emanuele. 📞
091-334 376. 🚇 104 (station).
🕐 7am–7pm daily. ✝ 9, 10
& 11am, 12.30 & 6pm hols.
Cathedral Treasury 🕐 9am–
noon, 4–5:30pm. ⬤ Sun. 📷

★ **Towers with Gothic double lancet windows**
The slender Gothic turrets with their lancet windows were added to the 12th-century Norman clock tower in the 14th–15th centuries.

The cupola, in Baroque style, was added in the late 1700s to a design by Ferdinando Fuga.

STAR FEATURES

★ **Catalan Gothic portico**

★ **Towers with double lancet windows**

The arched crenellation motif characteristic of Norman architecture runs along the right side of the Cathedral.

The exterior of the apses, decorated with interlaced arches, is the best preserved part of the original design.

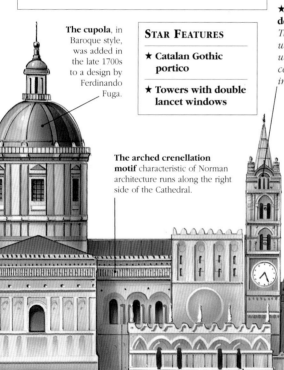

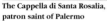

The lavishly decorated Baroque interior of the Chiesa del Gesù

San Giuseppe dei Teatini 8

Corso Vittorio Emanuele.
8:45–11:15am , 5–7pm Mon–Sat; 8:30am–1pm Sun.

THE THEATINE congregation spared no expense in the construction of San Giuseppe dei Teatini on a corner of the Quattro Canti (1612–45). Despite the fact that the façade was finished in 1844 in Neo-Classical style, the church exudes a Baroque spirit, beginning with the cupola covered with majolica tiles. The two-aisle nave is flanked by huge columns, the ceiling is frescoed and the walls are covered with polychrome marble decoration. On either side of the entrance are two marble stoups held up by angels. The chapels are richly decorated with stucco and frescoes, and the high altar is made of semiprecious stone.

Chiesa del Gesù and Casa Professa 9

Piazza Casa Professa.
091-606 71 11.
7:30–11:30am, 5–6:30pm.

THIS CHURCH perhaps represents the peak of Baroque decoration in Palermo. The late 16th-century façade was one of the sets for the film *Il Gattopardo* *(see p22)*. Work on the decoration began in 1597 and was interrupted permanently when the Jesuits were expelled in 1860. The grandiose interior is entirely covered with marble inlay – walls, columns and floor – in a profusion of forms and colours, blending in well with the fine stuccoes of Giacomo Serpotta *(see p33)*, the imitation bas-relief columns, and the various decorative motifs. The pulpit in the middle of the nave was the work of the Genoese school (1646). To the right of the church is the western section of the Casa Professa, with a 1685 portal and an 18th-century cloister affording access to the City Library.

Sant'Orsola 10

Via Maqueda. *8:30–11am. Oratory visits by request only.*

SANT'ORSOLA was built in the early 17th century by the Society of St Ursula, known as "Dei Negri" because of the dark habits the members wore during processions. The late Renaissance façade is decorated with figures of souls in Purgatory and angels. Three skulls lie on the architrave. The aisleless interior is an example of a light-filled Baroque church, with deep semicircular chapels linked by galleries. The vault over the nave is decorated with the fresco *The Glory of St Ursula* and two medallions depicting Faith and Charity. The painting *The Martrydom of St Ursula* by Pietro Novelli *(see p21)* is in the second chapel on the right, while frescoes of scenes of the saint's life are on the vault. Another work by Novelli, *Madonna with the Salvator Mundi*, is in the sacristy. From the sacristy there is access to the Oratorio di Sant'Orsola, decorated with 17th-century paintings and stucco sculpture.

The 18th-century cloister of the Casa Professa

An old commemorative postcard of the Teatro Massimo, Palermo's opera house

Chiesa del Carmine ⓫

Via Giovanni Grasso 13/a. 〖 091-651 20 18. ◯ 8am–noon, 4–6:30pm.

THE CHIESA DEL CARMINE, seat of the Carmelite friars, dates from the 17th century. It lies on a much higher level than the nearby Mercato del Ballarò and is topped by a cupola covered with multi-coloured majolica tiles supported by four Atlantes. The interior is dominated by an altar resting on pairs of spiral columns decorated with stuccoes by Giuseppe and Giacomo Serpotta (1683) of scenes from the life of the Virgin Mary. The painting by Pietro Novelli *(see p21), The Vision of Sant'Andrea Corsini*, is also worth a look.

The cupola with polychrome majolica tiles, Chiesa del Carmine

Teatro Massimo ⓬

Piazza Giuseppe Verdi.
〖 091-605 31 11.

R ECENTLY REOPENED after being closed for years, the Teatro Massimo has become one of the symbols of the rebirth of Palermo. It was designed in 1864 by Giovanni Battista Filippo Basile and finished in 1897. In order to make room for it, the city walls of Porta Maqueda, the Aragonese quarter, San Giuliano convent and church, and the Chiesa delle Stimmate di San Francesco and its monastery, were all demolished. Its 7,700 sq m (9,200 sq yd) make it one of the largest opera houses in Europe. The theatre now boasts five rows of boxes, a lavishly decorated gallery and a ceiling frescoed by Ettore Maria Bergler and Rocco Lentini. The entrance, with its Corinthian columns, is also monumental in style.

GUIDED TOURS OF THE MERCATO BALLARÒ

The Albergheria is one of the poorest and most run-down quarters in the old town, but it is also one of the most intriguing. Guided tours are organized by the San Francesco Saverio parish church and by the agency **Albergheria Viaggi**. The neighbourhood children, accompanied by bilingual guides for foreigners, will take you on the same itinerary once used by those making the Grand Tour. The first stop is the bell tower of San Francesco Saverio, a typical example of Sicilian Baroque, with a view of the cupolas and rooftops of Palermo. Then you will be able to observe how the local carob sweets are made and to see one of the last remaining decorators of authentic Sicilian carts, Pippino La Targia, at work. This tour also allows you to see monuments normally closed to the public, such as the 17th-century Oratorio del Carminello. But the highlight is the Mercato di Ballarò, one of the best markets in the city, a vivid combination of colours, smells and lively atmosphere.

Detail of a mural in the Albergheria quarter

Albergheria Viaggi
〖 091-21 83 44.

FURTHER AFIELD

T HE DESTRUCTION of the 16th-century defensive ramparts took place in the late 1700s, but it was only after the unification of Italy that Palermo expanded westwards past the city walls, which involved making new roads and demolishing old quarters. The heart of town shifted to Piazzas Verdi and Castelnuovo, where the Massimo and

Capital of a column at Monreale

Politeama theatres were built. This expansion also meant the disappearance of most of the lovely Arab-Norman gardens and parks the rulers had used for hunting and entertainment. Only a few, such as Castello della Zisa, have remained. At this time, "Greater Palermo" was created – an area that now includes Mondello and Monreale Cathedral.

SIGHTS AT A GLANCE

Galleries and Museums
Galleria d'Arte Moderna ❻
Museo Etnografico Pitré ❹

Historic Buildings
Palazzina Cinese ❸
Castello della Zisa ❽
La Cuba ❾
Ponte dell'Ammiraglio ⓮
Teatro Politeama ❺

Churches
Cripta dei Cappuccini ❼
Santo Spirito ⓬
San Giovanni dei Lebbrosi ⓭
Monreale Cathedral
pp74–5 ⓯

Parks and Gardens
Parco della Favorita ❷
Villa Giulia ❿
Orto Botanico ⓫

Beaches
Mondello ❶

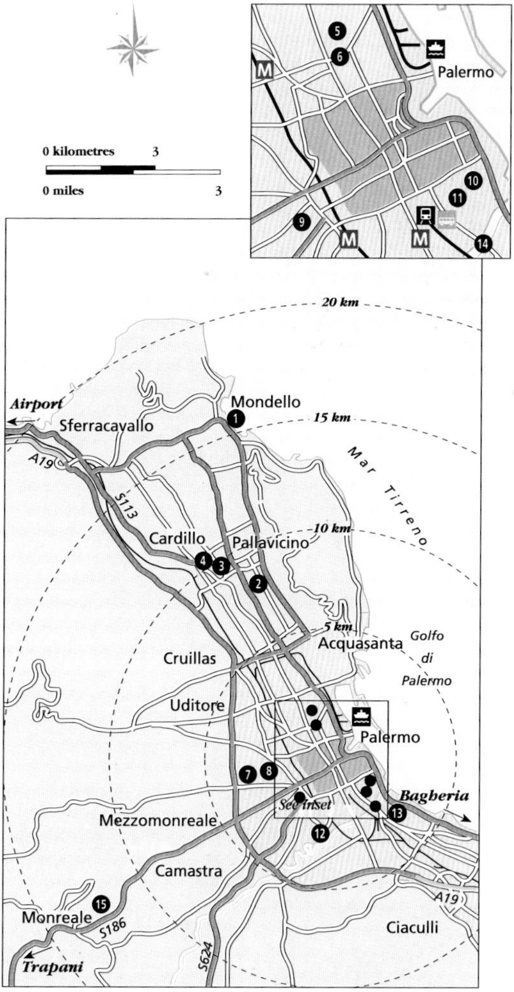

KEY

▨	Historic centre
☐	Urban area
▬	Motorway (Highway)
▬	Major road
▬	Minor road
▬	Railway line
🚉	Railway station
⛴	Ferry
M	Metro station
🚌	Bus station

0 kilometres 3

0 miles 3

20 km

15 km

10 km

5 km

Airport
Sferracavallo
Mondello ❶
Cardillo
Pallavicino
❹❸
❷
Cruillas
Uditore
Acquasanta
Golfo di Palermo
Palermo
❼ ❽
See Inset
Bagheria
⓭
Mezzomonreale
⓬
Camastra
Monreale ⓯
Trapani
Ciaculli
Mar Tirreno

❺
❻
Palermo
❿
⓫
❾
⓮

The lively fishing harbour at Mondello, filled with boats

Mondello **❶**

10 km (6 miles) north of Palermo.

A FAVOURITE WITH Palermitans, Mondello beach lies a short distance from the centre of the town, between the rocky promontories of Monte Pellegrino and Monte Gallo.

Mondello was once a small village of tuna fishermen, centred around a 15th-century square tower, but in the last 70 years it has become a residential area immersed in greenery. Mondello's golden age was at the turn of the 19th century, when a kind of garden-city was founded and well-to-do Palermitans had lovely Art Nouveau villas built there. The Kursaal bathhouse, built on piles in the sea a few yards from the beach, also dates from this period. Designed by Rudolph Stualket in the Art Nouveau style, it is decorated with mythological figures and sea monsters. Mondello is a popular town, perhaps even more on summer evenings, when the city dwellers come to escape from the heat and dine in one of the many fish and seafood restaurants lining the road in the old fishing quarter.

Parco della Favorita **❷**

Viale Ercole, Viale Diana.

THIS LARGE PUBLIC park, which is unfortunately in a state of neglect, extends for almost 3 km (2 miles) behind Monte Pellegrino. It was originally a hunting reserve, but King Ferdinand I (see p27) turned it into a garden in 1799, when he fled to Palermo with his retinue after being forced into exile from Naples by Napoleon's troops. The park has two large roads. Viale Diana, which goes to Mondello, is intersected by Viale d'Ercole, at the end of which is a marble fountain with a statue of Hercules, a copy of the famous *Farnese Hercules* that the king had wanted for himself in his court at Naples.

Most of the park is occupied by sports facilities (tennis courts, pools, stadium and racetrack). On the edge of the park there are many villas built in the 18th century as summer residences for the Sicilian nobility. The most interesting are the Villa Sofia, now a hospital; Villa Castelnuovo, an agricultural institute; Villa Niscemi, mentioned in di Lampedusa's novel *The Leopard (see p21)*, now the venue for cultural activities.

Palazzina Cinese **❸**

Via Duca degli Abruzzi. **☎** 091-740 48 85. **◯** for restoration.

The extravagant façade of the Palazzina Cinese

A T THE EDGE of the Parco della Favorita is the "little Chinese palace", the summer residence of Ferdinand I and his wife Maria Carolina during their period of exile in Sicily.

SANCTUARY OF SANTA ROSALIA ON MONTE PELLEGRINO

Period print of Santa Rosalia's float

On Monte Pellegrino, which dominates the city, is the Sanctuary dedicated to Santa Rosalia, the patron saint of Palermo. The daughter of the Duke of Sinibaldo, Rosalia decided to lead the life of a hermit in a cave. Five centuries after her death in 1166, the discovery of her remains coincided exactly with the end of the plague that had struck the city. Since then the saint has been venerated twice a year: on 11–15 July a triumphal float with her remains is taken in a procession through the city, and on 4 September the same procession goes to the Sanctuary. This was built in 1625; it consists of a convent and the saint's cave, filled with ex-votos.

It was designed by Venanzio Marvuglia in 1799 (it seems that the king himself had a hand in the design) and entertained such illustrious guests as Horatio Nelson and his wife, Lady Hamilton.

The Palazzina Cinese was the first example of eclectic architecture in Palermo, a combination of Chinese decorative motifs and Gothic, Egyptian and Arab elements. Overall it is an extravagant work, exemplified by details such as the repetition of bells in the shape of a pagoda on the fence, the cornices and the roof. The interior is equally flamboyant: Neo-Classical stuccoes and paintings are combined with 18th-century chinoiserie, scenes of Chinese life and Pompeiian painting.

Aerial view of the Neo-Classical Teatro Politeama

Museo Etnografico Pitrè ❹

Via Duca degli Abruzzi.
📞 091-740 48 93. ⭕ 9am–1pm.
⬤ Fri. 🖼

THE ETHNOGRAPHIC Museum, next to the Palazzina Cinese, has a collection of about 4,000 exhibits, documenting Sicilian life, traditions and folk art. The first rooms feature local embroidery and weaving and are followed by sections on traditional costumes and rugs. A great many display cases contain ceramics and glassware, as well as a fine collection of oil lamps. A further section displays traditional Sicilian carts, late 19th-century glass painting, and carts and floats dedicated to Santa Rosalia. The Sala del Teatrino dell' Opera dei Pupi has on display a number of rod puppets, which are traditional characters in Sicilian puppet opera, as well as playbills decorated with scenes taken from the puppeteers' works. The Sala dei Presepi features more than 300 nativity scenes, some by the 18th-century artist Giocanni Matera.

Teatro Politeama ❺

Piazza Ruggero VII.
📞 091-605 32 49 / 605 33 15.

THIS HISTORIC theatre is in the heart of modern-day Palermo, at the corner of Via Ruggero VII and tree-lined Viale della Libertà, the city's "outdoor living room". The Neo-Classical building was designed in 1867–74 by Giuseppe Damiani Almeyda. The façade is a triumphal arch whose attic level is decorated with sculpture crowned by a chariot. For years, until the re-opening of the Teatro Massimo, the Politeama was the centre of Palermo's cultural life, playing host to the opera and theatre seasons.

Galleria d'Arte Moderna ❻

Via Filippo Turati 10. 📞 091-588 951. ⭕ 9am–1pm Tue, Thu–Sun; 9am–1pm, 3–5:30pm Wed. ⬤ Mon. 🖼

THE GALLERY of Modern Art has been on the top floor of the Teatro Politeama since 1910. It contains a collection of works of art by 19th- and 20th-century sculptors and painters, the majority from Southern Italy. The best known are Renato Guttuso, Felice Casorati, Carlo Carrà, Fausto Pirandello, Domenico Purificato and Emilio Greco.

Entrance to the Museo Pitré, devoted to Sicilian folk art and customs

Cripta dei Cappuccini ❼

Via Cappuccini. ☎ 091-212 117.
◻ 9am–noon, 3–5pm.

THE CATACOMBS of the Convento dei Cappuccini contain the bodies – some mummified, others in the form of skeletons – of the prelates and well-to-do citizens of Palermo. They are divided according to sex, profession and social standing, wearing their best clothes, some of which are moth-eaten. Visitors can see the cells where the corpses were put to dry. **Embalmed body in the crypt**

At the end of the stairway is the body of the first friar to be "buried" there, Fra' Silvestro da Gubbio, who died in 1599. In 1881, interment in the catacombs ceased, but on display in the Cappella dell'Addolorata is the body of a little girl who died in 1920 and was so skilfully embalmed that she seems to be sleeping. In the cemetery behind the catacombs is the tomb of Giuseppe di Lampedusa.

Castello della Zisa ❽

Piazza Guglielmo il Buono.
☎ 091-652 02 69. ◻ 9am–1pm,
3–7pm Mon–Sat, 9am–noon Sun.

THIS REMARKABLE PALACE, built in 1165–67, once over-looked a pond and was surrounded by a large park with many streams and fish ponds. Sadly, the Zisa Castle now stands in the middle of an ugly fringe area of Palermo. After years of complete neglect, the castle has now been restored and once again merits the name given to it by the Arabs – *aziz*, or splendid. The handsome exterior gives the impression of a rectangular fortress; the blind arcades, which once enclosed small double lancet windows, lend it elegance. Two square towers stand on the short sides of the castle.

On the ground floor is the Sala della Fontana (Fountain Hall), one of the rooms with a cross plan and exedrae on three sides. The cross vault above is connected to the side recesses by means of a series of *muqarnas* (small stalactite vaults typical of Arab architecture). Along the walls is a fine mosaic frieze. Water gushing from the fountain runs along a gutter from the wall to the pavement and then pours into two square fish ponds. The air vents channelled the warm air towards the Sala della Fontana, where it then became cooler. On the second floor of the palace is a fine collection of Arab art.

La Cuba ❾

Corso Calatafimi 100.
☎ 091-590 299. ◻ 9am–1pm,
3–4:30pm daily.

WILLIAM II ORDERED this magnificent Fatimite-style Norman palace to be built in 1180. It too stood in a large park, the Genoardo, surrounded by an artificial pond, and served as a pavilion in which to spend the hot afternoons. This palace was so famous that Boccaccio used it as the setting for one of the tales in the *Decameron* (Day 5, no 6).

The rectangular construction acquires rhythm and movement from the pointed blind arcading. The interior ran around an atrium that may have been open to the air. The recesses under the small towers originally would have housed fountains.

Villa Giulia ❿

Via Abramo Lincoln.

DESPITE ITS NAME, the Villa Giulia is not a house but an impressive Italianate garden designed in 1778 outside the city walls by Nicolò Palma and then enlarged in 1866. It was named after Giulia Avalos Guevara, wife of the viceroy, and was the city's first public park. Its square plan is divided by roads decorated with statues, such as the marble image of the "Genius of Palermo" and the statues representing *Glory Vanquishing Envy* and *Abundance Driving Out Famine.* The roads converge centrally in an area with four Pompeiian-style niches by Giuseppe Damiani Almeyda decorated with frescoes in great need of restoration.

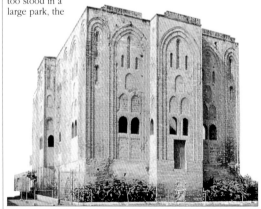

The Fatimite architecture of La Cuba, so renowned that Boccaccio used it as the setting for one of the tales in the *Decameron*

San Giovanni dei Lebbrosi, built in the Arab-Norman style

Orto Botanico ⓫

Via Abramo Lincoln 2B.
☏ 091-617 32 11. ☐ 9am–6pm Mon–Fri, 9am–1pm Sat, Sun.

THE BOTANICAL GARDEN lies next to the Villa Giulia. It was laid out in 1785 and has attained international fame thanks to the wealth and variety of its plant species: palm trees, bamboo, dracaenas, various cacti, euphorbias, spiny kapok trees with bottle-shaped trunks, pineapples and gigantic tropical plants. One of the marvels is a 150-year-old *Ficus magnolioides* fig tree with aerial roots. The Neo-Classical *Gymnasium* (now a museum), library and herbaria are by the entrance, a pond with waterlilies and papyrus is in the centre, and glasshouses line both sides.

Santo Spirito ⓬

Via Santo Spirito, Cimitero di Sant'Orsola. ☏ 091-422 691. ☐ 8am–2pm daily.

INSIDE THE Sant'Orsola Cemetery, this Norman church was founded by Archbishop Gualtiero Offamilio in 1178. It is also known as the "Chiesa dei Vespri" because, on 31 March 1282, at the hour of Vespers, a Sicilian uprising against the Angevin rulers *(see p31)* began right in front of the church. Simple and elegant, like all Norman churches, Santo Spirito has black volcanic stone inlay on its right side and on the apse. The two-aisle nave with three apses is bare but full of atmosphere. The wooden ceiling has floral ornamentation and there is a fine wooden crucifix over the high altar.

San Giovanni dei Lebbrosi ⓭

Via Cappello 38. ☏ 091-475 024.
☐ 4:15–6:45pm Mon–Sat, 7:30am–noon Sun.

ONE OF THE OLDEST Norman churches in Sicily lies in the middle of a luxuriant garden of palms. San Giovanni dei Lebbrosi was founded in 1071 by Roger I and, in 1119, a lepers' hospital was built next to it, hence its name. It was most probably constructed by Arab craftsmen and workers, as can be seen in the pointed arches crowned by arched lintels (also visible in San Giovanni degli Eremiti, *see pp62–3;* and San Cataldo, *see p53*). The façade has a small porch with a bell tower above. Inside the church there are three apses and a ceiling with trusses. Digs to the right of the church have unearthed remains of the Saracen Yahia fortress, which once defended southeastern Palermo.

Ponte dell'Ammiraglio ⓮

Via dei Mille.

THE ADMIRAL'S BRIDGE used to span the Oreto river before the latter was diverted. It is made of large cambered blocks of limestone resting on twelve pointed arches, five of them no more than small openings in the imposts. This beautiful and amazingly well-preserved bridge was built in 1113 by George of Antioch, Roger II's High Admiral (the *ammiraglio* of the name), but is now a rather incongruous sight, isolated without a river.

The impressive pointed arches of the 12th-century Ponte dell'Ammiraglio

Monreale Cathedral ⑮

Capital in the cloister

DOMINATING THE Conca d'Oro, the Cathedral of Monreale is the pinnacle of achievement of Arab-Norman art. It was founded in 1172 by William II and a Benedictine monastery was built next to it. The cathedral is famous for its remarkable interior with the magnificent gold mosaics representing episodes from the Old Testament. The cloister *(see p68)* has pointed Arab arches with geometric motifs, and scenes from the Bible are sculpted on the capitals of the 228 white marble twin columns.

★ Christ Pantocrator
The church, with a Latin cross plan, is dominated by the 12th–13th century mosaic of Christ in the middle apse.

Roman columns separate the sections of the nave

Cappella di San Placido

Gilded wood ceiling

Exterior of the apse
With its interlaced marble and tufa arches and multicoloured motifs, the exterior of the apse is the apogee of Norman decoration.

Entrance to the Cappella del Crocifisso and the Treasury

Choir pavement

The royal tomb of William II, sculpted in white marble, is next to the tomb of William I in a corner of the transept.

The bronze door by Barisano da Trani (1179), on the northern side, is under the porch designed by Gian Domenico and Fazio Gagini (1547–69).

★ The Mosaic Cycle
The stupendous 12th–13th-century mosaics occupy the entire nave and the aisles, the choir and the transepts. They illustrate scenes from the New and Old Testament.

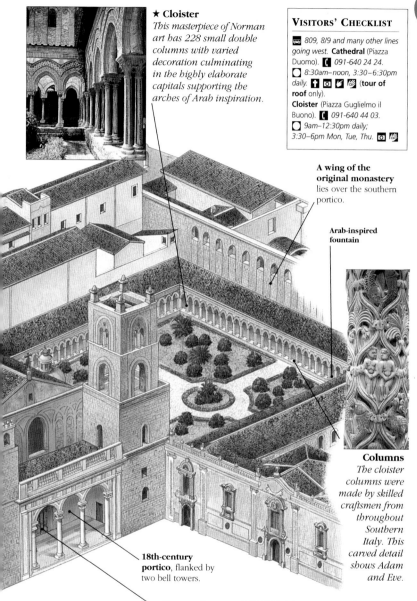

★ Cloister
This masterpiece of Norman art has 228 small double columns with varied decoration culminating in the highly elaborate capitals supporting the arches of Arab inspiration.

VISITORS' CHECKLIST

🚌 809, 8/9 and many other lines going west. **Cathedral** (Piazza Duomo). 📞 091-640 24 24. ⏰ 8:30am–noon, 3:30–6:30pm daily. 🚻 📷 ♿ (**tour of roof** only).
Cloister (Piazza Guglielmo il Buono). 📞 091-640 44 03. ⏰ 9am–12:30pm daily; 3:30–6pm Mon, Tue, Thu. 📷 ♿

A wing of the original monastery lies over the southern portico.

Arab-inspired fountain

Columns
The cloister columns were made by skilled craftsmen from throughout Southern Italy. This carved detail shows Adam and Eve.

18th-century portico, flanked by two bell towers.

Bronze door on the portal
This lovely door by Bonanno da Pisa (1185) has 42 elaborately framed Biblical scenes and other images. The lion and griffon were Norman symbols.

STAR FEATURES

★ **Cloister**

★ **The Mosaic Cycle**

★ **Christ Pantocrator**

SICILY
AREA BY AREA

Sicily at a Glance

THERE ARE FEW PLACES in the Mediterranean that can equal Sicily's striking landscapes and colourful history. There are noticeable differences between the eastern part of the island, culturally of Greek origin, and the Phoenician and Arab western side. However, Sicily is not simply an east and a west side – every village and town has its own unique story. Within a few kilometres of each other you may find splendid luxuriant coastline and arid, sun-parched hills, just as you can pick out different layers of civilization side by side or overlapping one another. It is not that unusual to see Greek, Arab, Norman and Baroque influences in the same site, sometimes even in the same building.

The Chiesa Matrice in Erice
(see pp96–7), *built in the 14th century, is a typical example of Norman religious architecture.*

Egadi Islands

The Sciacca thermae *(see pp114–5) date back to the distant past. The oldest bathhouse in Sicily, it is said to be the work of the mythical architect Daedalus.*

NORTHWESTERN SICILY
(see pp80–105)

SOUTHWESTERN SICILY
(see pp106–127)

Pelagic Islands

The Castello di Lombardia at Enna *(see p123) is one of the most important medieval fortifications in Sicily.*

◁ **Classical Greek theatre at Taormina, the second-largest of its kind in Sicily**

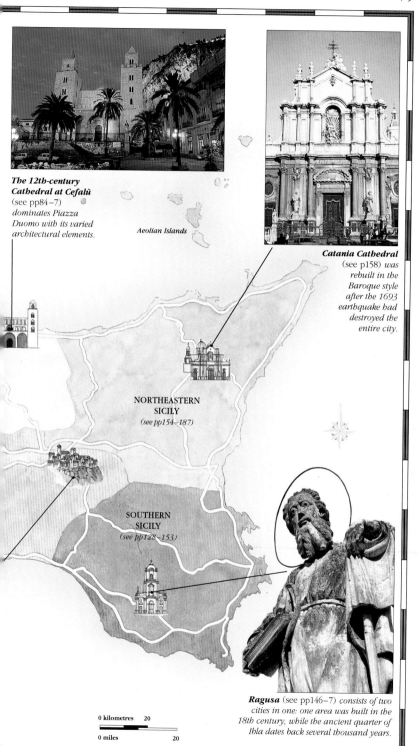

The 12th-century Cathedral at Cefalù (see pp84–7) *dominates Piazza Duomo with its varied architectural elements.*

Aeolian Islands

Catania Cathedral (see p158) *was rebuilt in the Baroque style after the 1693 earthquake had destroyed the entire city.*

NORTHEASTERN SICILY
(see pp154–187)

SOUTHERN SICILY
(see pp128–153)

Ragusa (see pp146–7) *consists of two cities in one: one area was built in the 18th century, while the ancient quarter of Ibla dates back several thousand years.*

0 kilometres   20

0 miles   20

NORTHWESTERN SICILY

O VER THE CENTURIES, *this area of Sicily has been particularly exposed to influences from different colonizing civilizations. The Phoenicians settled in Mozia and founded harbour towns at Palermo and Solunto. They were followed by the Greeks and then the Arabs, who began their conquest of the island at Marsala.*

These cultures are still very much alive in the names of the towns and sights, in the architecture and in the layout of the towns from Marsala to Mazara del Vallo. But, unfortunately, northwestern Sicily is also one of the areas most affected by the scourges of uncontrolled property development and lack of care for the environment. Examples of this are the huge area of unattractive houses between Palermo and Castellammare, which have disfigured what was one of the most fascinating coastlines in Sicily, and the squalidly reconstructed inhabited areas in the Valle del Belice, destroyed by the 1968 earthquake. They look forlorn and are not at all suited to their setting.

However, there are other towns pursuing a policy of preserving and reassessing their history. Erice is one of these; its medieval architecture and town plan have been preserved, and many of the churches have been converted into art and culture centres, instead of being left in a state of neglect. The same holds true for Cefalù, Nicosia, Sperlinga and the two Petralias. There is also a good deal of unspoiled scenery besides the nature reserves. The areas around Trapani and Belice are fascinating, as are the rugged valleys in the interior, characterized by villages perched on the top of steep cliffs with breathtaking views. Other beautiful sights include the Egadi Islands and Ustica.

The Palazzina Pepoli at Erice, converted into a villa in the 19th century

◁ **Typical Sicilian scenery: in the background is the Monte Cofano promontory near San Vito Lo Capo**

Exploring Northwestern Sicily

W̲ITH THE MAGNIFICENT ruins of Segesta, Selinunte, Solunto and Mozia, this area is full of archaeological fascination. The splendid medieval towns of Cefalù and Erice are also worth a visit in themselves. In the interior there are villages where time seems to have stood still, especially in the Madonie mountains. For those who prefer natural history, there are the crystal-clear waters of Ustica and the Egadi Islands, the Riserva Naturale Marina and the Riserva Naturale dello Zingaro between Scopello and San Vito Lo Capo.

㉗ USTICA

0 kilometres   2

0 miles   1

A windmill and outbuilding in the salt marshes near Trapani

EGADI ISLANDS ㉖

㉕ RISERVA DELLO ZINGARO

CASTELLAMMARE DEL GOLFO ⑭   SS187

TRAPANI ⑳

ALCAMO ⑬

A29 dir

⑯

⑲ ERICE   **SEGESTA**

MOZIA ㉒

SS115

⑱ SALEMI   A29

MARSALA ㉑   SS188   **㉗ GIBELLINA**

MAZARA DEL VALLO   **㉔ CASTELVETRANO**

㉕

㉓ SELINUNTE

MENFI   SS115

Ag

One of the statues on Caccamo Cathedral

KEY

▬▬ Motorway

▬▬ Major road

▭▭ Minor road

━━ River

🔆 Viewpoint

SEE ALSO

• *Where to Stay* pp195–6

• *Where to Eat* pp205–206

SIGHTS AT A GLANCE

GETTING AROUND

Northwestern Sicily has a very good road network. Toll-free *autostrada* (motorway) A29 links Palermo with Mazara del Vallo, while a connecting road goes to Trapani. Travelling eastwards, A29 ends at Cefalù and a toll is charged. The main roads along the coast and in the Valle del Belice are good, while those leading to the villages at the foot of the mountains are winding and slow and, in the winter, may be covered with snow or ice. There are frequent trains between Messina and Palermo, less frequently to Trapani, Marsala and Mazara. The bus network connects the main towns and smaller and more remote villages.

PALERMO

SOLUNTO **11**

BAGHERIA

TERMINI IMERESE

CEFALÙ **1**

SANTO STEFANO DI CAMASTRA **3**

CASTEL DI TUSA **2**

Messina

A19

A20

SS186

SS121

PIANA DEGLI ALBANESI **12**

CACCAMO **10**

PETRALIA SOPRANA **8**

PETRALIA SOTTANA **7**

GANGI **6**

POLIZZI GENEROSA **9**

SPERLINGA **5**

NICOSIA **4**

SS189

SS121

A19

Enna

Caltanissetta

0 kilometres 20

0 miles 10

The theatre at Segesta, on the top of Monte Barbaro, set in an extraordinary landscape. As with all Greek theatres, the scenery formed part of the stage set

Street-by-Street: Cefalù ❶

Founded on a steep promontory half way between Palermo and Capo d'Orlando, Cefalù has retained its medieval appearance around the Norman cathedral, which was built by Roger II in the 12th century. The narrow streets of the city centre are lined with buildings featuring elaborate architectural decoration. There are also numerous churches, reflecting the town's status as a leading bishopric. The fishermen's quarter, with its old houses clustered along the seafront, is very appealing, as is the long beach with fine sand, considered to be one of the most beautiful stretches on the northern coast.

Tonnaio Vase,
Museo
Mandralisca

★ Cathedral
Oversized compared with the rest of the city, this masterpiece of Norman art contains magnificent mosaics in the interior.

Seventeenth-century fortifications

VIA PORPORA

VIA CANDELORO

PIAZZA DUOMO

CORSO

PIAZZA CRISPI

VIA ORTOLANO

DI BORDONAR

The streets of Cefalù
The layout of the city is basically a grid plan crossed horizontally by Corso Ruggero and Via Vittorio Emanuele and intersected by alleys of medieval origin.

Capo Marchiafava rampart, 16th–17th centuries

Porta Marina
This striking city gate overlooking the sea is a Gothic arch. It is the only one remaining of the four that originally pierced the city wall, affording access to Cefalù.

KEY

▬ ▬ ▬ ▬ ▬ Suggested route

Chiesa del Purgatorio

Most of Cefalù's many churches date from the 17th century. The Chiesa del Purgatorio (1668), on Corso Ruggero, has a richly decorated Baroque doorway at the top of a double stairway.

VISITORS' CHECKLIST

Road Map D2. 🚶 *13,961.*
✈ *Falcone e Borsellino.*
🚆 *Messina–Palermo line (0921-942 11 69).* 🛈 *Corso Ruggero 77 (0921-421 050).*
🚌 *Sat.* 🎭 *Processione del Venerdì Santo (Good Friday Procession); Cefalù Incontri (Jul, Aug, Sep); Festa di San Salvatore (4–6 Aug); Le Città del Cinema (Oct); Vecchia Strina (31 Dec).*

★ Museo Mandralisca

This museum was founded by Enrico Piraino, the Baron of Mandralisca, and has a wide range of precious works of art, such as this 4th-century BC tragic mask.

0 metres 40

0 yards 40

Medieval fountain

This recently restored medieval stone fountain was used for washing clothes until a few years ago.

STAR SIGHTS

★ Cathedral

★ Museo Mandralisca

Exploring Cefalù

C EFALÙ IS MENTIONED for the first time in 396 BC in an account by Diodorus Siculus, but the city is more famous for its medieval monuments. Piazza Garibaldi (where you have to leave the car) is a good starting point for a walk around the town. Follow Corso Ruggero to reach the open space of Piazza Duomo, home to one of Sicily's most splendid cathedrals.

The medieval façade of the Cathedral of Cefalù

🔲 Piazza Duomo
This lively square, dominated by the sheer mass of the **Cathedral** and the steep **Rocca**, is the heart of Cefalù. It is surrounded by buildings constructed in different styles. On the southern side are the **Oratorio del Santissimo Sacramento**; **Palazzo Maria**, which was most probably Roger II's *Domus Regiae (see p27)*, decorated with an ogee portal and a Gothic window; and **Palazzo Piraino**, with its late 16th-century ashlar door. To the north, the square is bordered by the **Seminario**

and the **Palazzo Vescovile**, while to the west is the **Palazzo del Municipio** (Town Hall), which incorporates the former **Santa Caterina monastery**.

🏛 Cathedral
Piazza Duomo. 📞 0921-922 021. ⏰ 7am–noon, 3:30–6:15pm; summer: 7am–noon, 1:30–7pm. 🕐 7am, 9:30am, 11:30am, 6pm hols.
Cefalù Cathedral is one of Sicily's major Norman monuments. Building began in 1131 under Roger II. When he died work continued in fits and starts. The façade has two rows of blind arcades set over the three-arch outer narthex and is flanked by two masssive bell towers with single and double lancet windows. On the right-hand side you can see the interlaced arch motifs of the three side apses. The nave is divided by arches supported by marble columns. The wooden ceiling, with its painted beams, bears an obvious Islamic influence, while the presbytery is

Statue of a bishop, Cefalù Cathedral

covered with splendid mosaics. On high in the apse is the figure of Christ Pantocrator with the Virgin Mary, Archangels and the apostles; on the choir walls are saints and prophets, while cherubs and seraphim decorate the vault. A door on the northern aisle leads to the lovely cloister, long closed for restoration.

🔲 Corso Ruggero
This avenue goes all the way across the old town, starting from **Piazza Garibaldi**, where the **Porta di Terra** city gate once stood. A few steps on your left is **Palazzo Osterio Magno**, built in the 13th and 14th centuries, according to legend, as the residence of the Ventimiglia family. Almost opposite, a modern building houses the remains of the ancient Roman road. Visits can be made from 9am to 4:30pm. Continuing to the right, you will come to **Piazzetta Spinola**, with **Santo Stefano** (or Delle Anime Purganti), the Baroque façade of which is complemented by an elegant double staircase.

🏛 Museo Mandralisca
Via Mandralisca 13. 📞 0921-421 547. ⏰ summer: 9am–midnight daily; winter: 9am–12:30pm, 3:30–6pm daily. 🖼
This museum was founded by Enrico Piraino, the Baron of Mandralisca, in the 19th century and includes fine archaeological, shell and coin collections. It also houses an art gallery and a library with over 9,000 historic and scientific works, including incunabulae, 16th-century books and nautical charts.
Among the most important paintings are the *Portrait of a Man* by Antonello da Messina, *View of Cefalù* by Francesco Bevilacqua, *Christ on Judgment Day* by Johannes De Matta (mid-1500s), and a

Medieval fishermen's dwellings lining the seafront

Antonello da Messina, *Portrait of a Man* (1465)

series of icons on the second floor. Archaeological jewels include a late Hellenistic mosaic and a 4th-century BC krater with a figure of a tuna fish cutter. A curiosity exhibit is the collection of patience (solitaire) playing cards made out of precious materials.

⚏ Via Vittorio Emanuele

This street runs along the seafront, separated by a row of medieval houses facing the bay. Under one of these is the famous **Lavatoio**, the stone fountain known as *U' Ciuni*, or river, which was mentioned by the writer Boccaccio and was used for washing clothes until a few years ago. A stairway leads to the basin where water gushes from holes on three walls. The lovely **Porta Marina** is the only remaining city gate

of the four that once afforded access to the town. It leads to the colourful fishermen's quarter, where scenes were shot for the film *Cinema Paradiso (see p116)*.

⚏ La Rocca

From Piazza Garibaldi a path halfway up the hill offers a fine view of the old town and the sea and leads to the ruins of the fortifications (most probably Byzantine) and the prehistoric sanctuary known as the **Tempio di Diana**, a megalithic construction with a portal dating from the 9th century BC. On the top of the Rocca are the ruins of a 12th–13th-century castle.

ENVIRONS: Lying on the slopes of Pizzo Sant'Angelo is the **Santuario di Gibilmanna**, the sanctuary built in the 17th and 18th centuries and the most popular pilgrimage site in Sicily. The former convent stables house the **Museo dell'- Ordine**, the museum of the Capuchin friars with paintings, sculpture and vestments. The most interesting pieces are crêche figures, enamelled reliquaries, a 16th-century alabaster rosary, and a white marble Pietà by the local sculptor Jacopo Lo Duca, a pupil of Michelangelo.

A 16th-century statuette, Santuario di Gibilmanna

Castel di Tusa ➋

Road map D2. 🏠 *3,595*. 🚉 *0921-334 325*. 🛈 *0921-334 332*.

T HIS BEAUTIFUL swimming resort is dominated by the ruins of a 14th-century castle. The characteristic alleys with old stone houses and villas converge in the central square, which is paved with stone. To get to the little port you must go under the railway arches. The banks of the nearby Tusa River have been turned into an outdoor gallery with works by contemporary artists, including the sculptor Pietro Consagra. Only a few miles away are the **Ruins of Halaesa**.

⋔ Ruins of Halaesa

3 km (2 miles) on the road to Tusa. ☎ *0921-334 531*. ◷ *9am–1 hr before sunset*.

On a hill covered with olive trees and asphodels are the ruins of the city of Halaesa, a Greek colony founded in 403 BC, which prospered until it was sacked by the Roman praetor Verres. Excavations have started and you can see the Agora, remains of cyclopean walls and a Hellenistic temple. Near the archaeological site is the **Monastery of Santa Maria della Palate**.

Ruins of the Hellenistic temple of Halaesa, amid olive trees and asphodels

Santo Stefano di Camastra ❸

Road map D2. 🏛 5,164.
🚇 Messina–Palermo.
ℹ 0921-331 110 or 331 554.
🎭 Easter Week.

THIS TOWN FACING the Tyrrhenian Sea is one of the leading Sicilian centres for the production of ceramics. All the local craftsmen have their wares on display: vases, jugs, cornices and tiles with period designs such as those used in the **Villa Comunale**. In the centre of town stands the **Chiesa Madre**, or San Nicolò, with a Renaissance doorway and late 18th-century stucco decoration in the interior.

Nicosia ❹

Road map D3. 🏛 15,041.
🚌 129 km (80 miles) from Catania, 44 km (27 miles) from Enna. ℹ Piazza Garibaldi (0935-638 139, x239. 🎭 Easter Week, O' Scontro (Easter), Macaroni Festival (May), Palio (2nd week Aug), Nicosia da Vivere Festival (Jul–Sep).

SPRAWLED OVER four hills, Nicosia is dominated by the ruins of an Arab-Norman castle. Originally a Byzantine settlement, the town was re-populated in the Norman era by Lombard and Piedmontese colonists, who have left traces of their local dialects. The many churches and patrician mansions are a sign of the town's former splendour. Narrow streets and alleys run up the hills, often providing spectacular panoramic views.

The Villa Comunale, Santo Stefano di Camastra, with a tiled altar

Piazza Garibaldi is the heart of Nicosia, with the Gothic **San Nicolò Cathedral** and old buildings, including the current Town Hall. The **Salita Salomone** steps lead to Romanesque **San Salvatore**. There is a fine view of the old town from the porch. The church has a series of sundials which, according to tradition, were once used as the town's "clocks". **Via Salomone**, lined with aristocratic palazzi, leads up to **Santa Maria Maggiore**, just under the castle rock. The doorway is decorated with pagan statues of Jove, Venus and Ceres. In the interior is Charles V's throne, in memory of the emperor's visit here in 1535,

Detail of the ceiling of the Nicosia Cathedral

a gilded marble altarpiece by Antonello Gagini and a crucifix known as *Father of Mercy*. From here you can go up to the **Castle**, with its Norman drawbridge and the remains of the keep. At the foot of the castle is the Norman **Basilica of San Michele**, with its austere apses and majestic 15th-century bell towers.

🏛 Cathedral
Piazza Garibaldi. *Closed for restoration.*
The Cathedral is dedicated to the town's patron saint, San Nicolò. It was founded in the 14th century and partially rebuilt in the 19th century. What remains of the original structure are the 14th-century façade with porticoes running along the left-hand side and the bell tower with three sections, each distinguished by a different style, from Arab to Romanesque. The rebuilt interior has a crucifix attributed to Fra Umile de Petralia and a font by Antonello Gagini, while the choir was carved out of solid walnut by local artists. The vault, frescoed in the 19th century, conceals a fine Norman truss ceiling decorated in brilliant colours with scenes from the lives of the saints, hunting scenes, images of wild animals, a number of human heads, stylized flowers and geometric decorative motifs.

Nicosia, perched on a hill and once crucial to the area's defensive network

Panoramic view from the Norman castle at Sperlinga (c.1100)

Sperlinga **⑤**

Road map D3. 🏠 *1,038.*
🚌 *35 km (22 miles) from Enna.*
ℹ️ *0935-643 025 or 643 177.*
🎭 *Sagra del Tortone (16 Aug).*

SPERLINGA SEEMS to have been pushed against a spectacular rock face, its parallel streets on different levels connected by steps. In the eastern section, right up against the sandstone cliff, numerous troglodytic cave dwellings have been carved out. Until recently many of them were inhabited.

🏠 Norman Castle
Via Castello. 📞 *0935-643 198.*
🕐 *winter: 10am–1pm, 2:30–5:30pm (hols 9am–1pm); summer: 9am–1pm, 4–8pm.* 🎭 🚻
Sperlinga's castle was built by the Normans under Roger I around the year 1100 on the top of an impregnable rock face. It was later reinforced by Frederick II. It is linked with the Sicilian Vespers revolt (*see pp30–31*), when it was the last refuge of the Angevin rulers, who managed to resist attacks for a year. The events are commemorated by an inscription carved in the vestibule: *Quod Siculis placuit sola Sperlinga negavit* ("Sperlinga alone denied the Sicilians what they desired").

The numerous chambers in the castle make it a veritable stone labyrinth. The entrance hall, the Grotta delle Guardie (Guards' Grotto), is now an ethnographic museum with examples of cave dwellings and everyday work tools and objects. After passing through the second gate and crossing the Sala Riunioni, or assembly hall, you will find the stables, the prisons and the foundry (hewn entirely out of the rock). In the middle of the cliff is **San Domenico di Siria**, the nave of which has three side niches; next to this are the rooms used as a kitchen with the remains of two wood-burning ovens. Steep stairs lead to the top of the rock with magnificent views.

Gangi **⑥**

Road map D3. 🏠 *8,044.*
🚌 *51 km (32 miles) from Cefalù.*
🎭 *Sagra della Spiga (Aug).*

THE TOWN OF Gangi lies on the southwestern slope of Monte Marone, facing the Nebrodi and Madonie Mountains. The birthplace of painters Gaspare Vazano and Giuseppe Salerno has retained its medieval character, with winding streets and steps connecting the different levels. The towering **Chiesa Madre** has a 14th-century bell tower and a lovely *Last Judgment* by Salerno, inspired by Michelangelo's famous painting in the Sistine Chapel.

Petralia Sottana **⑦**

Road map D3. 🏠 *3,726.* 🚌
98 km (61 miles) from Palermo.
ℹ️ *0921-641 032.* 🎭 *Ballo della Cordella dance (1st Sun after 15 Aug).*

THIS VILLAGE is perched on a rock 1,000 m (3,300 ft) up, overlooking the Imera valley, and nestled at the foot of the tallest peaks in the Madonie mountains. Petralia Sottana is laid out around the **Via Agliata**, which ends in **Piazza Umberto I**, opposite the **Chiesa Madre**. The late Gothic church was partially rebuilt in the 1600s. Inside is a fine wooden triptych, *The Virgin Mary and Child between Saints Peter and Paul*. An arch connects the bell tower with the **Santissima Trinità**, which has a marble altarpiece by Domenico Gagini.

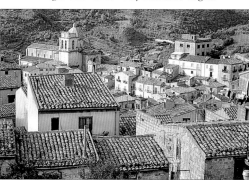

Petralia Sottana, in the middle of the verdant Valle dell'Imera

Petralia Soprana, the highest village in the Madonie mountains

Petralia Soprana 8

Road map D3. 🏘 *3,900.* 🚌 *104 km (65 miles) from Palermo.* ℹ *0921-649 491.*

THE HIGHEST VILLAGE in the Madonie mountains lies on a plateau 1,147 m (3,760 ft) above sea level, where the panoramic view ranges from the Nebrodi hills to the volcanic cone of Mount Etna. Petralia Soprana was an extremely important Greek and Phoenician city. Under Roman dominion ancient "Petra" was one of the largest wheat-producing *civitas* in the Empire. The city became *Batraliah* after the Arab conquest and a powerful defensive stronghold under the Normans. Later, the two Petralias (Soprana and Sottana) were taken over by noble families.

The village has preserved its medieval layout, with narrow paved streets, old stone houses, patrician residences and churches. The old **Chiesa Madre**, dedicated to Saints Peter and Paul and rebuilt in the 14th century, stands in an attractive square with a 17th-century double-column colonnade designed by the Serpotta brothers. In the interior is the first crucifix by Fra' Umile Pintorno (1580–1639), who also painted many other crucifixes throughout the island. **Santa Maria di Loreto** was built in the 18th century over the remains of a castle; it has a cross plan and the façade is flanked by two decorated bell towers.

Polizzi Generosa 9

Road map D3. 🏘 *4,637.* 🚌 *93 km (58 miles) from Palermo.* ℹ *0921-649 018.*

ON THE WESTERN slopes of the Madonie mountains, this village grew up around an ancient fortress rebuilt by the Normans. There are a great many churches, including the **Chiesa Madre**, with a fine 16th-century altarpiece, *Madonna and Child among Angels and Saints* by an unknown Flemish artist. A small museum illustrates the natural history of the Madonie mountains area.

ENVIRONS: From Polizzi, you can ascend to Piano Battaglia, part of the nature reserve, with footpaths in summer and ski runs in winter.

Caccamo 10

Road map C2. 🏘 *8,661.* 🚌 *48 km (30 miles) from Palermo.* ℹ *Corso Umberto 55 (091-810 32 40 or 810 31 11).* 🚆 Sat. 🌾 *Agricultural and gastronomic show (Dec–Jan), Investiture of the Chatelaine (Aug).*

CACCAMO lies under the castellated walls of its **Norman castle**, in a lovely setting of softly rolling hills only 10 km (6 miles) from the Palermo-Catania motorway. The town is laid out on different levels, with well maintained roads that open onto pretty squares. The most appealing of these is **Piazza Duomo**, with the **Chiesa Matrice** dedicated to San Giorgio, flanked by statues and two symmetrically arranged Baroque buildings: the **Oratorio della Compagnia del Sacramento** and the **Chiesa delle Anime Sante del Purgatorio**. The former was built by the Normans but was enlarged in the 17th century. Its richly decorated interior has a font by Gagini and his workshop. Not far away are the **Annunziata**, with twin bell towers, **San Marco** and **San Benedetto alla Badia**. The last is perhaps the loveliest of the three, with its Baroque stucco and majolica decoration, and a colourful floor depicting a ship sailing on the high seas, guarded by angels.

Coat of arms of Caccamo, founded in 1093

Interior of the impregnable Norman castle at Caccamo

*The **Gymnasium** at Solunto, with its Doric columns intact*

♣ Norman Castle

make appt with Signor La Rosa the day before your visit. 091-814 84 023.

This formidable Norman castle is truly impregnable. It was built on the top of a steep rock overlooking the valley and is protected by a series of walls. The first entranceway on the lower floor leads to a broad stairway flanked by castellated walls; this leads to the second entrance, where the guardhouse once stood. After crossing a drawbridge, you will find another door that leads to the inner courtyard. Through this you can reach the famous Sala della Congiura (Conspiracy Hall), so named because it was here in 1160 that the Norman barons hatched a plot against William I. The panoramic views from the large western terrace are breathtaking.

Solunto ⑪

Road map C2. Santa Flavia–Solunto–Porticello. 091-904 557. 9am–4:30pm, (summer: 9am–5pm). Mon.

THE RUINS of the city of Solunto lie on the slopes of Monte Catalfano in a stupendous site with a beautiful panoramic view of the sea. Solunto was one of the first Phoenician colonies in Sicily and was mentioned, together with Palermo and Mozia, by the Greek historian Thucydides. In 254 BC it was conquered by the Romans. By the 2nd century AD the city had been largely abandoned, and it was later almost destroyed by the Saracens. At the entrance there is a small exhibition (temporary, until the new museum is finished) with finds from the various digs, which began in 1826 and are still under way.

Solunto follows a traditional layout. The path leading to the site takes you to Via dell'Agorà, with a fired-brick pavement and gutters for drainage. This street makes a right angle with the side stairs, which mark off the blocks of buildings (insulae). Six Doric columns and part of the roof of one of these, the Gymnasium, are still standing. Other insulae have mosaic floors and plastered or even painted walls. At the eastern end is the Agora, with workshops, cisterns to collect rainwater and a theatre with the stage area facing towards the sea.

Panoramic view of Solunto

THE VILLAS IN BAGHERIA

In the 18th century Bagheria was the summer residence of the nobility of Palermo, who built luxurious villas surrounded by orange groves as retreats from the torrid heat of the capital. Prince Ettore Branciforti built the first, Villa Barbera, in 1657, followed by other aristocrats such as the Valguarnera and Gravina families. The most famous is Villa Palagonia, decorated with hundreds of statues of monsters and caricatures of mythological figures. Now in a state of utter neglect, the villa has retained only the Salone degli Specchi (Hall of Mirrors), where balls were held. The villas eventually proved to be too costly to maintain and were either abandoned or put to other uses. When the gardens were destroyed to make room for ugly (and illegal) housing units, the villas lost most of their fascination.

Façade of Villa Palagonia, the most famous villa in Bagheria

"Monster" at the Villa Palagonia

Typical Piana degli Albanesi costumes

Piana degli Albanesi

Road map B2. 6,114.
Comune di Piana degli Albanesi
(091-857 41 44). Santa Maria
Odigitria (Tue after Pentecost, 2 Sep).

DURING THE expansion of the Ottoman Empire in the Balkans, many groups of Albanians *(Albanesi)* fled to Italy. At the end of the 15th century, John II allowed an Albanian community to settle in this area, which originally took the name of Piana dei Greci, because the inhabitants belonged to the Greek Orthodox Church. The place was renamed Piana degli Albanesi in 1941. The town is famous for its colourful religious festivities, such as those during Epiphany and Easter. Try to catch the celebrations in honour of the patron saint Santa Maria Odigitria, which are followed by traditional folk festivities. **Piazza**

Vittorio Emanuele, in the heart of town, is home to the Municipio (Town Hall) and the Orthodox church of **Santa Maria Odigitria**, which has a beautiful iconostasis in the interior. Opposite the parish church is the oldest church in Piana degli Albanesi, **San Giorgio**, which was altered in the mid-1700s. Along the avenue named after the Albanian national hero Giorgio Kastriota Skanderbeg, is the cathedral, **San Demetrio**. As is customary in Orthodox churches, the apses are closed off by the iconostasis. On the vault is a fresco representing the Apostles, Christ and the four Orthodox patriarchs. Near the town is an artificial **lake** created by a dam built in the 1920s, containing 32 million cubic metres (1,129.6 million cu ft) of water.

Alcamo

Road map B2. 42,882.
Palermo–Trapani line.
Comune di Alcamo (0924-590 111).

DURING THE ARAB period the fortress of *Manzil Alqamah* was built as part of this area's defensive network. The town of Alcamo developed later, and between the 13th and 14th centuries centred around the Chiesa Madre and the castle. In recent decades, population

growth has led to the expansion of the town and the demolition of parts of the old city walls. In Piazza Ciullo is **Sant'Oliva**, built in 1723 over an earlier church, while the nearby **Chiesa del Rosario** boasts late 15th-century frescoes. Facing Piazza della Repubblica is **Santa Maria del Gesù**; with the so-called Greek Madonna altarpiece (1516), showing the Madonna with the Counts of Modica. But the most important church here is the **Chiesa Madre**, founded in 1332. Its Baroque façade, overlooking Piazza IV Novembre, has a 14th-century bell tower with double lancet windows and many paintings and sculptures can be seen in the chapels.

Castellammare del Golfo

Road map B2. 14,493.
Palermo–Trapani. 0924-590
111 or 30217.

THIS TOWN WAS the Greek port for Segesta and Erice, and then an Arab fortress. It became an important trading and tuna-fishing centre in the Middle Ages. In the heart of the town, on an isthmus, is the **Aragonese Castle**, and the old picturesque streets of the medieval quarter known as *castri di la terra*. On Via Garibaldi is the **Chiesa Madre**, frequently rebuilt in the 1700s and 1800s.

Castellammare del Golfo, on the Tyrrhenian Sea, a leading port town in the Arab-Norman period

Riserva dello Zingaro ⓯

Twenty kilometres (12 miles) from Erice, along the coast going towards Palermo, is the Riserva dello Zingaro, a nature reserve of about 1,600 ha (3,950 acres) sloping down to the sea. It is a paradise for birds, especially for raptors such as Bonelli's eagles, peregrine falcons and kites, and even, in recent years, golden eagles.

San Vito lo Capo ①
North of the reserve is this impressive promontory plunging into the sea.

SAN VITO LO CAPO ① MONTE ACCI
829 m, 2,720 ft

MONTE PASSO DEL LUPO
868 m, 2,847 ft

Contrada Acci

Contrada Uzzo •Ficarella

②

PIZZO AQUILA
759 m, 2,490 ft

Contrada Sugbero

MONTE SPEZIALE
913 m, 2,994 ft

③

Contrada Pianello PIZZO DEL CORVO
415 m, 1,360 ft
PIZZO PASSO DEL LUPO

Portella Mandra Nuova ⑥
A typical village 700 m (2,296 ft) above sea level.

610 m, 2,000 ft

④

Contrada Scardina

SCOPELLO

Grotta dell'Uzzo ②
Human skeletons over 12,000 years old have been found in this grotto.

Grotta del Sughero ③
Animals such as foxes, rabbits and porcupines live in these caves.

Contrada Capreria ④
Punta di Capreria, one of the loveliest parts of the reserve, lies in this area.

⑤

MONTE SCARDINA
680 m, 2,230 ft

Key

▬ Negotiable road

═ Path

☆ Viewpoint

Tips for Walkers

Road map C2.
Tour length: there are five marked footpaths. The shortest one is 6 km (4 miles) and goes from Scopello to Tonarella dell'-Uzzo, taking about 2 hours 20 minutes. The longest is 19 km (12 miles) and takes about 9 hours. The reserve can also be explored on horseback.

Baglio di Scopello ⑤
Scopello is a farming hamlet that grew up around an 18th-century fort.

0 kilometres   2

0 miles   1

Segesta ⑯

ACCORDING TO LEGEND, the ancient capital of the Elymians was founded on the rolling green hills of the Castellammare del Golfo area by exiles from Troy. Segesta was constantly at war with Selinunte and was frequently attacked. Yet the majestic Doric temple has miraculously survived sacking and the ravages of time, and stands in splendid and solemn isolation on the hill facing Monte Barbaro. The city of Segesta was built above the temple on the top of the mountain. Here lie the ruins of some buildings and the well-preserved 3rd-century BC theatre, where ancient Greek plays are performed every other summer.

Panorama
Ancient Segesta and the beautiful setting create an atmospheric scene.

The Temple
Built in the 5th century BC, the temple is still well preserved; 36 Doric columns support the pediments and entablatures.

Ruins of the city

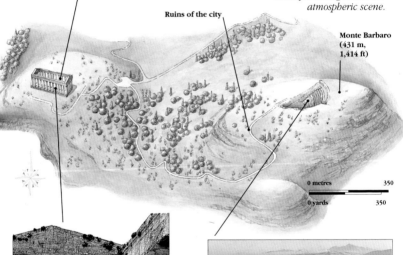

Monte Barbaro (431 m, 1,414 ft)

| 0 metres | 350 |
| 0 yards | 350 |

Interior of the Temple
The lack of architectural elements in the interior has led scholars to believe that the construction was interrupted by the war with Selinunte.

The Theatre
The Segesta theatre is a semicircle with a diameter of 63 m (207 ft) hewn out of the top of Monte Barbaro. A curious feature is that the stage area faces north, probably to allow a view of the hills and sea.

Gibellina

Road map B3. 🏛 *4,976.* 🚌 *89 km (55 miles) from Trapani.* ℹ️ *0924-67877 or 67428.* 🎭 *Oresteia (classical theatre, biennial, summer).*

I N 1968 A TERRIBLE earthquake destroyed all the towns in the Valle del Belice and the vicinity, including Gibellina. The new town was rebuilt, after years of bureaucratic delay, in the Salinella zone about 20 km (12 miles) from the original village. Thirty years after the event, the new Gibellina already seems old and rather sad. However, it is worth visiting because, thanks to the cooperation of contemporary architects and artists, the area has been enriched with many works of art, including a huge sculpture, *Stella* (Star) by Pietro Consagra, the city gate and symbol of Gibellina Nuova. Other interesting attractions are the **Torre Civica Carillon**, a tower in Piazza del Municipio, and the **Centro Culturale**, the cultural centre built over the remains of the 17th-century **Palazzo Di Lorenzo**.

The town of Salemi, dominated by its impressive medieval castle

Lastly, be sure to visit the **Museo Antropologico-Etnologico**, with everyday objects and tools illustrating local folk customs, and, above all, the **Museo Civico d'Arte Contemporanea**.

🏛 **Museo Civico d'Arte Contemporanea**
Via Segesta. ℹ️ *0924-67428.* ⏰ *9am–1pm, 4–7pm Tue–Sat; 10am–1pm Sun.*
This museum contains works by artists such as Fausto Pirandello, Renato Guttuso, Antonio Sanfilippo and Mario Schifano.

The Star of Gibellina, by Pietro Consagra

ENVIRONS: 18 km (11 miles) from the new town are the ruins of old Gibellina, which have been transformed by a disturbing and gigantic work of land art by Alberto Burri, who covered the ruins with a layer of white cement. The cracks cutting through this white expanse, known as *Burri's Crevice*, follow the course of the old streets, creating a labyrinth.

Salemi

Road map B3. 🏛 *12,230.* 🚌 *95 km (59 miles) from Palermo.* ℹ️ *Vigili urbani (0924-982 233).* 🛒 *Sat.* 🎉 *San Giuseppe (Mar).*

T HIS AGRICULTURAL town in the Valle del Delia dates from ancient times (it was probably the Halicyae mentioned by Diodorus Siculus). Despite the 1968 earthquake, the Arab town plan has remained, with a jumble of narrow streets at the foot of the three towers of the **Castle**. Here, on 14 May 1860, Garibaldi proclaimed himself ruler of Sicily in the name of King Vittorio Emanuele II *(see pp32–3)*. The castle was built in the 12th century by Frederick II and rebuilt in 1210.

In the old town, interesting sights are **Sant'Agostino** with its large cloister and the 17th-century **Collegio dei Gesuiti**, which houses the **Chiesa dei Gesuiti**, the **Oratorio del Ritiro** and the city museums, in particular the **Museo Civico d'Arte Sacra**.

🏛 **Museo Civico d'Arte Sacra**
Collegio dei Gesuiti. ℹ️ *0924-982 248.* ⏰ *8am–2pm, 4–6pm Mon–Fri; by appt Sun, hols.*
This museum of religious art has sculptures by Domenico Laurana and Antonello Gagini *(see p19)*, 17th-century paintings and wooden Baroque sculpture. The Risorgimento section features objects commemorating Garibaldi's feats.

The so-called *Burri's Crevice* covering part of the ruins of old Gibellina

Erice ⓳

Sign for an art gallery in Erice

THE SPLENDID TOWN of Erice, perched on top of Monte San Giuliano, has very ancient origins, as is shown by the cult of the goddess of fertility, Venus Erycina. Laid out on a triangular plan, the town has preserved its medieval character, with fine city walls, beautifully paved streets, stone houses with decorated doorways, small squares and open spaces with numerous churches – including the medieval Chiesa Matrice – many of which have recently become venues for scientific and cultural activities.

🛡 Cyclopean walls

These extend for 700 m (2,296 ft) on the northern side of the town, from Porta Spada to Porta Trapani.

The lower part of the wall, with its megalithic blocks of stone, dates back to the Phoenician period; the letters *beth*, *ain*, *phe* of the Phoenician alphabet are carved in it. The upper part and the gates were built by the Normans. The **Porta Spada** gate owes its name to the massacre of the local Angevin rulers during the Sicilian Vespers (*spada* means sword) (*see pp30–31*). Nearby are **Sant'Antonio Abate** and **Sant'Orsola**. The latter houses the 18th-century "Mysteries", sculptures borne in procession on Good Friday.

♟ Castello Pepoli e Venere

Via Conte Pepoli. 🄲 0923-860 042. 🄾 winter: 8:30am–4:30pm; summer: 8:30am–8:30pm (hols: 8:30am–1pm).

This Norman castle was built on an isolated rock over the ruins of the **Temple of Venus Erycina**. Entrance is gained via a tower, the only remaining original part of the castle, with Ghibelline castellation. It was used as a prison and watchtower. Above the entrance, with its pointed arch, is a plaque with the coat of arms of the Spanish Hapsburgs, surmounted by a 14th-century double lancet window. Inside are a sacred well and the ruins of the Temple of Venus Erycina, a Phoenician house and a Roman bath. The castle is the starting point of a system of fortifications including the **Torri del Balio**, formerly the headquarters of the Norman governor. Further down, on a ledge over the Pineta dei Runzi pine forest, is the **Torretta Pepoli** (*see p81*), built as a hunting lodge in 1872–80 and one of the symbols of Erice. In front of the castle are the 19th-century public gardens, **Giardini del Balio**, which link this zone with the eastern side of Erice.

The Norman castle, built on the site dedicated to Venus Erycina in ancient times

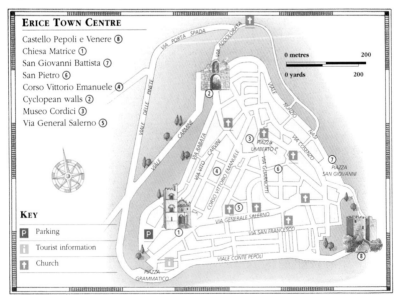

ERICE TOWN CENTRE

Castello Pepoli e Venere ⑧
Chiesa Matrice ①
San Giovanni Battista ⑦
San Pietro ⑥
Corso Vittorio Emanuele ④
Cyclopean walls ②
Museo Cordici ③
Via General Salerno ⑤

0 metres   200
0 yards   200

KEY

P   Parking

ℹ   Tourist information

✝   Church

The austere exterior of the Chiesa Matrice in Erice

Chiesa Matrice
Piazza Matrice. 0923-869 123. 9am–1pm, 3:30–7pm.
This church is dedicated to Our Lady of the Assumption. It was built in 1314. The austere façade has a portico with pointed arches surmounted by a beautiful rose window; it faces the detached campanile with double lancet windows, which was built in 1312

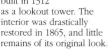

Plaque commemorating the Sicilian scientist Ettore Majorana

as a lookout tower. The interior was drastically restored in 1865, and little remains of its original look.

Corso Vittorio Emanuele
The Corso, the main street in Erice, begins at **Porta Trapani**, one of the three gates through the massive city walls, and goes uphill. The street is lined with Baroque patrician residences and tempting pastry shops selling local specialities. To the left is **San Salvatore**, which once had a monastery annex and boasts a 15th-century portal. At the end of the Corso, formerly called Via Regia, is **Piazza Umberto I**, redesigned in the 19th century, and the **Palazzo del Municipio** (town hall), which houses the **Museo Comunale Cordici**.

Museo Cordici
Piazza Umberto I. 0923-869 258. 8:30am–1:30pm.
This museum features finds from the necropolis, coins, terracotta items and a small head of Venus. Some rooms also exhibit vestments and old paintings and sculpture such as the *Annunciation*, a marble group by Antonello Gagini.

San Pietro
Via Filippo Guarnotti.
Founded in the 14th century in the middle of Erice, this church was rebuilt in 1745, and a fine Baroque portal added. The nearby convent is now one of the bases for the **Centro di Cultura Scientifica Ettore Majorana**. This centre, founded in the early 1960s to honour the brilliant Sicilian scientist who died in mysterious circumstances before World War II, runs courses and conferences on subjects ranging from medicine to mathematical logic. The centre makes use of abandoned buildings such as the former convents of San Domenico, San Francesco and San Rocco.

Via General Salerno
This street its noble palazzi connects **Corso Vittorio Emanuele** with the castle area. Immediately to the left is **San Martino**, a Norman church with a Baroque portal and interior, where there is a fine 17th-century wooden choir. The sacristy takes you to the **Oratorio dei Confrati del Purgatorio**, built in the animated Rococo style, with a carved altar decorated with gilded stucco. Further along the street is **San Giuliano**, which looks over a square made even more spectacular by the pink colour of the façade. The church was begun in 1080 by Roger I but was radically altered in the 1600s. It was closed when the vault caved in on the central section of the nave; now restored, it is used as a cultural and artistic centre.

An example of the lovely paved streets in Erice

San Giovanni Battista
Piazzale San Giovanni. 0923-869 171. only for events.
This white-domed church is probably the oldest in Erice, despite the many alterations that have changed its appearance. The last refurbishing phase took place in the 1600s, when the nave was totally rebuilt. The church is now used only as an auditorium, but interesting works of art remain. These include the statue of St John the Baptist by Antonio Gagini and the 14th-century frescoes moved here from the deconsecrated church of Santa Maria Maddalena.

ENVIRONS: On the slopes of Monte San Giuliano, in the restored Baglio Cusenza, is the **Museo Agroforestale**, with an exhibition of farm equipment. Old ploughs, presses, barrows and a limestone millstone are on display in the courtyard.

Museo Agroforestale
Località San Matteo. 0923-869 532. 8:30am–1pm, 3–5pm winter; 8:30am–1pm, 3–6pm summer (9am–1pm hols).

Boats anchored in the large port of Trapani

Trapani ⑳

Road map A2. 🏔 *69,854.*
✈ *Vincenzo Florio a Birgi (0923-841 222).* 🚊 *0923-28071.* 🚌 *0923-28900.* ℹ *Via San Francesco d'Assisi (0923-545 511).* 🚢 *Thu.* 🎭 *Processione dei Misteri (Good Friday).*

T HE TOWN WAS built on a narrow, curved promontory (hence the name, which derives from the Greek word *drepane*, or sickle) that juts out into the sea opposite the Egadi Islands. In ancient times Trapani was the port town for Erice *(see pp96–7)*. It flourished under the Carthaginians and languished under the Vandals, Byzantines and Saracens. The economy has always been linked to the sea and reached its peak in the 1600s and 1700s with shipyards and tuna fishing. The town now extends beyond the promontory to the foot of Monte San Giuliano and the edge of the salt marshes.

🏛 Museo Pepoli
Via Conte Agostino Pepoli 200.
📞 *0923-553 269.* 🕐 *summer: 9am–1:30pm, 3–7pm daily; winter: 9am–1:30pm Mon, Wed, Fri, Sat; 9am–1:30pm, 3–6:30pm Tue, Thu; 9am–12:30pm Sun & hols.* ♿
This museum was opened in 1906 in the former Carmelite monastery, thanks to Count Agostino Pepoli, who donated his private collection. A broad polychrome marble staircase leads to the first floor, which has archaeological finds, 12th–18th century Sicilian painting, jewellery and ceramics. The art produced in Trapani is interesting: wooden 16th-century angels, an 18th-century coral and alabaster nativity scene, jewellery, clocks with painted dials, tapestries with coral and majolica from Santa Maria delle Grazie.

🚩 Via Garibaldi
This is the street that leads to the old town. It begins in **Piazza Vittorio Veneto**, the heart of the city with **Palazzo d'Alì**, now the Town Hall. The street is lined with 18th-century patrician residences such as **Palazzo Riccio di Morana** and **Palazzo Fardel-la Fontana**. Almost directly opposite the 1621 Baroque façade of **Santa Maria d'Itria** are the steps leading to **San Domenico**, built in the 14th century and restructured in the 18th. In the interior is the sarcophagus of Manfred, natural son of Frederick II *(see p27)*.

🚩 Corso Vittorio Emanuele
This is the main street in the old town, lined with late Baroque buildings and **San Lorenzo Cathedral**, which has a fine portico. The main features of the interior are the painted ceiling, stucco decoration and, in the right-hand altar, a *Crucifixion* attributed to Van Dyck.

🅰 Santuario di Maria Santissima Annunziata
Via Conte Agostino Pepoli.
📞 *0923-539 184.* 🕐 *winter: 7am–noon, 4–7pm including hols; summer: 7am–noon, 4–8pm (7am–1pm, 4–8pm hols).* 🕐 *8 & 9am, 6pm.*
Known as the Madonna di Trapani, this church was built by the Carmelite fathers in 1224. The portal and part of the rose window are the only original elements remaining, as the rest of the church is Baroque, thanks to the restoration effected in 1714. Inside are the Cappella dei Pescatori, the

---

THE SALT MARSHES

The Stagno and Trapani salt marshes were exploited in antiquity and reached the height of their importance in the 19th century, when salt was exported as far away as Norway. The long periods of sunshine (five or six months a year) and the impermeable nature of the land made these marshes very productive,

Windmills, used for draining water from the basins

A workman at the Stagnone salt marsh

although activity has declined in the last 20 years. At one time, windmills supplied energy for the Archimedes screws used to take water from basin to basin; some of them have now been restored. At Nubia the Museo delle Saline (Salt Marsh Museum) is now open, and the Stagnone area will soon become a fully-fledged nature reserve. The seawater will be protected from pollution, and the age-old tradition of salt extraction will survive.

Bell tower of the Santuario dell'Annunziata in Trapani

Cappella dei Marinai, and the Cappella della Madonna di Trapani with the *Madonna and Child* by Nino Pisano, one of the most important Gothic sculptures in Sicily.

🔓 Chiesa del Purgatorio

Via San Francesco d'Assisi.
📞 0923-21321. ⏱ 10am–noon Tue;10am–noon, 5–7pm Fri (10am–noon, 4–7pm daily in Lent).
This church is well known because it houses unusual 18th-century wooden statues with precious silver decoration representing the Stations of the Cross *(Misteri)*. At 2pm on Good Friday, they are carried in a 24-hour procession, a ceremony dating from the 18th century.

🏛 Museo di Preistoria

Torre di Ligny. 📞 0923-22300.
⏱ 9:30am–12:30pm. 📷 🎫
At the tip of the peninsula, the **Torre di Ligny** (1671) affords a fine view of the city and its port. The tower is now used as an archaeological museum, with objects from the Punic Wars and from the shipwrecks that occurred on the ancient trade routes, and amphoras used to carry wine, dates and garum, a highly prized fish sauce.

🏛 Museo delle Saline

Contrada Nubia, Paceco. 📞 0923-867 422. ⏱ 9am–noon, 4–6pm.
⚫ Sun & hols.
From Trapani to Marsala the coast is lined with salt marshes. The area is now a

nature reserve, a unique habitat for migratory birds. The landscape, with its salt marshes and windmills, is striking. A museum illustrates the various stages of the ancient practice of salt extraction.

Marsala ㉑

Road map A3. 🏘 80,419. 🚌 124 km (77 miles) from Marsala and 31 km (19 miles) from Trapani. 🛈 0923-714 097. 🚌 Tue. 🎭 Maundy Thursday procession.

Sicily's largest wine-producing centre was founded by the colonists from Mozia who survived the destruction of the island by Dionysius of Syracuse in 397 BC. It then became a major Carthaginian city, but in the first Punic War it was conquered by the Romans, who made it their main Mediterranean naval base. The city plan is basically Roman, other quarters being added by the Arabs, who conquered the city in 830 and made it a flourishing trade centre. **Piazza della Repubblica**, bounded by **Palazzo Senatorio** and the **Cathedral**, dedicated to St Thomas of Canterbury, is the heart of town. The Cathedral was founded by the Normans and completed in the 1900s. It boasts sculptures by the Gaginis and their school. Behind the apse is the **Museo degli Arazzi Fiamminghi**, with eight 16th-century Flemish tapestries depicting Titus' war against the Hebrews. They were donated by Philip II of Spain to the Archbishop of Messina and later taken to Marsala Cathedral.

🏛 Museo degli Arazzi Fiamminghi

Piazza della Repubblica, Duomo.
📞 0923-712 903. ⏱ 9am–1pm, 4–6pm. ⚫ Mon. 🎫

🏛 Museo Archeologico

Baglio Anselmi. 📞 0923-952 535.
⏱ 9am–2pm, 4–7pm (9am–2pm Mon, Thu; 9am–1pm, 3–6pm Sun).
This archaeological museum features prehistoric and ancient finds from digs in the area, including the mosaics from the Roman ruins at Capo Boeo and a 3rd-century BC Punic shipwreck.

Mozia

Road map A2–3. 🚤 from Trapani and Marsala (dawn to sunset).
🛈 APT di Trapani (0923-25946 or 27077.

The prosperous Phoenician city of Mozia was built on the island of San Pantaleo, a very short distance from the shores of Sicily. The ancient site is linked with Joseph Whitaker, the son of an English wine merchant who made his fortune from Marsala wine. He became owner of the island in the early 1900s, began archaeological digs in 1913, and founded a museum that houses the statue of the "young man from Mozia". You can also visit the dry docks, which, together with those in Carthage, are the most ancient in the Mediterranean.

Punic head, Mozia museum

Ruins of the northern gate on the island of Mozia, destroyed in 397 BC

Selinunte ㉙

THE RUINS OF SELINUNTE, overlooking the sea, are among the most striking archaeological sites in the Mediterranean and a supreme example of the fusion of Phoenician and Greek culture. Founded in the 7th century BC by colonists from Megara

Attic vase found in Selinunte

Hyblaea, Selinunte soon became a powerful city with flourishing trade and artistic activity. A rival to Segesta and Mozia, it was destroyed by Carthage in 409 BC and largely forgotten. Excavations (still under way in the oldest parts of the Selinunte ruins) have brought to light eight temples with colossal Doric columns, as well as a fortification system.

★ **Temple C (580–550 BC)**
Decorated with metopes now kept in Palermo, this was the largest and oldest temple on the acropolis, dedicated to Heracles or Apollo.

**Temple A
(480–470 BC),**
perhaps dedicated to Leto.

Sanctuary of Malophoros

Ruins of ancient city

**Temple D
(570–550 BC)** was perhaps dedicated to Aphrodite.

**Temple O
(480–470 BC),**
sacred to Artemis.

Temple B (c.250 BC) was probably the only one built in the Hellenistic age.

★ **Acropolis**
This was the hub of public life. It centred around two main streets that divided it into four quarters protected by a wall 1,260 m (4,132 ft) long.

VISITORS' CHECKLIST

Road map B3.
✈ *Palermo Punta Raisi
(Falcone Borsellino).*
🚌 *Castelvetrano.* ℹ️ *924-904
654.* 🕐 *9am– sunset.* 🅿️

Temple F (560–530 BC)
was dedicated to Athena and
is the most ancient temple on
the eastern hill. Sadly it is
totally in ruins.

★ Temple E (490–480 BC)
*This temple, located at the top of an eight-stepped
base (crepidoma), was partly rebuilt in the
1960s. It was probably sacred to Hera and is
considered one of the finest examples of Doric
architecture in Sicily.*

The harbour area lay at the
junction of the Cotone river
and the road connecting the
Acropolis to the eastern hill.

**Eastern
hill**

**Temple G
(540–480 BC)**
*This temple is also
completely in ruins but
is still an important
monument because, at
6,120 sq m (65,850 sq ft),
it was one of the largest
temples in antiquity. It
reached a height of 30 m
(98 ft) when complete.*

STAR FEATURES

★ **Acropolis**

★ **Temple C**

★ **Temple E**

0 metres	130
0 yards	130

Exploring Selinunte

Y OU WILL NEED at least two hours to visit the archaeological site of Selinunte. The excavated area is
divided into four zones, starting off from the east: the
eastern hill with its group of temples; the Acropolis; the
ancient city; and the Sanctuary of Malophoros. Besides
its great cultural interest, the surrounding landscape is
very beautiful, and there are lovely views of the sea.

The metopes on Temple C are now in Palermo museum *(see p54)*

⋔ Acropolis

This lies on a bluff right over
the sea, between the Selino
river to the west and the
Gorgo Cotone river to the
east. Their mouths once
formed the city harbour,
now silted up. The
Acropolis was
surrounded by
colossal stone walls
3 m (10 ft) high,
with two gates,
the larger one on
the northern side.
This area contained
the public buildings
and temples, all
facing east. From
the southern end,
the first places are
the sparse ruins of
**Temples O and
A**, close together and much
alike. This similarity is
perhaps due to the fact that

they were both dedicated to
Castor and Pollux. There
were originally 6 columns
along the short sides and 14
on the longer ones. Further
on you come to the small
Hellenistic **Temple B**,
which was perhaps
dedicated to Empedo-
cles, the philosopher
and scientist from
Agrigento who may
have supervised
the drainage
operations in
the area.
Temple C
is the most
ancient on the
Acropolis. It was
dedicated to Apollo
and had 6 columns on
the short sides and 17
on the long ones. The pediment was decorated with
superb metopes, three of

**Hellenistic vases,
Museo
Archeologico,
Palermo (see p54)**

which are now kept in the
Museo Archeologico in
Palermo *(see p54)*.

In 1925–6, 14 columns on
the northern side and on part
of the architrave were reconstructed. Seeing these among
the other blocks of massive
columns placed here and
there around the ancient
sacred precinct is quite an
impressive sight.

Temple D is also reduced
to a state of fragmentary
ruins. The Acropolis
area was divided by
two main perpen-
dicular streets, which
can be reached
by means of
stone steps.

⋔ The
eastern hill

The sacred
precinct has remains
of three temples set
parallel to one
another at the
entrance to the
archaeological zone.
In ancient times it
was surrounded by
an enclosure.
The partially
reconstructed
Temple E was
built in the
pure Doric
style. An   **The bronze
inscription   ephebus, Selinunte**
on a votive stele found in
1865 shows that it was
dedicated to Hera (Juno). Its
68 columns still support part
of the trabeation.

An eight-step stairway leads
to **Temple F**, the smallest and
most badly damaged of the
three. It was built in the

Temple E, one of the best examples of Doric architecture in Sicily

The Collegio dei Gesuiti at Mazara del Vallo, home to a Museo Civico

archaic style, surrounded by 36 columns which were more than 9 m (29 ft) high. The vestibule had a second row of columns, and the lower part of the peristyle was enclosed by a wall.

The size of **Temple G** was 110.36 by 50.10 m (362 by 164 ft). Today it is only a huge mass of stones, in the middle of which stands a column, which was restored in 1832. It was dedicated to Apollo, but its construction was never completed.

⌂ The Ancient City
On the Collina di Manuzza hill north of the Acropolis, the ancient city has been the subject of archaeological excavations only in recent years. After the destruction of the city in 409 BC, this ancient part was used as a necropolis by those inhabitants who remained.

⌂ Malophoros Sanctuary
Situated west of the Selino river, about a kilometre (half a mile) away from the Acropolis, the Malophoros Sanctuary is extremely old and perhaps was founded even before the city itself.

The main building in this sanctuary is enclosed by walls and was dedicated to a female divinity, Malophoros (meaning "bearer of pomegranate"), the goddess of fertility, many statuettes of whom have been found in the vicinity. According to experts, the sanctuary was a stopping point on the long, impressive funeral processions making their way to the Manicalunga necropolis.

Castelvetrano ㉔

Road map B3. 🏛 30,264.
🚌 73 km (45 miles) from Trapani, 110 km (68 miles) from Palermo. 🛈 Corso Vittorio Emanuele 64 (0924-46251. 🚌 Tue. 🎭 Funzione dell'Aurora (Easter).

THE CENTRE consists of three linked squares. The main one is **Piazza Garibaldi**, where the mainly 16th-century **Chiesa Madre** has an interesting medieval portal. Inside are stuccoes by Ferraro and Serpotta, and a *Madonna* by the Gagini school. By the church are the **Municipio** (Town Hall), the **Campanile** and the Mannerist **Fontana della Ninfa**. Close by is the **Chiesa del Purgatorio**, built in 1624–64, its façade filled with statues, and the neo-Doric **Teatro Selinus** (1873).

ENVIRONS: At **Delia**, 3.5 km (2 miles) from town, is Santa Trinità, a church built in the Norman period.

Mazara del Vallo ㉕

Road map A3. 🏛 49,019.
🚌 50 km (31 miles) from Trapani, 124 km (77 miles) from Palermo.
🛈 0923-941 727. 🚌 Wed.
🎭 Festino di San Vito (Aug).

FACING THE Canale di Sicilia, at the mouth of the Mazarò river, the town, a colony of Selinunte, was destroyed in 409 BC by the Carthaginians, passed to the Romans and then became a prosperous city under the Arabs, who made it the capital of one of the three "valleys" into which they divided Sicily (*see p30*). In 1073 Mazara was conquered by Roger I, who convened the first Norman Parliament of Sicily there.

In **Piazza Mokarta** remains of the castle can be seen. Behind this is the **Cathedral**, of medieval origin but rebuilt in 1694. It houses the *Transfiguration*, a sculpture group by Antonello Gagini. The left side of the Cathedral closes off Piazza della Repubblica, with the façade of the **Seminario dei Chierici** and the **Palazzo Vescovile**. On Lungomare Mazzini you will see the **Collegio dei Gesuiti**, seat of the **Museo Civico** and can enter the old Arab town.

⌂ Museo Civico
Piazza Plebiscito. 📞 0923-940 266.
🕗 8:30am–2pm. ⛔ Sun & hols.
The former Collegio dei Gesuiti, with its Baroque door with 4 telamons, contains archaeological finds, sculpture and medieval paintings.

Mazara del Vallo, one of the most important fishing harbours in Italy

Egadi Islands

Road map A2. 👥 4,698. 🚢 from
Trapani (0923-24073); (0923-21754).
✈ Trapani Birgi (0923-841 124).
ℹ Consorzio Turistico Egadi (0923-
921 342); APT Trapani (0923-
29000).

THE SICILIAN islands
of Favignana,
Levanzo and Marettimo
were connected to
mainland Sicily 600,000
years ago. As the sea
level gradually rose, the
links were submerged,
slowly changing the islands
into an archipelago in the
centre of the Mediterranean.
The islands are now popular
as places for vacations and
swimming as they are easily
reached from Trapani.

A stretch of the Favignana coastline

Favignana

This island has two distinct
parts. The eastern side is flat,
with pastureland and farm-
land, while the other half is
craggy and barren. In the
middle is the small town of
Favignana, which was rebuilt
in the 1600s over its original
medieval layout. Sights worth
visiting are the **Chiesa
Matrice** (dedicated to the
Immaculate Conception), the
buildings constructed during
the height of the tuna fishing
industry and the 19th-century
Villino Florio, which is now
the Town Hall. The so-called
Bagno delle Donne (Ladies'
Bath), a Roman bath with
traces of mosaics, is worth a
look.

    The boat tour of the island
is to be recommended. It
departs from the port and visits
Punta Faraglione, **Punta
Ferro** and **Punta Sottile**,
where there is a lighthouse.

It continues to the small
islands of **Galera** and **Galeot-
ta**, **Punta Fanfalo** and **Punta
Calarossa**, where
there are heaps of
tufa from the island
quarries. The tour
ends here, taking you
back to the port.

Levanzo

The smallest of the
Egadi Islands has a
wilder aspect than
Favignana: the tall,
rocky coastline is
dominated by a
cultivated plateau.
There is only one
small village, **Cala Dogana**,
and the landscape is barren
and desolate, interrupted here
and there by the green
maquis vegetation. A series of
footpaths crosses the island
and provides very pleasant
walks to the beautiful **Cala
Tramontana** bay.

    Northwest of Cala Dogana
is the **Grotta del Genovese**,
which can be reached on foot
in about two hours or by
boat. The grotto has a series

of carved Palaeolithic
drawings of human figures,
animals and idols, some in a
rather naturalistic style, others
rendered more schematically.

Marettimo

The rugged, mountainous and
varied landscape of Marettimo, the first island in the
group to break off from the
mainland, is very striking. The
paths crossing the island –
there are no roads or hotels
here – will introduce you to a
world of limestone pinnacles
and caves leading up to
Monte Falcone (686 m,
2,250 ft). The island has many
rare plant species that grow
only here – caused by the
long isolation of Marettimo –
as well as some introduced
moufflon and boar. The
Punta Troia fort housed a
Bourbon penal colony where
the Risorgimento hero,
Guglielmo Pepe, was held for
three years. Not far from the
tiny village of Marettimo there
are some ancient Roman
buildings and, in the vicinity,
a small Byzantine church.

The little harbour at Cala Dogana, the only village in Levanzo

The Grotta Azzurra, a major attraction on boat tours around Ustica

Ustica ㉗

Road map B1. ∭ *1,184.* ⛴ *from Palermo 091-607 01 81; in summer from Naples (081-580 03 40).* ✈ *Palermo Punta Raisi 091-591 663.* ℹ *Pro Loco di Ustica 091-844 91 90; APT Palermo (091-586 122).*

USTICA IS the result of ancient volcanic eruptions: its name derives from the word *usta* (burned) and the land is made up of sharp black volcanic rock, which lends it its unique appearance. The emerged part of the gigantic submerged volcano, about 49 km (30 miles) from the Sicilian coast, is only 8.6 sq km (3.32 sq miles), but its extremely fertile lava terrain is ideal for the cultivation of grapes, wheat and vegetables. The steep and rocky coasts and the landscape of the island make it an ideal spot for underwater sports. Because of the importance of the sea beds, the first **Marine Reserve** in Italy was established here on 12 November 1986; it is run by the local authorities. The park is divided into three sections, and the degree of protection ranges from total (from Caletta to Cala Sidoti) to partial. Guided tours are organized by the Marine Reserve itself, and in July the island plays host to a series of international skin- and scuba-diving programmes. A particularly interesting underwater excursion is the one that starts off at **Punta Gavazzi**, with what could be described as an archaeo-

logical diving tour of the ancient Roman amphorae, old anchors, and traces of the passage of sailors since the beginning of human history in this part of the sea.

The village of **Ustica** is dominated by the **Capo Falconara** promontory, where the Bourbon rulers built a little fort offering a splendid view as far as the Sicilian coast. Ustica was founded in the mid-1700s and is still inhabited. Local life revolves around Piazza Umberto I, where there is a whitewashed parish church. Age-old human presence on the island is visible in a number of interesting sites,

such as the prehistoric village of **Faraglioni** and the Phoenician tombs at **Falconara**, which were used at different times by the Greeks, the Romans and the Byzantines.

The main feature of a boat tour of the island is the great number of underwater caves in the rocky coastline: the **Grotta Azzurra**, whose large caverns are preceded by an imposing natural arch, the **Grotta delle Colonne**, with a cliff of the same name, and the **Grotta Blasi**, **Grotta dell'Oro** and **Grotta delle Barche** (where fishermen used to moor their boats during storms), are only a few of the many caves to be seen.

The sea bed at Ustica, where archaeological treasures may still lie

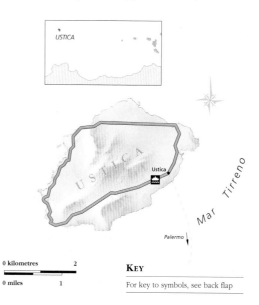

0 kilometres 2
0 miles 1

KEY

For key to symbols, see back flap

SOUTHWESTERN SICILY

THIS CORNER OF SICILY *is only a stone's throw from North Africa. The landscape is varied, much of it hilly or mountainous, with rugged cliffs along parts of the coast and arid, barren plateaus inland. The Greeks built classically beautiful temples at Agrigento, and the Romans left an extensive villa at Piazza Armerina, saved for posterity by being buried under mud for centuries.*

Along the coast, steep craggy cliffs alternate with flatter, stretches of sand. This southern shore was a favourite landing place for travellers plying the Mediterranean, with their ships putting in at places like Agrigento, Eraclea and Sciacca.

Agrigento became an important Greek centre, and an entire valley of temples still remains as evidence of their skills. Some are still in good condition 2,000 years later. The mud-preserved Roman mosaics at the Villa del Casale at Piazza Armerina are in marvellous condition and provide an excellent picture of Roman life.

The land rises away from the sea to become soft, rolling hills and then, quite abruptly, rugged mountains. Rivers may emerge for only a few weeks each year. Around the towns of Enna and Caltanissetta lies the stony heart of the island, exploited for its sulphur mines and quarries for centuries. Inland, Southwestern Sicily is a totally different world from the coast. Towns like Enna seem to perch precariously on hilltops. Many of the people of these rather isolated towns have retained an austere and deep-seated religious faith, which is expressed in the colourful processions held during Easter Week *(see p122)*. The flatter land and slopes nearer to the sea were once the domain of ancient feudal estates with their olive and orange groves, vividly described in Giuseppe de Lampedusa's novel *The Leopard*. This, perhaps the most truly "Sicilian" part of Sicily, was also the birthplace of the great Italian writer Pirandello.

A boar being captured in one of the fine hunting scene mosaics in the Villa del Casale, at Piazza Armerina

◁ The beautifully preserved Temple of Concord (c.430 BC) in the valley of the Temples at Agrigento

Exploring Southwestern Sicily

A GOOD STARTING point for a visit to this corner of Sicily is Agrigento, as it is within easy reach of the eastern coast, with Palma di Montechiaro and Licata, and the western coast, moving towards Megara and Sciacca. Major communications routes travel into the interior towards Caltanissetta and Enna on the one hand and, westwards, into the hinterland towards Palermo. From the port at Agrigento there is a regular boat service to the islands of Lampedusa and Linosa.

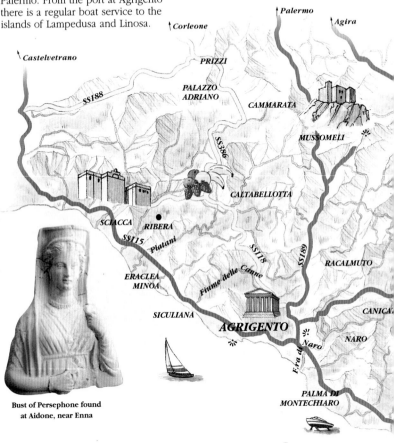

Palermo

Agira

Corleone

Castelvetrano

PRIZZI

PALAZZO ADRIANO

CAMMARATA

SS188

SS386

MUSSOMELI

CALTABELLOTTA

SCIACCA   **RIBERA**

SS115

Platani

ERACLEA MINOA

Fiume delle Canne

SS118

SS189

RACALMUTO

SICULIANA

AGRIGENTO

Fra di Naro

NARO

CANICA

Bust of Persephone found
at Aidone, near Enna

PALMA DI MONTECHIARO

GETTING AROUND

You can visit the sights of Agrigento by public transport if you choose to, but if you want to see the interior you will need a car. The main roads in this area are the SS189 Agrigento–Palermo, the SS640 to Caltanissetta (from Caltanissetta to Enna it becomes the SS117b and returns to the coast via Piazza Armerina and Gela) and lastly the SS115, which runs along the entire southwestern coastline of Sicily.

PANTELLERIA

P E L A G I E
I S L A N D S

LINOSA

LAMPEDUSA

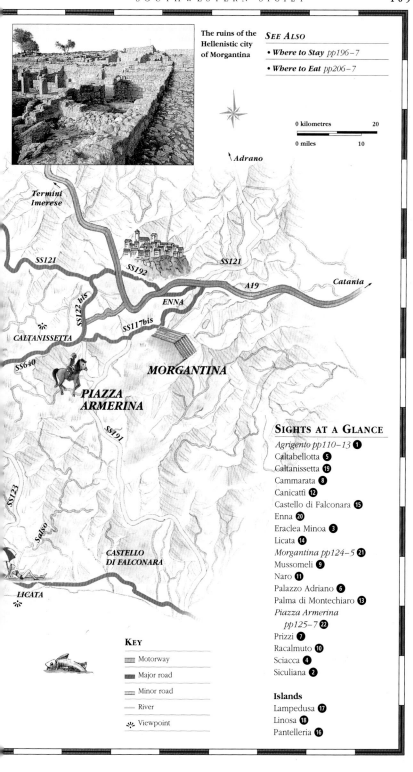

The ruins of the Hellenistic city of Morgantina

SEE ALSO

• *Where to Stay* pp196–7

• *Where to Eat* pp206–7

0 kilometres 20

0 miles 10

Adrano

Termini Imerese

SS121

SS192

SS121

A19

Catania

SS122 bis

ENNA

SS117bis

CALTANISSETTA

SS640

MORGANTINA

PIAZZA ARMERINA

SS191

SS123

Salso

CASTELLO DI FALCONARA

LICATA

KEY

	Motorway
	Major road
	Minor road
	River
☀	Viewpoint

SIGHTS AT A GLANCE

Agrigento pp110–13 ❶
Caltabellotta ❺
Caltanissetta ❿❾
Cammarata ❽
Canicattì ⓬
Castello di Falconara ⓯
Enna ⓴
Eraclea Minoa ❸
Licata ⓮
Morgantina pp124–5 ㉑
Mussomeli ❾
Naro ⓫
Palazzo Adriano ❻
Palma di Montechiaro ⓭
Piazza Armerina pp125–7 ㉒
Prizzi ❼
Racalmuto ❿
Sciacca ❹
Siculiana ❷

Islands
Lampedusa ⓱
Linosa ⓲
Pantelleria ⓰

Agrigento

T HERE ARE TWO main sights in Agrigento: the magnificent remains of the Greek colony in the Valle dei Templi *(see pp112–3)* and the rocky hill where the medieval town was built. The city of Akragas was founded by the Greeks, then conquered by the Romans in 210 BC, who gave it the name of Agrigentum. During a period of barbarian invasions the town moved from the valley to the rock. It was then ruled by the Byzantines and for some time by the Arabs, whose dominion came to an end with the Normans in 1087.

Detail of San Nicola, Museo Archeologico

Façade of Agrigento Cathedral (11th century)

🔒 Cathedral and Museo Diocesano

Piazza Don Minzoni. **Museo Diocesano** 🕐 *0922-401 352.* ☐ *daily.*
The Cathedral was founded in the 12th century and enlarged and altered subsequently, as can be seen in some of the exterior details. For example, the bell tower has a series of Catalan Gothic single lancet windows, while others are in the original style. Inside is the Cappella di San Gerlando, named after the bishop who founded the church, with an elegant Gothic portal. The ceiling has both painted and coffered sections, dating from the 16th and 17th centuries respectively. There is also a curious acoustic phenomenon here, known as the *portavoce:* if you stand under the apse you can clearly hear the whispering of people at the other end of the nave, 80 m (262 ft) away. The **Museum** has some Roman sarcophagi and a series of frescoes taken from the Cathedral walls in 1951.

🎭 Teatro Pirandello

Piazza Pirandello. 🕐 *0922-20391.*
Founded in 1870 and originally called Teatro Regina Margherita, the theatre is part of the Town Hall. It was designed by Dionisio Sciascia, and the decoration was executed by Palermo architect Giovanni Basile.

🏛 Museo Civico

Piazza Pirandello. 🕐 *0922-597 198.* 📷 ● *Mon.*
The city museum, which lies opposite the Municipio (Town Hall), contains a collection of medieval paintings and sculpture.

🔒 San Lorenzo

Piazza del Purgatorio.
☐ *daily.*
Very little remains of this old church (also known as Chiesa del Purgatorio), which was rebuilt in the Baroque style in the 1600s. The stately two-stage façade has an interesting portal flanked by two large spiral columns and a large bell tower. Both interior and exterior have a series of allegorical statues representing the Christian Virtues, executed in the early 1700s by Giuseppe and Giacomo Serpotta, and a Madonna of the Pomegranate attributed to Antonello Gagini.

Near the church, under a stone lion, is the Ipogeo del Purgatorio (Hypogeum of Purgatory), a network of underground conduits built in the 5th century BC by the Greek architects to supply water to the city's various quarters.

AGRIGENTO

Cathedral and Museo Diocesano ①
Convento di Santo Spirito ⑤
Museo Civico ③
Piazza Vittorio Emanuele ⑥
San Lorenzo ④
Teatro Pirandello ②
Valle dei Templi (see pp112–3) ⑦

0 kilometres   1

0 miles   1

The arched coupled windows in the Convento di Santo Spirito (1295)

⛪ Convento di Santo Spirito

Salita Santo Spirito. ◯ *daily.*

This abbey complex is of ancient origin. The church and adjacent Cistercian monastery were founded in the 13th century by the Countess Prefoglio of the powerful Chiaramonte family. They were altered several times, particularly the façade, which, however, still has a Gothic portal and rose window. For centuries the church was the most important in the Agrigento area and was known as the Badia Grande. In the 18th century the nave was decorated with lavish and fantastic stuccowork that mirrors the shapes of the church; the motif is also developed in sculpted panels. Next to the church is the monastery, now city property, where the cloister is well worth a visit. The impressive chapter-house is lined with Gothic arcades.

⛪ Piazza Vittorio Emanuele

This large, lively, traffic-filled square connects the old town of Agrigento with the more recently built part, which developed in the 19th century. The two areas, Girgenti to the west and Rupe Atenea to the east, were once separated by a valley that was filled in during the late 19th century, blocking what was traditionally known as "Empedocles' opening", through which the north wind passed, cooling the valley below.

KEY

FS	Railway station
P	Parking
i	Tourist information
†	Church

ENVIRONS: Below Agrigento, towards the sea and Porto Empedocle, is the parish of Kaos, which is worth visiting to see the **Birthplace of Luigi Pirandello**, the house of the great dramatist and novelist *(see pp20–23)*. The winner of the 1934 Nobel Prize for Literature once lived here; it is now a small museum with interesting memorabilia. Nearby, in a crack in a rock next to an old pine (recently blown down by the wind) facing the sea, is the urn containing Pirandello's ashes.

Proceeding from Agrigento down to the sea you come to the port town of **Porto Empedocle**, an important outlet for the mining activity in the interior. In the old harbour is the impressive Bastione di Carlo V (Rampart of Charles V), while there is a constant bustle of fishing boats around the more industrialized area.

In contrast, by heading north from Agrigento and turning off SS189 at the Comitini crossroads, two kilometres (one mile) of dirt road to the south will take you to a place famous for an extremely curious geological phenomenon: little volcano-shaped cones known as the **Vulcanetti di Macalube** emit methane gas bubbles and brackish watery mud in the middle of a lunar landscape made sterile by this pseudo-volcanic activity.

⛪ Birthplace of Pirandello

◯ 9am–1pm, 3–6pm.
● Fri, Sat am, Sun.

The eerie landscape of the Vulcanetti di Macalube

Valle dei Templi

Agrigento was founded in 581 BC by colonists from Gela, who named the town Akragas *(see p28)*. Yet only a century later the population had grown to 200,000 and the Greek poet Pindar described it as "the fairest city inhabited by mortals". It was ruled briefly by the Carthaginians. The Valley of Temples is the site of the main temples (dedicated to Olympian Zeus, Heracles, Concord and Hera), minor shrines (Sanctuary of the Chthonic Divinities) and the Archaeological Museum.

The Ephebus of Agrigento

Sanctuary of the Chthonic Divinities (6th–5th century BC)
A shrine dedicated to Demeter and Persephone (also known as Kore), with altars and sacred precincts.

Temple of Hephaistos (5th century BC)

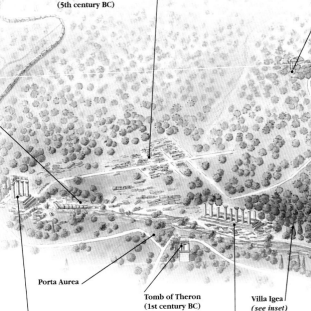

Temple of Olympian Zeus (5th century BC)
Only fragmentary ruins remain of this temple, except for this Telamon now on display in the Museo Archeologico.

Porta Aurea

Tomb of Theron (1st century BC)

Villa Igea *(see inset)*

Temple of Castor and Pollux (5th century BC)
The four surviving columns, a symbol of the Valley of Temples, were restored in the 19th century.

Temple of Heracles (6th century BC)
These eight columns, put back in place in 1924, belonged to the oldest temple dedicated to the hero worshipped by both the Greeks and Romans (as Hercules). The archaic Doric structure has an elongated rectangle plan.

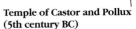

★ Museo Archeologico
The Archaeological Museum was opened to the public in 1967. The 13 rooms display objects ranging from prehistoric times to the early Christian period, including pieces from the Classical era.

The Hellenistic-Roman quarter is all that remains of the large post-Classical age settlement.

EARLY CHRISTIAN CATACOMBS

The niches, hewn along the floors and walls

The Valle dei Templi is famous for its splendid monuments of the Magna Graecia civilization, but it also has Early Christian ruins. The Ipogei of Villa Igea (also known as the Grotta di Frangipane), between the Temple of Heracles and the Temple of Concord, were cut out of the rock to house the bodies of the first Christians here. A series of niches, closed off by stone slabs, alternated with chapels that still bear traces of wall painting.

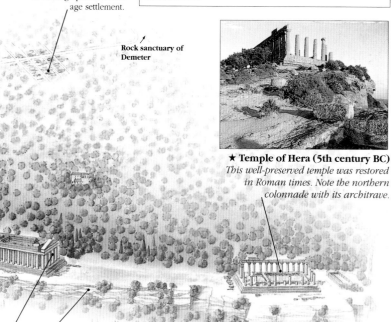

Rock sanctuary of Demeter

★ Temple of Hera (5th century BC)
This well-preserved temple was restored in Roman times. Note the northern colonnade with its architrave.

Line of fortifications

★ Temple of Concord (5th century BC)
With its 34 columns, this is one of the best preserved Doric temples in the world, partly thanks to alterations made in the 4th century AD, when it became a Christian basilica. It was restored to its original classical form in 1748.

0 metres	200
0 yards	200

STAR FEATURES

★ Temple of Concord

★ Temple of Hera

★ Museo Archeologico

Siculiana ②

Road map C4. 🏛 5,021. 🚆 from Palermo and Trapani to Castelvetrano, then 🚌 ℹ️ Comune di Siculiana (0922-815 105 or 167-219 267).

THE PRESENT-DAY town of Siculiana was built on the site of an Arab fort destroyed by the Normans in the late 11th century. The new lords – the Chiaramonte family from Agrigento – rebuilt the fortress in the 1300s and it was altered several times afterwards. Despite all the changes, Siculiana has retained some Arab features.

In central Piazza Umberto I is the Baroque **Chiesa Madre**, dedicated to San Leonardo Abate, dominating the square at the top of a flight of steps. In the old centre, divided into large blocks, you can glimpse entrances to courtyards and alleys, which were once part of the covered Arab town.

Siculiana, built on a hill during Arab rule

The archaeological site at Eraclea Minoa, close to the rocky shore

Eraclea Minoa ③

Road map B4.
Digs ◯ 9am–1 hr before sunset.

THIS ANCIENT settlement was founded during the Mycenaean age and then developed by Spartan colonists who arrived in the 6th century BC and gave it its present name. After being fought over by Agrigento and Carthage, Eraclea became a Roman colony. Today it is a stone's throw from the craggy coast jutting out into the sea. Eraclea is a wonderful combination of a lovely setting and atmospheric ruins, above all the **theatre**. The theatre is well preserved – excavations began in the 1950s – and hosts special performances of Greek theatre, although the overall impression is marred somewhat by the plastic used to protect it in bad weather. All around the theatre are the ruins of the ancient city with its defence system, as well as some necropolises.

Sciacca ④

Road map B3. 🏛 31,365. 🚆 from Palermo and Trapani. ℹ️ Corso Vittorio Emanuele 84 (0925-21182 or 22744); Azienda Regionale Terme di Sciacca, Viale delle Terme (167-881 079).

FROM A DISTANCE, Sciacca seems to be overwhelmed by Monte San Calogero, with its thermal waters and steam vapours, which have made the town famous over the centuries. Although the hot springs had been used since prehistoric times, Sciacca was founded as a mere military outpost for Selinunte during the interminable warfare with the city of Agrigento, and was called *Thermae Selinuntinae* (Selinunte baths) by the Romans. It developed rapidly under Arab rule (Sciacca derives from *as-saqah*) and many traces of their culture can be seen in the old Rabato and Giudecca-Cadda quarters, with their blind alleys and maze of roofed courtyards.

THE ORANGES OF RIBERA

Orange decoration for the festival

The real home of orange-growing is the plain around Mount Etna, but oranges play an important role in the southwestern corner of Sicily, too. At Ribera, an agricultural town where the statesman Francesco Crispi was born (see p34), they grow a special type of navel orange that was brought to Sicily from America by emigrants returning home. These enormous and delicious oranges are celebrated in an annual orange festival during which the public gardens are filled with sculptures made of fruit. A short distance from Ribera, the impressive ruins of the Poggio Diana castle tower above the wooded gullies of the Verdura river.

Locally grown oranges, still harvested by hand in this area

The rusticated façade of the Catalan-Gothic Palazzo Steripinto

The town was further fortified by the Normans, who quickly recognized its strategic importance in controlling the trade routes. Much fought-over in the years that followed, the town was fortified again and again, in particular against the assault of Charles I of Valois.

In the middle of town is **Palazzo Steripinto**, built in Catalan-Gothic style in 1501 with a rusticated façade. The church of **Santa Margherita** has a splendid Gothic portal; note the bas-relief sculpture in the lunette representing Santa Margherita, the Arch-angel Gabriel, Our Lady of the Assumption and saints Calogero and Maddalena. Don't miss the cloister of the former **Convent of San Francesco** and the unfini-shed Baroque façade of the **Chiesa del Carmine**, with its 14th-century rose window. In central Piazza Don Minzoni stands the **Cathedral**, dedica-ted to Santa Maria Maddalena. It was rebuilt in 1656, but retains three Norman apses.

However, the main attractions in Sciacca are Monte San Calogero and its thermal pools. From the large square at the summit, with the sanctuary dedicated to the evangelist San Calogero, who in the 5th century eliminated pagan rites in the mountain caves, the panorama is breathtaking. The summit is almost 400 m (1,312 ft) high, and on a clear day there is a commanding view from Capo

Bianco to Capo Lilibeo, with the limestone ridge of Calta-bellotta in the background and Pantelleria island before you. The older spas are on the slopes of the mountain, while new ones have been built closer to the seaside.

Sciacca is also known for its ceramics, which were mentioned in antiquity by Diodorus Siculus. Local production thrived during the period of Arab rule, and another golden age came in the 16th century. The tradition is being maintained today by the local craftsmen.

Sculpture at the Hermitage of San Pellegrino

Caltabellotta ❺

Road map B3. 🚶 5,283.
ℹ️ Comune di Caltabellotta (0925-951 013 or 167-215 558).

VISIBLE from most of the hilly area of Sciacca, the rocky crest of Caltabellotta (950 m, 3,116 ft) has been inhabited for millennia, as can be seen in the many ancient necropolises and hypogea. The site was fortified at different stages until the arrival of the Arabs, who gave the castle its definitive form, calling it *Kal'at–at–al ballut* (rock of the oak trees). The county capital, Caltabellotta witnessed the signing of peace between Charles I of Valois and Frederick II of Aragon in 1302 (see pp26–7), who took over the whole of Sicily. Perched on the ridge above the houses of the Torrevecchia quarter are the ruins of the **Nor-man castle** and **San Salvatore**, while on the other side of the rock is the **Chiesa Madre**, now being restored, founded by Roger I to celebrate his victory over the Arabs. On the western slope, the **Hermitage of San Pellegrino**, which consists of a monastery and a chapel, dominates the city.

The town of Caltabellotta at the foot of Monte Castello

The façade of San Nicolò, in the upper part of Palazzo Adriano

Palazzo Adriano ❻

Road map C3. 👥 *2,790.*
ℹ *Comune di Palazzo Adriano.*
📞 *091-834 81 65.*

Aᴌᴍᴏsᴛ 700 m (2,296 ft) above sea level, on the ridge of Cozzo Braduscia, is Palazzo Adriano, founded in the mid-15th century by Albanian refugees who fled from the Turkish conquerors. Central Piazza Umberto I boasts two important churches: Greek Orthodox **Santa Maria Assunta**, built in the 16th century and then rebuilt (the interior has a lovely iconostasis and an icon of Our Lady of the Assumption); and **Santa Maria del Lume**, which is Catholic and was founded in the 18th century. In the middle of the square, bordered by **Palazzo Dara**, now the Town Hall, and **Palazzo Mancuso**, there is a lovely octagonal fountain sculpted in 1607. Further up the hill, in the oldest part of Palazzo Adriano, the red dome of the 15th-century **San Nicolò** overlooks the alleyways of this quarter, which were built around the castle that stood here before the town was founded.

Prizzi ❼

Road map C3. 👥 *6,845.*
ℹ *Comune di Prizzi (091-834 67 83 or 167-016 681).*

Tʜᴇ sʟᴏᴘᴇs ᴏf wind-blown Mount Prizzi overlooking the surrounding valleys have been inhabited since ancient times. There was once a fortified Arab town here, but present-day Prizzi mostly reflects the influence of the Middle Ages. The maze of alleys winding up the slopes to the summit (960 m, 3,149 ft) is crowned by the ruins of the medieval castle. Along the narrow streets you will see **San Rocco**, a large stretch of open space with **Santa Maria delle Grazie**, and the 18th-century **Chiesa Madre** dedicated to St George and bearing a fine statue of the Archangel Michael.

Cammarata ❽

Road map C3. 👥 *7,002.* 🚆 *from Palermo & Agrigento.* ℹ *Comune di Cammarata (0922-902 709).*

Tʜᴇ ᴇᴀʀʟɪᴇsᴛ ʜɪsᴛᴏʀɪᴄ records for this town date from the Norman period, when Roger I donated the fief to Lucia de Cammarata. The **Chiesa Madre**, San Nicolò di Bari, and the **Dominican monastery**, whose church was rebuilt in the 1930s, are all worth a visit. But the fascination of Cammarata lies in the overall layout: a labyrinth of alleys and steps – narrow or wide, depending on the natural slope of the rock – offering an unforgettable view of the valleys below this medieval hill town.

Cɪɴᴇᴍᴀ Pᴀʀᴀᴅɪsᴏ

In 1990 the film *Cinema Paradiso* by the Sicilian director Giuseppe Tornatore *(see p22)* won an Oscar for the best foreign film. The film tells the story of the arrival of cinema (the "Nuovo Cinema Paradiso") in an isolated village in Sicily and the effect the big screen has on the main character, a young boy. *Cinema Paradiso* was filmed in the streets and squares of Palazzo Adriano and used many of the locals as extras, conferring fame on the village. The weeks the film unit and the inhabitants of Palazzo Adriano spent working together are commemorated on a majolica plaque on a corner of Piazza Umberto I.

The plaque commemorating the filming of *Cinema Paradiso*

The characteristic stone trough at Piazza Fontana, in Racalmuto

Convent, now the Town Hall, and the **Teatro Regina Margherita**, founded in 1879 by Dionisio Sciascia. Further up the hill, at the far end of the steps is the **Sanctuary of Santa Maria del Monte**, where an important annual festival is held on 11–14 July. Inside the sanctuary is a statue of the Virgin Mary from 1503. Other churches worth visiting are the Carmelites' (with canvases by Pietro D'Asaro), the Itria and San Giuliano, which was once the chapel of the **Sant'Agostino Convent**. A short walk from the centre takes you to **Piazza Fontana**, with a stone drinking trough, and, further along, Piazza San Francesco, where there is the monastery complex of the Conventual friars, rebuilt in the 1600s.

Mussomeli ⓿

Road map C3. 11,638.
0934-956 203. **Castello Manfredano** 9:30am–1pm, 3:30–5pm.

IN THE 14TH CENTURY, Manfredi III Chiaramonte founded the town of Mussomeli and the large fortress that still towers over what has since become a large agricultural centre. The **castle**, called Manfredano in honour of its founder and built over the remains of a Hohenstaufen fortification, was altered in the 15th century by the Castellar family. It has a second walled enclosure in the interior as well as the Sala dei Baroni, with noteworthy portals. From the outer walls there are lovely panoramic views of the valleys and hills of the interior of the island.

Racalmuto ⓾

Road map C4. 10,244.
from Catania and Palermo (via Caltanissetta). Comune di Racalmuto (0922-948 111).

THE TOWN OF Racalmuto (the name derives from the Arab *rahalmut*, or destroyed hamlet) was founded by Federico Chiaramonte (head of the powerful Sicilian Chiaramonte family) over an existing fortification. For centuries the growth of the town went hand in hand with the development of various monastic orders (Carmelite, Franciscan, Minor and Augustines), but the place still bears traces of the typical Arab layout marked by courtyards and alleys. For centuries Racalmuto thrived on the mining of rock salt and sulphur. The town is also the birthplace of author Leonardo Sciascia *(see p21)*. Today it is a famous agricultural centre, especially known for its dessert grapes.

In the middle of town, in Piazza Umberto I, is the 17th-century **Chiesa Madre dell'Annunziata**, its interior decorated with lavish stucco, as well as **San Giuseppe** and the ruins of the 13th-century **Chiaramonte castle**. Steps lead to Piazza del Municipio, with the **Santa Chiara**

Naro ⓫

Road map C4. 11,273. Comune di Naro (0922-956 368).

NARO LIES ON a hill in the middle of a water-rich area. Its name derives from ancient Greek and Arab origins – the Greek word for river is *naron*, and *nahr* is the Arab translation of the same.

A "resplendent" royal city during the reign of Frederick II Hohenstaufen, it was fortified at different times. Besides the Baroque churches and the remains of monasteries, there are the ruins of the medieval **Chiaramonte castle**, which is always closed, 14th-century Santa Caterina and the 16th-century Chiesa Madre.

The Chiaramonte castle at Naro, built in the 14th century

The 15th-century Castello di Montechiaro, overlooking the sea

Canicattì ⑫

Road map C4. 🏚 33,784.
🛈 *Comune di Canicatti (0922-73411 or 167-012 303).*

THE LARGE agricultural town of Canicattì owes its fame to the production of dessert grapes (a festival in celebration is held each autumn). Known to Arab geographers as *al-Qattà*, this town became a part of documented Sicilian history in the 14th century, when it was registered as the fief of the Palmieri family from Naro. The late 18th century marked a period of prosperity and growth under the Bonanno family, who commissioned numerous buildings and public works.

In the centre of town are the ruins of the **Castello Bonanno** and the **Torre dell'Orologio**, rebuilt in the 1930s. Economic prosperity is confirmed by the many churches – **San Diego**, rebuilt in the Baroque period with stucco decoration; the **Chiesa del Purgatorio**, with a statue of the Sacred Heart; the **Chiesa del Carmelo**, rebuilt in the early 20th century with funds donated by the local sulphur mine workers – and civic works such as the **Fountain of Neptune** and the recent **Teatro Sociale**. The **Chiesa Madre** is dedicated to San Pancrazio. It was rebuilt in the early 20th century. The new façade is the work of Francesco Basile and among its many interesting sculptures and paintings is the *Madonna delle Grazie*, sculpted in the 16th century in Byzantine style. Along the main street in the upper town there are three monasteries.

Baroque decoration on a building in Licata

Palma di Montechiaro ⑬

Road map C4. 🏚 24,681.
🛈 *Comune di Palma di Montechiaro (0922-799 111).*

FOUNDED IN 1637 by Carlo Tomasi, the Prince of Lampedusa, Palma owes its name to the palm tree on the coat of arms of the De Caro family, relatives of the Tomasi. The town was the property of the Tomasi di Lampedusa family up to the early 19th century, but the family name became really famous only after the publication of the novel *Il Gattopardo (The Leopard)* in 1958.

Palma was created with a town plan, partly the inspiration of the 17th-century astronomer Giovanni Battista Odierna, and loosely based on that of Jerusalem. The layout revolves around **Piazza Provenzani**, with the church of **Santissimo Rosario** and a Benedictine monastery. Further up is the monumental stairway leading to Piazza Santa Rosalia, with the **Chiesa Madre**, built in the late 1600s with an impressive two-stage façade flanked by twin bell towers. On Sundays and holidays this square is the hub of city life.

A walk through town reveals a number of interesting Baroque buildings.

IL GATTOPARDO

Tomasi di Lampedusa's famous novel *(see pp21–2)* was a great success when it was published posthumously in 1958, selling over 100,000 copies. It was later made into a highly acclaimed film by Luchino Visconti. The novel was published thanks to the efforts of novelist Giorgio Bassani, who met Tomasi di Lampedusa in 1954, three years before he died. Most of the novel is set in Palermo, but there are recognizable descriptions of the villages and landscape in this part of Sicily, with which the author had strong bonds.

Giuseppe Tomasi di Lampedusa (1896–1957)

A typical square in Licata

A few miles away, not far from the sea, are the evocative ruins of **Castello di Montechiaro**, founded, according to tradition by Federico III Chiaramonte. Although it is now closed for restoration, it is worthwhile visiting the site of this 15th-century castle because of the wonderful views of the coastline from its walls.

Licata ❹

Road map C4. 👥 *42,828.* 🚆 *from Syracuse, Palermo & Catania, via Caltanissetta (0922-774 122).* ℹ️ *167-211 275.*

LICATA IS ONE of the chief market garden towns in southern Sicily. It was built in the Greek period – according to tradition it was founded by the tyrant of Agrigento, Phintias, in 280 BC and was named after him – and under Roman dominion became the port for the shipment of local produce. Evidence of the town's former wealth can be seen in the many rock-hewn Byzantine churches. After the period of Arab rule, in 1234 Frederick II made it part of the public domain, building fortresses which over the centuries have disappeared (Castel Nuovo was destroyed by the Turks at the end of the 1561 siege). Licata again became a part of history on 10 July 1943, when the Allied troops landed nearby and advanced northwards in their conquest of Italian territory. The centre of town life is Piazza Progresso, where there is the art deco **Municipio** or Town Hall, designed in 1935 by Ernesto Basile, which houses some interesting art works, including a statue of the *Madonna and Child* and a 15th-century triptych. Also worth visiting is the **Museo Civico**, which has exhibits of prehistoric artefacts from the Palaeolithic to the Bronze Age, archaic Greek (particularly funerary objects) and Hellenistic archaeological finds, and a series of medieval statues representing the Christian virtues. Along Corso Vittorio Emanuele, which leads towards the coast, there are some patrician mansions such as **Palazzo Frangipane**, which has an 18th-century façade decorated with reliefs. On the Corso you can also see the **Chiesa Matrice di Santa Maria la Nova**, which, according to local legend, the Turks tried to burn down in 1553. Founded in the 1500s, it houses a 16th-century crucifix and a 17th-century Flemish Nativity scene. The harbour is almost exclusively given over to fishing boats since the decline of sulphur mining drastically decreased its industrial importance.

🏛 **Museo Civico**
Piazza Linares 7.
📞 *0922-868 111.*

Castello di Falconara ❺

Road map D4. 🕐 *by appt only.*
📞 *0934-347 929.*

NOT FAR FROM Licata, on the road towards Gela, is the village of Falconara, famous most of all for the impressive castle towering above the sea from the top of a rocky bluff. The Castello di Falconara was built in the 15th century. It is usually closed, but you can make an appointment to view with the custodian.

Towards Licata is the Salso river, the second largest in Sicily. Its name derives from the many outcrops of rock salt which make its waters salty (*salso* means saline). The river flows through the Sommatino plateau, a mining area, and down a series of gullies before meandering across the coastal plains.

Castello di Falconara, constructed in the 15th century, set among greenery at the water's edge

Pantelleria ⑯

Road map A5. 7,717.
Comune di Pantelleria (0923-911 077); Pro Loco (0923-911 838).

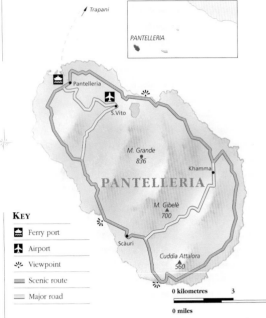

KEY

🚢 Ferry port

🛬 Airport

☼ Viewpoint

▭ Scenic route

— Major road

PANTELLERIA, the largest island off the Sicilian coastline, is also closer to the Tunisian coast (Capo Mustafà is 70 km or 44 miles away) than to Capo Granitola in Sicily (100 km, 62 miles). Despite this isolation, Pantelleria was colonized by the Phoenicians and then by the Greeks. It was controlled by the Arabs for almost 400 years (in fact, its name derives from *Bent el-Rhia*, "daughter of the wind") and was then conquered and fortified in 1123 by Roger I. Since that time its history has run in parallel to the vicissitudes of Sicily.

The strong wind that blows here all year round has forced the inhabitants to protect their plants and kitchen gardens with enclosures and walls, and to prune the olive trees so that they grow almost horizontally, close to the ground. Wind is also responsible for a typical style of building called *dammuso*, a square, whitewashed peasant's house with walls almost 2 m (6 ft) thick and tiny windows in order to provide the best insulation. Water is scarce on the island, so the roofs of these homes are shaped to collect rainwater. The coastal road is 45 km (28 miles) in length; it starts at the town of Pantelleria and goes past the

archaeological zone of Mursia (with a series of megalithic structures called *sesi* in local dialect) and then goes up to high ground. The main sights here are **Punta Fram**, **Cala dell'Altura** and **Punta Tre Pietre**, where another road takes you to the village of **Scauri**. The coast is steep and craggy with some inlets (like the **Balata dei Turchi**, a favourite landing place for Saracen pirates, or the lovely **Cala**

Walled gardens on Pantelleria

Rotonda) up to the **Punta Tracino** promontory– with a striking rock formation in front of it – which separates the **Tramontana** and **Levante inlets**. After the village of Gadir and the lighthouse at Punta Spasdillo the road descends to the **Cala Cinque Denti** inlet or the **Bagno dell'Acqua** hot springs and then back to its starting point. The town of **Pantelleria**, at the foot of the **Barbacane Castle**, was almost destroyed by Allied bombings in World War II. Life revolves around **Piazza Cavour** and the new **Chiesa Madre**, both facing the sea. Renting a bicycle is a very pleasant way of getting to know the island and the local way of life, as well as the handicrafts, the famous *Moscato passito* dessert wine and the locally grown capers.

Arco dell'Elefante, one of the most beautiful spots in Pantelleria

Baia dei Conigli in Lampedusa, where the rare sea turtle still survives

Lampedusa ⑰

Road map A4. 🏛 *(with Linosa)*
5,192. 🚢 ✈ 🚉 *APT Agrigento
(0922-401 352); Consorzio Albergatori 35° Parallelo (0922-971 906).*
🎏 *22 Sep.*

THE LARGEST ISLAND in the
Pelagie (the archipelago
that includes Linosa and the
small island of Lampione),
Lampedusa is 200 km (124
miles) from Sicily and 150 km
(93 miles) from Malta. The
Greek name *Pelaghiè* reflects
their chief characteristic –
isolation in the middle of the
sea. Inhabited for a little more
than a century – from the
time Ferdinand II of Bourbon
sent a group of colonists and
prisoners there – Lampedusa
was soon deforested, which
in turn brought about the
almost total degradation of
the soil and any possibility of
cultivating it. Human settlements have also led to a
dramatic decrease in local
fauna, and the Baia dei Conigli nature reserve was set
up to create a safe refuge for
sea turtles (*Caretta caretta*).
The island's main beaches are
Cala Maluk, **Cala
Croce**, **Baia dei
Conigli**, **Cala Galera**
and **Cala Greca**, and
diving is one of the
many popular sports.
Near the town of
Lampedusa (almost
completely destroy-
ed in 1943) is the
**Madonna di Lam-
pedusa Sanctuary**,
where on 22
September the
Bourbon takeover is
commemorated.

**Entrance to a
house in Linosa**

Linosa ⑱

Road map A4.
🏛 *(with Lampedusa) 5,192.* 🚢
🚉 *APT Agrigento (0922-401 352);
Consorzio Albergatori 35° Parallelo
(0922-971 906).*

ANCIENT Aethusa, 40 km (25
miles) from Lampedusa, is
a small volcanic
island where life
centres around the
village of Linosa,
with its brightly
coloured houses.
Thanks to the natur-
ally fertile volcanic
soil, agriculture
thrives on the island.
One of the best ways
of exploring Linosa
is by leaving the
road behind and
rambling around the craters
and the fenced-in fields.

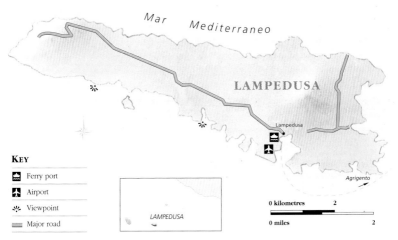

Caltanissetta

Road map D3. 👥 *62,069.* **FS** *from Catania & Palermo (0934-25047).* ℹ *Corso Vittorio Emanuele 109 (0934-530 411).*

ONE OF THE EARLIEST traces of a settlement in this area is the **Badia di Santo Spirito**, a Norman abbey commissioned by Roger I and his wife Adelasia in the late 11th century and consecrated in 1153. It is still one of the most interesting sights in Caltanissetta and its immediate vicinity. In common with other hill towns in the interior, Caltanissetta was surrounded by medieval walls and then expanded towards the monasteries, built around the city from the 15th century on. The centre of a thriving mineral-rich area, it became prosperous after the unification of Italy thanks to the **sulphur and rock salt mines**. It was during this period that the look of the town changed with the construction of buildings and public works. In the heart of town, in Piazza Garibaldi, are the Baroque **San Sebastiano** and the **Cathedral** (dedicated

The Baroque façade of San Sebastiano, completed in the 1800s

to Santa Maria la Nova and San Michele). A brief walk down Corso Umberto I will take you to **Sant'Agata** – or Chiesa del Collegio – built in 1605 for the Jesuits of Caltanissetta, next to their seminary. The rich decoration inside includes a marble statue of *St Ignatius in Glory* on the left-hand transept altar, the altarpiece *San Francesco Saverio* in a side chapel and a canvas of the *Martyrdom of Sant'Agata*. Not far from the **Castello di Pietrarossa**, probably a former Arab

fortress, is the **Museo Civico**, where the sections are given over exclusively to archaeology and to modern art.

The **Museo Mineralogico, Paleontologico e della Zolfara**, established by the local Mineralogy School, has a fine and extensive collection of minerals and fossils.

🔒 **Badia di Santo Spirito**
◯ *9am–noon, 4–6pm daily.*
🏛 **Museo Civico**
Via Colajanni 3. 📞 *0934-25936.*
◯ *9am–1pm Mon–Fri.* 📷

ENVIRONS: About 5 km (3 miles) along the main road to Enna is the site of the ancient city of **Sabucina**, which gives you the opportunity to see a prehistoric village and cave tombs dating from the 12th–10th centuries BC. The city became a Greek colony, but subsequently declined and was later abandoned.

🔒 **Sabucina**
◯ *8am–2pm, 4pm–sunset.*

The Badia di Santo Spirito, one of the major Norman churches in Sicily

EASTER WEEK

In the interior of Sicily the celebrations of the *Misteri*, or statues of the Stations of the Cross, during Easter Week, are of the greatest importance. At Enna they begin on Palm Sunday. For four days, the 15 city confraternities take part in processions through the streets to the Cathedral; on Good Friday a huge torchlit procession bears the statue of the Madonna of the Seven Griefs, the Reliquary of Christ's Thorn and the Dead Christ's Urn through the city; then on Easter Sunday the Resurrected Christ and the Virgin Mary statues meet in Piazza Duomo. At Caltanissetta, celebrations begin on Wednesday with the Procession of the Holy Sacrament, followed by the representatives of the 11 city confraternities. On Maundy Thursday the large statues of the Passion of Christ are taken through the city and on Good Friday the Passion of the Black Christ ends the celebrations.

Part of the colourful Easter Week celebrations

The Sulphur Mines
Ente Parco Minerario Floristella, Grottacalda (0935-958 105).

For centuries the Floristella sulphur field was one of the most important sources of wealth in the Sicilian hinterland. Mining activity ceased in 1988, but now work is under way to turn this yellow-stained land into a mining park, which will probably be unique in Sicily. Extraction reached its height during the 19th century – when Palazzo Pennisi, the residence of the mine owners, was built – and involved hundreds of workers in the mines and at the furnaces, where the sulphur was separated from the limestone rock.

Enna ⑳

Road map D3. 🏛 29,013.
FS *from Catania and Palermo (0935-500 91 10).* 🚌 *Viale Generale Muscarà 13 (0935-680 535).*

A MOUNTAIN TOWN – at 931 m (3,054 ft) the highest provincial capital in Italy – in antiquity Enna was first Greek, then Carthaginian and finally Roman. It remained a Byzantine stronghold even after the Arab conquest of Palermo, and was then conquered by general Al-Abbas Ibn Fadhl in 859 and was wrested from the Muslims only in 1087. From that time it was repeatedly fortified around the strongholds of Castello di Lom-

Enna Cathedral, built in the 15th century and rebuilt after a fire

The Castello di Lombardia, built over an Arab fortification

bardia and Castello Vecchio (present-day Torre di Federico). The defensive walls, no longer visible, were the basis of the city's plan, while all the principal sites of religious and civic power were constructed on what is now Via Roma. Because of its altitude, Enna has a climate unique in the interior of Sicily and even during summer the temperature is pleasant. The town's exceptional position means splendid views. Going up Via Roma, you first come to Piazza Vittorio Emanuele, site of **San Francesco d'Assisi**, the only

The " Madonna's Crown", Museo Alessi in Enna

original part of which is the fine 15th-century bell tower. In Piazza Colajanni you will see the façade of **Palazzo Pollicarini**, which has many Catalan Gothic features on the side next to the stairway, as well as the former church of **Santa Chiara**.

In 1307 Eleonora, wife of Frederick II of Aragon, founded the **Cathedral** of Enna. The building was destroyed by fire in the mid-1400s and subsequently rebuilt. A fine 16th-century doorway – with a bas-relief depicting *St Martin and the Beggar* – leads to the Latin cross interior with two aisles. The cathedral is richly decorated with an assortment of statues and paintings.

Just past the Gothic apse are the rooms housing the **Museo Alessi**, which includes the Cathedral Treasury with its candelabra and vestments, a fine collection of coins and an art gallery featuring *St John the Baptist*, part of a 16th-century wooden triptych.

Almost directly opposite the entrance of the Museo Alessi is the **Museo Archeologico**,  with a fine display of prehistoric, Greek and Roman archaeological items found in the city, in the area around and near Lake Pergusa. But the pride and joy of Enna are its two fortresses. The **Castello di Lombardia**, built by the Hohenstaufens and altered in the Aragonese era, is one of the most important in Sicily. A tour here includes the three courtyards, the Torre Pisana and the Rocca di Cerere. In the public gardens is the octagonal **Torre di Federico II**, the only remaining part of the original defences.

🏛 **Museo Alessi**
📞 *0935-24072.* ⏰ *9am–1pm.* 🚫 *Mon.* 🚫
🏛 **Museo Archeologico**
⏰ *9am–1:30pm, 3:30–6:30pm (9:30am–12:30pm hols).* 🚫
♙ **Castello di Lombardia**
⏰ *9am–1pm, 3–6:30pm.*
♙ **Torre di Federico II**
⏰ *9am–1pm, 3–6:30pm.*

Morgantina ㉑

Sᴵᴛᴜᴀᴛᴇᴅ ᴀʙᴏᴜᴛ 4 km (2 miles) from Aidone, the ancient city of Morgantina was founded by the so-called Morgeti, a population from Latium who settled here around 1000 BC. The city was then occupied by Greek colonists. Its golden age, when the city was a strategic trade centre between the north and south of Sicily, was in the Hellenistic and Roman periods. From the top of a hill the large site affords visitors a fine view of what remains of the theatre, as well as the city streets and the agora, all set in lovely countryside.

The Gymnasium
This was a large area for athletic exercises, with baths (in the photo), dressing rooms and rooms with equipment for the athletes.

RECONSTRUCTION OF MORGANTINA

This drawing shows the city as it appeared around 300 BC. The reconstruction is based on studies made by archaeologists from Princeton University in the United States.

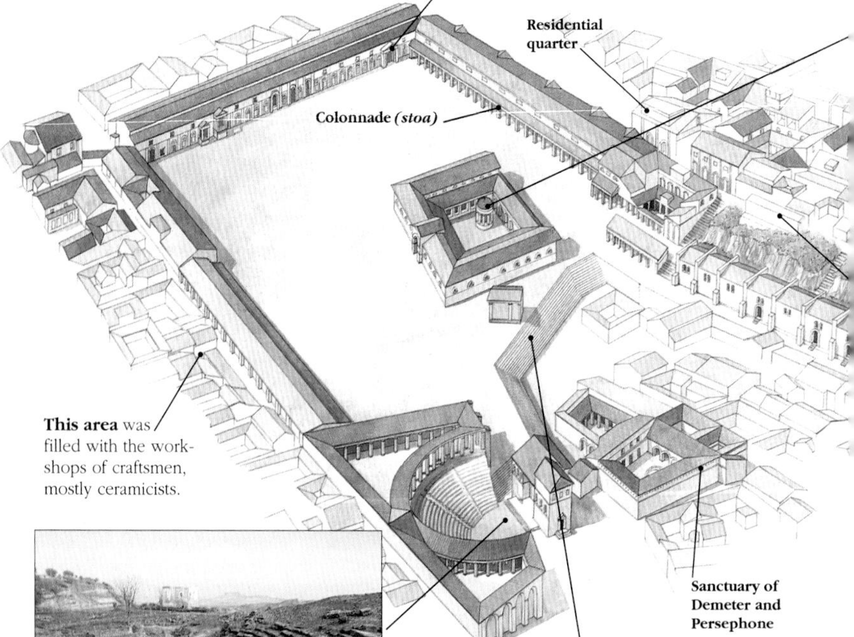

Residential quarter

Colonnade *(stoa)*

This area was filled with the work-shops of craftsmen, mostly ceramicists.

Sanctuary of Demeter and Persephone

★ Theatre
Constructed at the end of the 4th century BC, the theatre at Morgantina was carved out of the slope of a hill and could seat about a thousand spectators.

| 0 metres | 50 |
| 0 yards | 50 |

★ Agora
Unusually, the agora, or forum, was divided into two parts, one above the other, linked by a trapezoidal, 14-step stairway.

The Market
This lay in the middle of the upper agora. Above is the tholos, a round structure which had a number of different functions.

Street Paving
In the eastern residential quarter, the remains of the paved street leading out of the city walls are still visible.

STAR FEATURES

★ **Theatre**

★ **Agora**

Piazza Armerina ㉒

Road map D4. 🏛 *22,207.* ⓘ *AAST, Piazza Armerina, Via Cavour 15.* ⓒ *0935-680 201.* 🎪 *Palio dei Normanni (13–14 Aug).*

IN THE MIDDLE of an area inhabited since the 8th century BC, Piazza Armerina developed in the Middle Ages, a period marked by frequent clashes between the local population – strongly influenced by the centuries of Arab domination – and the Latin conquerors. After the huge devastation wrought in the 12th century by battles between these two factions, Piazza Armerina was recreated around the Colle Mira hill (in the middle of the present-day Monte quarter) and was populated by a colony of Lombards from Piacenza. A new, massive defensive wall system was built in the late 14th century, but the city soon spread well beyond this into the surrounding hills and slopes.

In the heart of town is a large **Aragonese Castle**, built by King Martin I in the late 14th century, whose massive towers dominate the **Cathedral**. Dedicated to Our Lady of the Assumption, the Cathedral is flanked by the campanile of another church which had been built on the same site in the 14th century. Inside, look out for the choir, built in 1627, and a wooden crucifix painted in the late 15th century. The Cathedral also affords access to the small **Museo Diocesano,**

The Cathedral at Piazza Armerina, with its 14th-century bell-tower

which has vestments, monstrances and reliquaries on display. Elsewhere in the town are many other interesting attractions. **Piazza Garibaldi** is the heart of town life, boasting the Baroque **Palazzo del Senato** and two palatial mansions belonging to the barons of Capodarso. The whole of the historic centre deserves further exploration on foot, through charming medieval alleys, steps and lanes.

Not far from town, at the end of Via Tasso, is the **Chiesa del Priorato di Sant'Andrea**, founded in 1096 and then acquired by the Knights of the Order of the Holy Sepulchre. This magnificent example of Sicilian Romanesque architecture has a commanding view over a valley. Do not miss seeing the series of 12th- to 14th-century frescoes in the interior (visits are allowed only on Sundays, when mass is celebrated).

View of Piazza Armerina, which developed around the Colle Mira hill

Villa del Casale

Autumn, from the Hall of the Seasons

THIS FAMOUS VILLA was part of a 3rd-4th century AD estate, and is one of the most fascinating attractions in archaeologically rich Sicily. The exceptionally beautiful mosaics that decorated every one of the rooms of the landowner's apartments have been preserved through the centuries, thanks to a flood that buried them in mud in the 12th century. The villa was discovered in the late 19th century. A logical sequence for a visit to the site is as follows: the thermae, the large peristyle, the long corridor with hunting scenes and, lastly, the owners' private apartments.

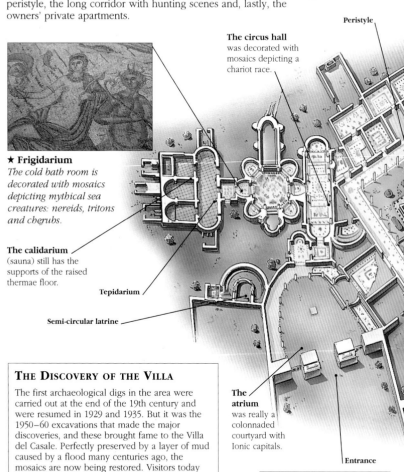

Peristyle

The circus hall was decorated with mosaics depicting a chariot race.

★ Frigidarium
The cold bath room is decorated with mosaics depicting mythical sea creatures: nereids, tritons and cherubs.

The calidarium (sauna) still has the supports of the raised thermae floor.

Tepidarium

Semi-circular latrine

The atrium was really a colonnaded courtyard with Ionic capitals.

Entrance

THE DISCOVERY OF THE VILLA

The first archaeological digs in the area were carried out at the end of the 19th century and were resumed in 1929 and 1935. But it was the 1950–60 excavations that made the major discoveries, and these brought fame to the Villa del Casale. Perfectly preserved by a layer of mud caused by a flood many centuries ago, the mosaics are now being restored. Visitors today may come across expert archaeologists working on the tesserae of what have been called "the most exceptional Roman mosaics in the world".

The exterior of the Villa del Casale

STAR FEATURES

★ Frigidarium

★ Corridor with hunting scenes

★ The Myth of Arion

★ Hall of the Female Gymnasts in Bikinis

★ Corridor with hunting scenes
This passageway contains splendid mosaics representing wild game hunting. Ferocious beasts such as boar and lions are being loaded onto ships after capture.

Northern area
The vestibule in the private apartments of the villa has a large mosaic depicting Ulysses and Polyphemus.

0 metres	10
0 yards	10

★ The Myth of Arion
In the colonnaded semicircular atrium leading to the dome-roofed hall, Arion, threatened by her sailors, is saved by a dolphin.

Aqueduct

★ Hall of the Female Gymnasts in Bikinis
The ten gymnasts seen in the mosaics in this hall are a rare and precious record of the Roman fashions of the time.

Triclinium
The mosaics in the dining room feature the Labours of Hercules and other mythological subjects.

SOUTHERN SICILY

D OMINATED BY *Mount Etna, Southern Sicily's permanent backdrop, this area is a curious mixture of fertile land and intensive cultivation, ancient monuments and utter neglect. Many towns and monuments built by the ancient Greeks still survive, most notably in the town of Syracuse, birthplace of Archimedes.*

Southern Sicily, which the Arabs called the Val di Noto, presents another facet of Sicily. It is very different from the eastern end of the island, although the topography is equally varied. The south has Phoenician Palermo, the former Greek Syracuse. One of Sicily's most important sights is the stony-tiered Greek theatre in Syracuse. The tradition of performing ancient Greek plays was revived in 1914, and now every other summer the great works of the ancient tragedians come to life in their natural setting. This part of Sicily is also home to the ancient Greek ruins of Megara Hyblaea, now sadly dominated by the eerie landscape of the refineries of Augusta.

Inland, the rebuilding of towns following the terrible earthquake of 1693 has resulted in a number of Baroque gems. The churches, buildings and balconies of Ragusa, Modica, Scicli, Noto and Chiaramonte are a triumph of the Sicilian Baroque style, with their majestic steps, detailed ornamentation and curving façades. Ibla, the medieval quarter of Ragusa, should be included on a tour of the towns of the interior: rocky Caltagirone is an important ceramics centre, and Chiaramonte and Vizzini also have their charms. In complete contrast you can also experience the natural silence of the rock-cut necropolises in the cliffs of Ispica and Pantalica.

Fishing boats anchored in Ortygia harbour in Syracuse

◁ The majestic Baroque portal of Ragusa Cathedral, dedicated to St John the Baptist

Exploring Southern Sicily

AN ALMOST OBLIGATORY starting point for any visit to the southern tip of Sicily is Syracuse, with its exceptional artistic and cultural heritage. It lies about 60 km (37 miles) from Catania airport and is a two-hour drive from Messina, along a scenic route with the Ionian Sea of Taormina to your left and the massive presence of Mount Etna to your right. Besides Syracuse, the most popular sights in this area are the old cities in the interior – Noto, Modica, Caltagirone, Ragusa and ancient Ibla. The mountains conceal an impressive testimony to the ancient history of southern Sicily in the crevices of Pantalica, Ispica or Palazzolo Acreide and Lentini.

SEE ALSO

• **Where to Stay** pp190–97

• **Where to Eat** pp200–208

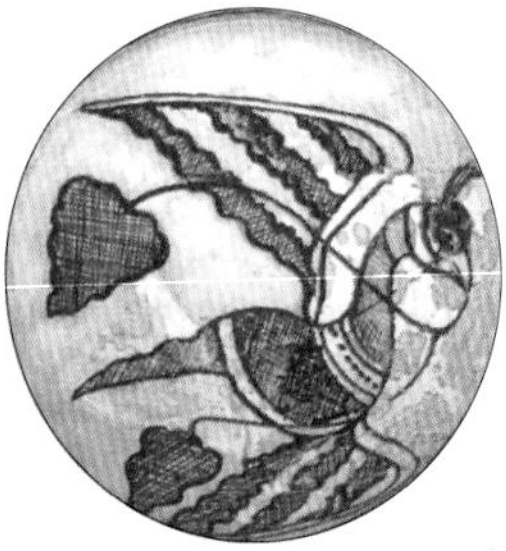

↑ *Caltanissetta*

CALTAGIRONE ⑭

SS117bis

Agrigento ←

GELA ⑩

SS115

VITTORIA ⑨

Ippari

Ceramic plate produced in Caltagirone

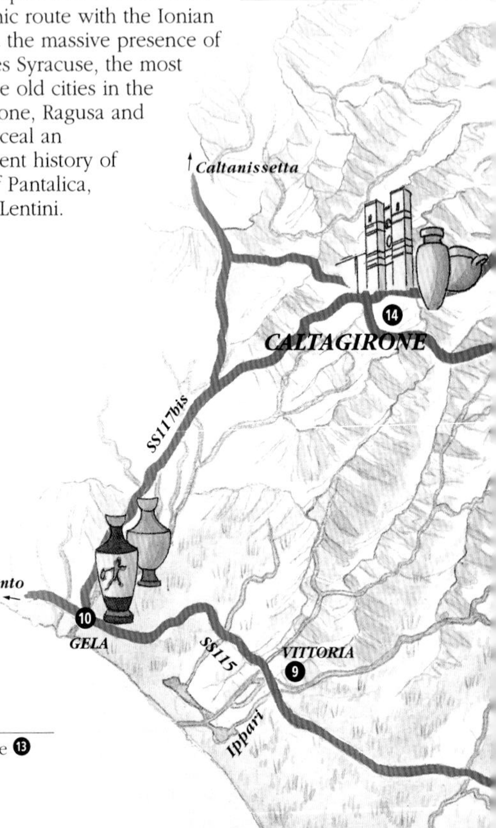

Sights at a Glance

Augusta ⑰
Caltagirone pp150–51 ⑭
Capo Passero ④
Cava d'Ispica ⑤
Chiaramonte Gulfi ⑪
Gela ⑩
Lentini ⑮
Megara Hyblaea ⑯
Modica ⑧
Noto pp140–43 ②
Pachino ③

Palazzolo Acreide ⑬
Pantalica ⑱
Ragusa pp146–7 ⑦
Scicli ⑥
Syracuse pp132–9 ①
Vittoria ⑨
Vizzini ⑫

Key

▨ Motorway

▬ Major road

▭ Minor road

— River

❋ Viewpoint

Irminio

The Baroque façade of the Basilica di San Giorgio in Ragusa

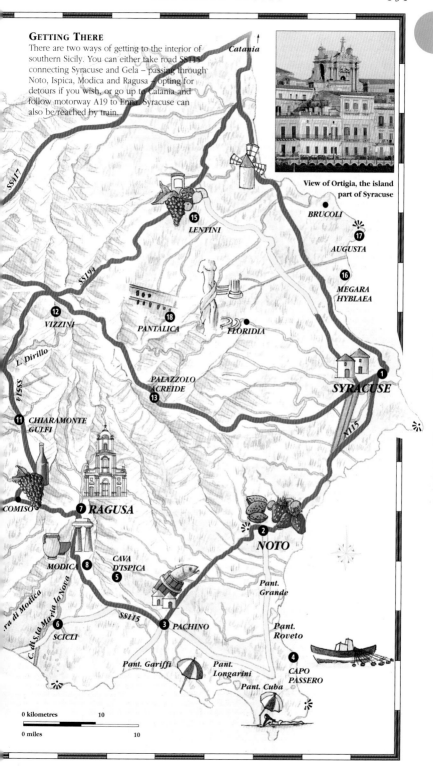

GETTING THERE

There are two ways of getting to the interior of
southern Sicily. You can either take road SS115
connecting Syracuse and Gela – passing through
Noto, Ispica, Modica and Ragusa – opting for
detours if you wish, or go up to Catania and
follow motorway A19 to Enna. Syracuse can
also be reached by train.

Catania

View of Ortigia, the island
part of Syracuse

BRUCOLI

17

AUGUSTA

16

*MEGARA
HYBLAEA*

SS417

15

LENTINI

SS194

12

VIZZINI

18

PANTALICA

FLORIDIA

L. Dirillo

SS514

*PALAZZOLO
ACREIDE*

13

1

SYRACUSE

N115

11

*CHIARAMONTE
GULFI*

COMISO

7 *RAGUSA*

MODICA

8

*CAVA
D'ISPICA*

5

2

NOTO

*Pant.
Grande*

C.ra di Modica

C. di S.ta Maria la Nova

6

SCICLI

SS115

3 *PACHINO*

*Pant.
Roveto*

Pant. Gariffi

*Pant.
Longarini*

Pant. Cuba

4

*CAPO
PASSERO*

0 kilometres   10

0 miles   10

Syracuse ●

OR 27 centuries the city of Syracuse, in modern Italian, Siracusa, has been of great economic and cultural importance. From the prehistoric populations to the Corinthians who founded the Greek city, to the introduction of Baroque architecture, the history of Syracuse is an open book, clearly visible in many streets and buildings. The Greek theatre survives in good condition, and you can still see the stone quarries, or Latomie, which provided stone for many of the ancient monuments, but also served as prisons.

Goddess, Museo Archeologico

⋔ The Neapolis Archaeological Area
Viale Paradiso. ☎ 0931-66206.
🕓 9am–2 hrs before sunset.
⬤ Mon. 🎫
The Neapolis archaeological area was established in 1955 with the aim of grouping the antiquities of Syracuse within one site, enabling visitors to make an uninterrupted tour of the city's most remote past. Not far from the ticket office for the park is medieval **San Nicolò dei Cordari**, built over a reservoir *(piscina)* cut out of the rock, which was used for cleaning the nearby Roman amphitheatre.

⋔ Greek Theatre
See pp134–5.

🎭 Latomies
A huge hollow separates the theatre area and the southern section of the archaeological site. This is the area of the Latomies – stone quarries – from which Syracuse architects extracted millions of cubic metres of stone for building. The enormous caves were also used as prisons for centuries. The Ear of Dionysius (**Orecchio di Dioniso**), is one of the most impressive

Entrance to the Orecchio di Dioniso, in the Latomie area

quarries. According to legend, thanks to the extraordinary acoustics of this cave, the local tyrant Dionysius could hear the whispers of his most

SYRACUSE

Altar of Hieron II ③
Catacombs of San
  Giovanni Evangelista ⑥
Greek Theatre pp134–5 ②
Latomies ①
*Museo Archeologico
  Regionale pp136–7* ⑦
Museo del Papiro ⑧
Ortygia pp138–9 ⑨
Roman Amphitheatre ④
Tomb of Archimedes ⑤

KEY

🚆 Railway station

🅿 Parking

ℹ️ Tourist information

✝ Church

⛴ Ferry service

0 metres   600
0 yards   600

The large Grotta dei Cordari, the most interesting of the Latomie caves

VISITORS' CHECKLIST

Road map F4. 🚌 *120,949.*
🚆 *from Messina, Naples, Rome, Milan, Turin (0931-67964).*
📮 🚌 ℹ️ *APT (0931-67710 or 461 477); Via Maestanza (0931-67964). SAIS (0931-66710).*
🎉 *13 Dec, Santa Lucia; first Sunday in May, Santa Lucia delle Quaglie.*

dangerous prisoners and thus take due precautions. There are other huge adjacent caves, including the **Grotta dei Cordari**, which until recent times was used by local rope makers *(cordari)*, the **Latomia Intagliatella** and the **Latomia Santa Venera**. All are closed for restoration work intended to reverse the centuries of neglect that have made the ancient caves unsafe.

⌂ Tomb of Archimedes

In the northwestern corner of the Neapolis site there is an area that was used as a burial ground until the Hellenistic era. This is known as the **Necropoli Grotticelli**. One of the largest tombs here is traditionally called the **Tomb of Archimedes**. Archimedes was a native of Syracuse and one of the greatest scientists in antiquity *(see p26)*.

⌂ Altar of Hieron II and Roman Amphitheatre

These lie on the other side of the road that cuts the Neapolis area in two. Although only the foundations remain of the **Altar of Hieron II**, its impressive size (198 x 23 m, 649 x 75 ft) is clear. This monument was dedicated to Zeus and was used for public sacrifices, in which as many as 400 bulls were put to death at one time. A huge public work undertaken in the early years of the Empire, the **Roman Amphitheatre** (outer diameter, 140 x 119 m, 459 x 390 ft) is only slightly smaller than the Arena in Verona. The walls in the interior were part of the underground section, used to house the stage scenery. Beneath the tiers were corridors through which the gladiators and wild beasts entered the arena.

🏛 Museo Archeologico Regionale

See pp136–7.

⌂ Catacombs of San Giovanni Evangelista

Via di San Giovanni. ☐ *mid-Mar–mid-Nov: 9am–noon, 3–6pm; mid-Nov–mid-Mar: 9am–1pm.*
This underground complex – which dates back to 315–360 BC – housed hundreds of loculi, or rooms, which were used to bury the followers of the new Christian religion in Roman times.
  The main gallery of the catacombs, which was made by enlarging a former Greek aqueduct, leads to a series of round chapels that still bear traces of frescoes.

🏛 Museo del Papiro

Viale Teocrito 66. 📞 *0931-61616.* ☐ *9am–2pm.* ● *Mon.*
This museum is devoted to the *Cyperus papyrus* plant. The largest European colony of the papyrus plant thrives on the banks of the Ciane river near Syracuse.

The stepped base of the Altar of Hieron II, giving an idea of the impressive size of the original sacrificial site

The Greek Theatre

T HIS IS ONE OF THE MOST important examples of ancient theatre architecture anywhere, and for centuries it was the centre of Syracusan life. The Greek theatre was a much more complex construction than today's ruins might indicate; in 1520–31, Emperor Charles V had much of the stone transported to build the walls around Ortygia *(see pp138–9)*. Designed in the 5th century BC by the Greek architect Damacopos, the theatre was enlarged in the 3rd and 2nd centuries BC by Hieron II. From the 5th century BC onwards, the great Greek playwrights, including Aeschylus who premiered some of his tragedies here, wrote and staged their works in this magnificent setting.

Votive niches
To the west of the grotto near the ancient colonnade, the wall is punctuated by a series of rectangular niches that might have housed votive paintings or tablets in honour of Syracusan heroes.

Grotta del *Museion*
This cave, hewn out of the rock wall above the theatre, has a rectangular basin where the aqueduct flowed.

The *cavea* (auditorium) is over 138 m (453 ft) wide with 67 tiers, divided into 10 vertical blocks (or "wedges"). Each block was served by a flight of steps and was indicated by a letter, a custom that survives in modern theatres today.

The diazoma divided the auditorium into two parts.

Classical Greek theatre
In even-numbered years, the Greek theatre in Syracuse hosts a summer programme of classical theatre.

VISITORS' CHECKLIST

Greek Theatre and Neapolis Archaeological Zone Viale Paradiso. ☏ 0931-66206. ○ 9am–2 hrs before sunset. ● Mon.

Istituto Nazionale del Dramma Antico (INDA)
Corso Matteotti 29. ☏ 0931-67415 or 65373.

Galleries
Called criptae, *the galleries were cut out of the rock in the Roman period to replace the more ancient passageways of the* cavea, *which had been removed to create more seating space.*

The stage area was greatly enlarged in the Roman period.

Two enormous pillars of rock stood either side of the stage area.

0 metres 10
0 yards 10

On the orchestra was a monument to Dionysus, around which the chorus acted, danced and sang.

Logo dell'INDA di Siracusa

THE ISTITUTO NAZIONALE DEL DRAMMA ANTICO

On 16 April 1914, the tradition of performing ancient Greek theatre was revived at Syracuse, and now a season of plays first performed here over 2,500 years ago is put on every other year. The Istituto Nazionale del Dramma Antico (National Institute of Ancient Drama), was set up in 1925. The Scuola Professionale di Teatro Antico (Professional School of Ancient Theatre) joined as partners in 1983.

Playbill of Aeschylus' *Libation Bearers* **designed by Duilio Cambellotti (1921)**

Museo Archeologico Regionale Paolo Orsi

6th–5th century BC theatre mask

FOUNDED IN 1967 (and opened to the public in 1988), in order to establish a proper home for the enormous quantity of material excavated from digs throughout southeastern Sicily, the Regional Archaeological Museum is divided into three main sections with over 18,000 pieces on display. The museum is named after the eminent archaeologist Paolo Orsi, head of the Antiquities Department of Sicily from 1888, who was instrumental in fostering interest in the island's past and was personally responsible for many important excavations and discoveries. The collections named after him have been reorganized since the museum moved from its Ortygia site.

★ **Funerary statue**
This came from the digs at Megara Hyblaea, dating from 560–550 BC. The inscription on the right thigh shows it was dedicated to the physician Sambroditas.

Syracuse

Megara Hyblaea

Chalcidian colonies

Proto

Prehistory

Preh

Prehistory

GUIDE TO THE MUSEUM
The museum is divided into three sections. Section A features the geological history of Sicily and then the prehistoric, protohistoric and Siculan cultures. Section B is given over to the Greek colonies, and includes the Landolina Venus and the friezes from the Temple of Apollo. Last, Section C has material from the subcolonies founded by the Syracusans in 663–598 BC and from digs in the Hellenized towns in the interior. Finds from Gela and Agrigento complete the exhibition.

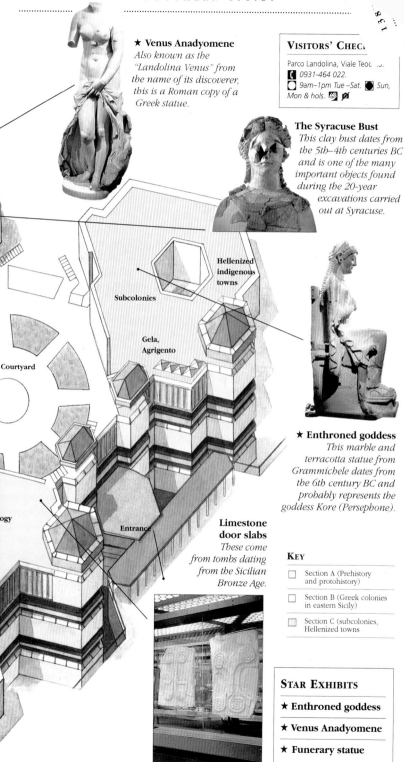

★ Venus Anadyomene
Also known as the "Landolina Venus" from the name of its discoverer, this is a Roman copy of a Greek statue.

The Syracuse Bust
This clay bust dates from the 5th–4th centuries BC and is one of the many important objects found during the 20-year excavations carried out at Syracuse.

Hellenized indigenous towns

Subcolonies

Gela, Agrigento

Courtyard

★ Enthroned goddess
This marble and terracotta statue from Grammichele dates from the 6th century BC and probably represents the goddess Kore (Persephone).

...logy

Entrance

Limestone door slabs
These come from tombs dating from the Sicilian Bronze Age.

KEY

☐	Section A (Prehistory and protohistory)
☐	Section B (Greek colonies in eastern Sicily)
☐	Section C (subcolonies, Hellenized towns

STAR EXHIBITS

★ Enthroned goddess

★ Venus Anadyomene

★ Funerary statue

Exploring Ortygia

T HE ISLAND OF ORTYGIA has always been the focal point of Syracuse. A stronghold until the end of the 19th century, it separates the city's two harbours (connected by the dock canal). Ortygia (in Italian, Ortigia) is now linked to the mainland by the Umbertino bridge. The town's long history is visible in many buildings, going back as far as the 6th-century BC Temple of Apollo.

Façade of Palazzo Beneventano del Bosco, opposite the Cathedral

Lungomare di Levante
This is the promenade that overlooks the **Porto Piccolo**, or small port, and is still the maritime heart of town. By going southwards along the promenade you reach **Spirito Santo**, with an 18th-century façade dramatically facing the sea. This church was the seat of the Holy Spirit Confraternity, hence its name.

Temple of Apollo
A good part of Piazza Pancali, as you enter Ortygia, consists of the ruins of the Temple of Apollo, which were discovered in 1860 inside the old Spanish barracks. The temple was built in the early 6th century BC, which makes it the oldest extant Doric temple in Western Europe. It is of an imposing size – 58 x 24 m (190 x 79 ft). On the top step of the base, an inscription to Apollo provides proof that the building was dedicated to the god. Over the centuries the temple has served as a Byzantine church, a mosque, again a Christian church under the Normans, and a military stronghold.

Palazzo Greco
On Corso Matteotti, an avenue created by demolition during the Fascist era, only one old building has survived: Palazzo Greco, founded in the mid-14th century and now serving as the home of the Istituto Nazionale del Dramma Antico (*see p135*). It has a lovely Gothic double lancet window and a loggia.

Palazzo Beneventano del Bosco
Piazza Duomo is home to Palazzo Beneventano del Bosco, built in 1779 by architect Luciano Alì. The façade, with its doorway supporting a lovely balcony, is an impressive sight. The interior is also interesting; a broad staircase leads up to the private apartments filled with **Decorative coat of arms on the Duomo façade** Venetian furniture, where Admiral Horatio Nelson and King Ferdinand III of Bourbon once stayed.

Duomo
Piazza Duomo. ☐ *8am–noon; 4–7pm.*
In Piazza Duomo, next to the **Palazzo del Senato**, now the Town Hall, is the city's Cathedral, built in 1728–53. It was designed by Andrea Palma, and incorporates an ancient Temple of Minerva, which in turn had been built over the site of a 6th-century BC monument, which Gelon had dedicated to Athena. The intact ancient structures can be best seen by skirting the outer northern side of the church, where a series of massive columns from the temple are clearly visible. Initially a temple, and then a

The ruins of the Temple of Apollo, in the heart of Ortygia

The Baroque façade of the Duomo, designed by Andrea Palma (1728–53)

Christian church, the building became a Muslim mosque and finally a glorious example of Sicilian Baroque religious architecture. The Duomo contains a 13th-century font, Norman era mosaics, and many fine paintings and sculptures. The sacristy has 16 wooden choir stalls carved in 1489.

🏛 Galleria Regionale di Palazzo Bellomo

Via Capodieci. 📞 0931-69617 or 65343. ⏲ 9am–2pm Mon, Wed, Thu, 9am–2pm Tue & Fri, 9am–1pm Sun. ⬛ Mon. 🈺

This museum, housed in the **Parisio** and **Bellomo** palazzi, has both interesting architecture (much of the original Hohenstaufen construction still stands) and artworks on display. The first rooms contain medieval and Renaissance sculpture. The courtyard, decorated with coats of arms, leads to the first floor, with the jewel of the collection, Antonello da Messina's *Annunciation* (1474, *see p21*). In the next room is a display of Christmas cribs. The exhibition ends with Arab and Sicilian ceramics and jewels.

🏯 Fonte Aretusa

On Largo Aretusa, facing the **Porto Grande**, the waters of this spring still gush just as they did in Greek times. According to the myth made famous by Pindar and Virgil, Arethusa was a nymph transformed into a spring by the goddess Artemis.

🏠 San Filippo Apostolo

In the heart of the Giudecca – the Jewish quarter of Syracuse – is **San Filippo Apostolo**, which was built over the old synagogue. In the crypt you can still see the basin of holy water in which the Jewish women purified themselves.

🏯 Palazzo Margulensi-Montalto

A stone's throw from central **Piazza Archimede**, with the 19th-century **Fountain of Artemis**, a walk along Via Montalto takes you to Palazzo Margulensi-Montalto, one of the most interesting medieval buildings in Syracuse. Built in 1397, as indicated by the inscription over the portal, this palazzo has preserved some original elements: the Gothic windows of the façade supported by spiral columns, the staircase and the arcade.

♣ Castello Maniace

This castle is on the southern tip of Ortygia, where tradition says the temple of Hera and the villa of the Roman governor once stood. It was built by Frederick II in the 1200s and over the centuries had various functions: royal residence, fortress and even storehouse. The name derives from the Byzantine general Maniakes, who took the city from the Arabs. The castle is square, with four corner towers.

ENVIRONS: On the hill overlooking the city is the most important work of military architecture in the Greek world, the **Castello Eurialo**, built by Dionysius the Elder in 402 BC to protect Syracuse from the Carthaginians. Two rock-cut moats and a tower protected the fortress on the eastern side, a 15-m (49-ft) keep was built in the middle of the fortification, the walls and towers overlooked the sea.

⌂ Castello Eurialo

8 km (5 miles) from Syracuse. 📞 0931-711 773. ⏲ 9am–1 hr before sunset.

The ruins of the extensive Castello Eurialo

Street-by-Street: Noto **❷**

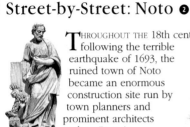

Sculpture in the Cathedral

THROUGHOUT THE 18th century, following the terrible earthquake of 1693, the ruined town of Noto became an enormous construction site run by town planners and prominent architects such as Rosario Gagliardi, Vincenzo Sinatra and Antonio Mazza. Today Noto's magnificent Baroque architecture is unique in Sicily, despite an unmistakable air of decay. Partly because of neglect and partly because of the fragile stone used, many buildings are deteriorating or quite badly damaged.

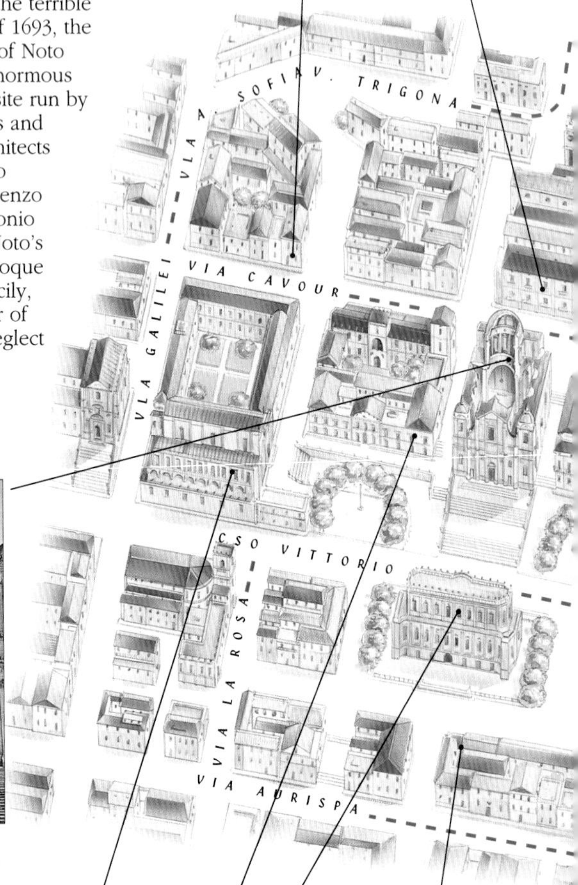

Montevergine church

Palazzo Astuto lies behind the Cathedral.

VIA SOFIA — V. TRIGONA

VIA GALILEI — VIA A

VIA CAVOUR

CSO VITTORIO

VIA LA ROSA

VIA AURISPA

★ Cathedral
Dedicated to San Nicolò, the Cathedral looks down on three flights of steps. The cupola collapsed in 1996.

Palazzo Nicolaci

Palazzo Landolina (Sant'Alfano)

Palazzo Ducezio
This building, now the Town Hall, stands opposite the Cathedral. The façade, with its lovely round arches, has been described as "a triumph of columns".

★ San Carlo al Corso
Formally called San Carlo Borromeo, this church is called "al Corso" because it lies on the city's main avenue, Corso Vittorio Emanuele.

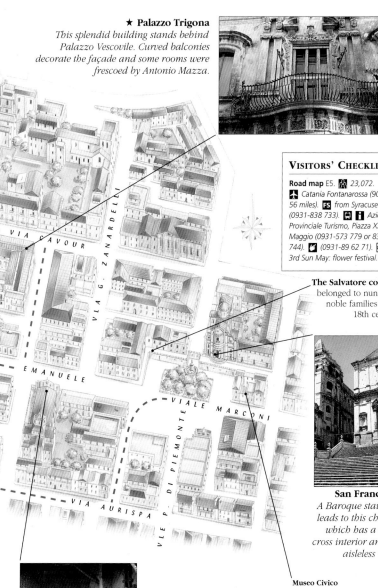

★ Palazzo Trigona
This splendid building stands behind Palazzo Vescovile. Curved balconies decorate the façade and some rooms were frescoed by Antonio Mazza.

VISITORS' CHECKLIST

Road map E5. 🏠 *23,072.*
✈ *Catania Fontanarossa (90 km, 56 miles).* 🚆 *from Syracuse (0931-838 733).* 🚌 🛈 *Azienda Provinciale Turismo, Piazza XXIV Maggio (0931-573 779 or 836 744).* 🎫 *(0931-89 62 71).* 🎪 *3rd Sun May: flower festival.*

The Salvatore convent belonged to nuns from noble families in the 18th century.

San Francesco
A Baroque staircase leads to this church, which has a Latin cross interior and an aisleless nave.

Museo Civico

Santa Chiara
The church was designed by Rosario Gagliardi. It is built on an oval plan and is richly decorated. This 19th-century altarpiece of San Benedetto and Santa Scolastica is by the Palermo artist Lo Forte.

KEY

------- Suggested route

STAR SIGHTS

★ **Cathedral**

★ **San Carlo al Corso**

★ **Palazzo Trigona**

0 metres		70
0 yards		70

Exploring Noto

THE HEART OF the town is the main avenue, modern Viale Marconi, which becomes Corso Vittorio Emanuele at the monumental Porta Reale (or Ferdinandea) city gate, and passes through Piazza XXIV Maggio, Piazza Municipio (a good starting point for a visit) and Piazza XXX Ottobre. Steps lead to the upper town, with marvellous views of the landscape around.

The Cathedral prior to 1996

The Cathedral as it is today

🔒 Cathedral
In the winter of 1996, a loud rumble signalled the collapse of the Cathedral cupola, leaving a noticeable scar in the heart of Noto. It was a great loss to Sicilian Baroque art. The church was originally completed in 1776, and dedicated to San Nicolò. It stands at the end of a spectacular three-flight staircase designed by Paolo Labisi, the façade bearing twin bell towers and a bronze portal. The interior has a wealth of frescoes and other decoration, especially in the side chapels. The dome and the two-aisle nave are being rebuilt and should be finished by the year 2000.

🏛 Palazzo Ducezio
This palazzo, which stands opposite the Cathedral, was built in 1746 by Vincenzo Sinatra. The façade is decorated with an impressive series of columns. In the interior, which now houses the offices of the Town Hall, there is a huge drawing room decorated in the French Louis XV style, with gold and stucco decorative elements and a fine fresco on the vault by Antonio Mazza.

🏛 Museo Civico
Corso Vittorio Emanuele 34.
📞 0931-836 462.
The Civic Museum (some rooms of which are closed for restoration) features ancient and medieval material from the old town, Noto Antica, and from many nearby places such as the town of Eloro.

🔒 San Francesco
On the wide stretch of Piazza XXX Ottobre, a monumental stairway leads to San Francesco, which was once part of a convent, and is now a high school. The church, with fine stucco decoration, was built in the mid-18th century and contains some paintings of interest as well as a wooden statue of the Virgin Mary (1564), which probably came from one of the churches in the old town, Noto Antica.

Statue on the Cathedral façade

🏛 Palazzo Trigona
This palazzo is perhaps the most "classically" Baroque building in Noto. The façade with its curved balconies blends in with the adjacent religious and civic buildings, in line with the schemes of the architects who rebuilt Noto. The drawing rooms of the palazzo were frescoed by Antonio Mazza.

BAROQUE ARCHITECTURE AND ART IN NOTO

After the devastation left by the 1693 earthquake, an ambitious programme of reconstruction was introduced throughout eastern Sicily in the first half of the 18th century. The architects entrusted with this task elaborated upon the achievements of 17th-century Baroque architecture and adopted recurrent features that can still be seen in the streets of Noto. The façades of both churches and civic buildings became of fundamental importance in the hands of these men. Some of them, like Rosario Gagliardi, who designed the churches of Santa Chiara, Santissimo Crocefisso and San Domenico in Noto, were originally craftsmen themselves. Their skills can be seen in the great attention paid to decorative detail in façades and balconies. Rebuilding made the large monastery complexes – which together with the mansions of the landed gentry were the economic and social backbone of 18th- and 19th-century Noto – even more grandiose than before.

An 18th-century Baroque balcony on Palazzo Nicolaci in Noto

🔒 San Carlo

Along Corso Vittorio Emanuele, San Carlo (also called Chiesa del Collegio because of the attached former Jesuit monastery) has a slightly convex façade with three levels – Doric, Ionic and Corinthian. The impressive Latin cross plan interior is decorated with frescoes.

🔒 San Domenico

Looking over Piazza XXIV Maggio, the church of San Domenico is part of a group of buildings that includes the **Dominican Convent**, worth visiting because of its splendid entrance with a host of friezes. Like other buildings of this kind, the convent was abandoned after the elimination of all congregational orders, decreed by the Italian government in 1866. The lovely façade of the church, with its convex central part, was designed by the architect Rosario Gagliardi. The portal gives way to a rounded church interior, which is crowned by five cupolas with fine stucco decoration.

The convex façade of San Domenico, designed by Gagliardi

🏛 Palazzo Nicolaci Villadorata

On nearby Via Nicolaci, one of the most striking streets in Noto, stands Palazzo Nicolaci del Principe di Villadorata. The façade has six balconies supported by corbels which are decorated – in keeping with the pure Baroque style – with complex wrought-iron

Palazzo Landolina, former residence of the Norman Sant'Alfano family

work and grotesque and mythological figures: lions, sirens, griffons and cherubs. The interior is interesting because of the fresco decoration in the lavish rooms, the most striking of which is the Salone delle Feste (Hall of Festivities). The palazzo also houses the **Biblioteca Comunale**, or City Library, founded in the mid-19th century, with numerous old volumes and the architects' original designs for Noto.

🏛 Palazzo Landolina

To the right of the Cathedral is the 19th-century **Palazzo Vescovile** (Bishop's Palace), while to the left is Palazzo Landolina, residence of the marquises of Sant'Alfano, an old and powerful family of the Norman aristocracy. Once past the elegant Baroque façade you enter a courtyard where two sphinxes flank the stairway leading to the main floor and frescoed rooms.

🔒 Chiesa del Crocefisso

In the heart of Noto Alta, at the end of a stairway that begins at Piazza Mazzini, is this church, built at the end of the street

Detail of Baroque decoration

that leads upwards from Piazza Municipio and the Cathedral. The façade – designed by Gagliardi but never finished – has a large Baroque door. The Latin cross plan interior boasts a magnificent Renaissance statue by Francesco Laurana, known as the *Madonna della Neve* (Madonna of the Snows, 1471) which miraculously survived the earthquake. At the end of the left-hand aisle is Cappella Landolina. The Romanesque statues of lions also come from the old town. The church is surrounded by palazzi, convents and churches. Among others, the façades of **Sant'Agata**, the **Badia della Santissima Annunziata** and **Santa Maria del Gesù** are well worth a longer look.

The unfinished façade of the Chiesa del Crocefisso in the upper town, Noto Alta

The road leading to Pachino, one of the most important agricultural towns in southern Sicily

Pachino ❸

Road map E5. 🕍 *21,850.* ℹ️
Pachino Town Hall (0931-846 753).

THE TOWN of Pachino,
founded in 1758 by the
princes of Giardineli and
populated by a few dozen
families, has evolved into a
large agricultural and wine-
producing centre. Despite
inroads made by modern
architecture, there are still
some traces of the original
town plan: a series of courtyards and alleys reveals an
Arab influence.

To Italians, however, Pachino
is also synonymous with
tomatoes, or rather, a variety
of small red tomato used for
sauces and salads, which has
become familiar throughout
the country. Besides the
pachini tomatoes, the area –
close to the sea and seaside
resorts – is famous for the
production of red wine.

Capo Passero ❹

Road map E5.

**Fishing boats on the beach at
Capo Passero**

AT THE SOUTHERN TIP of Sicily,
on the Capo Passero
headland, lies the small town
of **Portopalo di Capo
Passero**, a centre for agricultural produce and fishing.
Portopalo, together with the
nearby town of **Marzamemi**,
has in recent years become a
popular summer tourist spot.

Just off the coast is the small
island of **Capo Passero**,
which, because of its strategic
position, has always been
considered an excellent
observation point. Proof is
provided by the 17th-century
watchtower, which replaced a
series of military installations
and fortifications, some of
which were of ancient origin.

The southernmost point
on the headland is **Capo
delle Correnti**. Opposite the
point a lighthouse stands on
an island called **Isola delle
Correnti**. Near here – or
more precisely, close to
Portopalo – Allied troops
landed on 10 July 1943 with
the aim of establishing a
bridgehead on Sicily.

North of Portopalo you can
see a tuna fishery *(tonnara)*
and a fish processing plant. In
nearby Marzamemi the town
also grew up around a tuna
fishery and the residence of
the noble Villadorata family,
who are still the proprietors
of the local *tonnara*.

The waters of the central
Mediterranean are still
populated by large schools of
tuna fish which migrate
annually. Enticed towards the
tonnara, the fish become
trapped in a complicated
network of tuna fishing nets.
Tuna caught using this
traditional method is prized
and considered highly
superior to tuna caught out
on the open sea, because the
method of killing (which
involves very rapid loss of
blood) seems to enhance the
flavour of the meat.

Portopalo di Capo Passero, a fairly recent tourist attraction

Byzantine fresco in the Ipogeo di San Michele, in the Cava d'Ispica gorge

Cava d'Ispica ❺

Road map E5. *Access from SS115 from Ispica to Modica, right-hand turn-off at Bettola del Capitano, follow the branch for 5.5 km (3.5 miles) as far as the Cavallo d'Ispica mill.* ▣ *Syracuse–Ispica (0932-951 884).* ○ *9am–6pm (summer), 9am–5pm (winter).*

AN ANCIENT RIVER carved the Cava d'Ispica out of the rock and the gorge has developed into an open-air monument. The sides of the canyon are perforated with the tombs of a necropolis, places of worship, and cave dwellings where religious hermits went through mystical experiences. It was an Egyptian hermit, Sant'Ilarione, who initiated the monasticism in the canyon, which was used only as a burial site in antiquity.

New, improved access has made it possible to visit the **Larderia Necropolis**, although since the establishment of a new enclosure, it is much more difficult to gain an overall idea of the complex of caves that have made Cava d'Ispica such a

world-famous attraction for decades. While the Larderia necropolis is an impressive network of catacombs (there is also a small museum), not far from the entrance you can visit – on request – the **Ipogeo di San Michele**, a cave with a Byzantine fresco of the Madonna, or the small Byzantine church of **San Pancrati**, set in a claustrophobically narrow enclosure. Despite the difficult terrain, the unfenced part of the gorge is also well worth visiting. Every step of the way you will be well rewarded for the strenuous climb.

Scicli ❻

Road map E5. ▦ *25,121.* ▣ *from Syracuse (0932-832 445).* ▤ *from Noto.* ▯ *Scicli Town Hall (0932-839 111).* ▨ *Festa delle Milizie: last Sun in Jun.*

THE TOWN LIES at the point where the Modica river converges with the valleys of Bartolomeo and Santa Maria la Nova. Scicli once played a major role in controlling communications between the coast and the uplands. It was an Arab stronghold and then became a royal city under the Normans. It was totally rebuilt after the 1693 earthquake, and Baroque streets, façades and churches emerged from the devastated town.

For visitors arriving from Modica along the San Bartolomeo valley (where the panoramic views are splendid), the first stop is San Bartolomeo followed by the new town centre, built on the plain after the old hill town was abandoned. In the centre is the church of **Santa Maria la Nova**, rebuilt several times and now with Neo-Classical features, **Palazzo Beneventano** with its Baroque motifs, the former **Convent of the Carmelites** and the adjoining **Chiesa del Carmine**. Lastly is the **Chiesa Madre**, in Piazza Italia. This has a papier mâché statue – the Madonna dei Milici – depicting the Virgin Mary on horseback subduing two Turks, which represents the famous 1091 battle between Christians and Arabs. Higher up are the ruins of **San Matteo**, the old cathedral, at the foot of the ruined **castle** built by the Arabs.

Santa Maria la Nova, at Scicli, rebuilt in the Neo-Classical style

Ragusa ❼

Baroque decoration, Duomo

THIS ANCIENT CITY was founded as Hybla Heraia when the Siculi moved into the interior to escape from the Greek colonists. Ragusa is divided into two communities: new Baroque Ragusa, built on the plateau after the 1693 earthquake, and quiet Ibla, which is linked to the modern town by a rocky crest and is very atmospheric. A visit to Ragusa therefore involves two stages.

The Duomo of Ibla in the heart of the old town

Exploring Ragusa

The new town was designed to suit the needs of the emerging 17th-century landed gentry as opposed to the old feudal nobles, who preferred to stay entrenched in old Ibla. It was laid out on an octagonal plan, the result of detailed planning following the earthquake of 1693.

⚐ Cathedral

Piazza San Giovanni. ◯ *8am–noon, 4–7pm.*
The Cathedral was built in 1706–60 in the middle of the new town, preceded by an impressive porticoed terrace and with a massive cusped bell-tower and a lovely monumental portal *(see p128).* It is dedicated to St John the Baptist. The interior has a Latin cross plan with two side aisles and fine stucco decoration.

🏛 Museo Archeologico Ibleo

Via Natalelli. 📞 *0932-622 963.* ◯ *9am–1:15pm, 4–7:15pm Mon–Sat, 9am–1pm, 4–7pm Sun & hols.* 🈯
The Archaeological Museum is divided into six sections and is devoted to the cultures that have dominated the province of Ragusa. The first section has prehistoric finds from Modica, Pantalica and Cava d'Ispica. The second one is given over to Kamarina, the Syracusan subcolony founded on the banks of the Ippari river on a coastal site not far from present-day Vittoria. Kamarina once enjoyed important trade links with ancient Ibla. On display here are many examples of

ceramics, statues and terracotta figurines from the recent excavations at Kamarina, organized and sponsored by the Syracuse Archaeological Office. The third section of the museum features the Siculi cultures, followed by an exhibit of Hellenistic finds – especially from Scornavacche, a very important trade and caravan centre – including an interesting reconstruction of a potter's oven. The fifth section focuses on the Roman epoch, while the last one illustrates the growth of this area in the Byzantine age, with finds from the ancient port of Caucana.

⚐ Santa Maria delle Scale

This church stands at the top of a flight of 340 steps connecting Ibla and Ragusa, hence the name, *scale* meaning stairs. Santa Maria delle Scale was built in the 14th century over a Norman convent and was rebuilt after the 1693 earthquake. The original Gothic doorway and external pulpit of the campanile are still intact.

Exploring Ibla

The hill of Ibla has probably been inhabited since the 3rd millennium BC and is rich in history. However, in recent years its economic importance has waned compared with the "new" town of Ragusa.

🏛 Duomo (San Giorgio)

The Cathedral stands at the top of a stairway that begins at **Piazza Duomo**, the real centre of Ibla. It was built over the foundations of San Nicolò, which was destroyed by the 1693 earthquake. The new church was designed by Rosario Gagliardi and built in 1738–75. The huge façade is immediately striking, with its three tiers of columns which, together with the vertical lines of the monumental stairway leading to the church, accentuate the vertical thrust of the building. An impressive Neo-Classical cupola dominates the nave. The interior contains a series of paintings from different periods (including a 16th-century *Enthroned Madonna and Child*) and 13 stained glass windows.

Statue of San Giuseppe

🏛 Circolo di Conversazione

If you go down Corso XXV Aprile, you will see the Neo-Classical Circolo di Conversazione (Conversation Club), on your left. This private club has a plush Neo-Classical interior, steeped in the atmosphere of 19th-century Ibla.

🏛 San Giuseppe

Also along Corso XXV Aprile, at Piazza Pola you come across the Baroque **San Giuseppe**, which is in many ways similar to the Duomo, San Giorgio, and for this reason is also attributed to the architect Gagliardi. The oval-shaped interior has a large cupola decorated with Sebastiano Lo Monaco's fresco *Glory of St Benedict.* After leaving this church, turn down Corso XXV Aprile and you will come to an extremely interesting series of monuments. First there are the ruins of the Norman church of Santa Maria la Nova. Then there is San Francesco all'Immacolata, which was built over Palazzo Chiaramonte and incorporates its Gothic portal. Last is

The façade of San Giuseppe, with its Corinthian columns

San Giorgio Vecchio, which was for the most part destroyed by the 1693 earthquake. A splendid portal survives – it is Catalan-Gothic and its lunette has a bas-relief of St George killing the dragon and, above, the eagles from the House of Aragon coat of arms.

🌳 Giardino Ibleo

This delightful 19th-century public garden has a fine view of the area. It also contains a number of churches, including the 14th-century San Giacomo and the Chiesa dei Cappuccini. In the simple aisleless nave there are some interesting 15th-century altarpieces, including one by Pietro Novelli.

IBLA

VIA DEL MERCATO
VIA CHIARAMONTE
VIA STEFANO
LARGO CAMERINA
PIAZZA SOLARINO
PIAZZA DUOMO
VIA PATERNO
VIA AREZZO
CORSO XXV APRILE
VIA GIARDINO
SS194
SS115

0 metres 300
0 yards 300

RAGUSA AND IBLA

KEY

🚉 Railway station
🅿 Parking
ℹ Tourist information
🏛 Church

The Duomo at Modica, a remarkable example of Sicilian Baroque

Modica ❽

Road map E5. 🚶 *49,192.* **FS** *from Syracuse (0932-941 192).* ℹ️ *Comune di Modica (0932-759 111).*

INHABITED SINCE the era of the Siculi culture, Modica rebelled against Roman rule in 212 BC and, thanks to its strategic position on a rocky promontory, became one of the most important towns in medieval and Renaissance Sicily. Peter I of Aragon made it an area that roughly corresponds to the present-day province of Ragusa, and it was later ruled by the Chiaramonte and Cabrera families. Perched on the rocky spurs dominating the large "Y" formed by the confluence of the Janni Mauru and Pozzo dei Pruni rivers, Modica grew, occupying the valley where the rivers were filled in after a disastrous series of floods.

Modica Alta is built on the hill and is connected to the lower town, Modica Bassa, via flights of steps. Some of these are monumental, such as the 250-step flight built in the 19th century which descends from San Giorgio. Alleys and lanes evoke the walled town, which from 844 to 1091 was an important Arab city known as *Mohac*.

Sculpture on Corso Umberto I

🔒 Duomo (San Giorgio)

It is worthwhile making the effort to climb up the hill to see the Cathedral. It is dedicated to St George and was built by Count Alfonso Henriquez Cabrera on the site of a 13th-century church which had been destroyed by an earthquake. The magnificent façade (which, because of its similarity to several churches in Noto, is attributed to the architect Rosario Gagliardi) rises upwards elegantly with three ranks of columns. In the interior are ten 16th-century wooden panels with scenes from the New Testament. **Corso Regina Margherita**, the main street in Modica Alta, has many fine and 19th-century palazzi.

🔒 Santa Maria di Betlem

By going up the road following one branch of the confluence of the valley rivers, now called Via Marchesa Tedeschi, you will come across the façade of Santa Maria di Betlem, a 16th-century church which was rebuilt after the 1693 earthquake. At the end of the right-hand aisle is the beautiful Cappella del Sacramento, a splendid example of late Gothic-Renaissance architecture. It was commissioned by the Cabrera family.

🚌 Corso Umberto I

There are many interesting churches and other buildings along the city's main street. The former **Monastero delle Benedettine** (a convent for Benedictine nuns now used as a courthouse), the 19th-century **Teatro Garibaldi**, the 18th-century **Palazzo Tedeschi**, **Santa Maria del Soccorso** and **Palazzo Manenti**, whose corbels are decorated with figures of all kinds: knights with plumes in their hats, lovely girls and grotesque monsters.

🔒 San Pietro

Also on Corso Umberto I, is a flight of Baroque **monumental steps**, flanked by statues of the Apostles, which leads to the entrance of **San Pietro**. This church was built after the 1693 earthquake on the site of a 14th-century church. The two-aisle interior has a number of paintings and statues. The *Madonna dell'Ausilio*, a Gagini-school statue, stands in the second chapel in the right-hand aisle.

San Pietro stands at the top of a monumental Baroque staircase

🏛 Museo Civico

Largo Mercè. 📞 *0932-945 081.* ⏰ *10am–1pm, 4:30–8pm daily (summer: 10am–1pm, 5–11pm Thu & Sat).* 🖼️ Craftsmen and their tools are featured in this ethnographic museum, with workshops reconstructed in the cells of the former monastery of the Mercedarian friars. You can make an appointment to see the various local artisans (saddle-makers, smiths, basket weavers, shoemakers and stone-cutters) demonstrating their ancient skills.

The ruins of the Greek walls at the Capo Soprano headland, Gela

Vittoria ❾

Road map D5. ⚔ *54,237.*
ℹ *0931-862 606.*

FOUNDED BY Vittoria Colonna in 1603, this agricultural town lies on the plain between the Ippari and Dirillo rivers. In the central Piazza del Popolo are the **Teatro Comunale** (1877) and **Santa Maria delle Grazie**, a Baroque church built after the disastrous 1693 earthquake.

Gela ❿

Road map D4. ⚔ *79,188.*
FS *from Syracuse (0933-911 546).*
ℹ *AAST (0933-923 268).* **Excavations at Capo Soprano** ◯ *9am–1 hr before sunset.* **Museo Archeologico Comunale and Acropolis excavations** ◯ *9am–2pm; 9am–1pm hols.* ● *Mon.*

THE GREEK historian Thucydides recorded that Gela was founded in 688 BC, 45 years after Syracuse. The city prospered and in the 6th century BC founded Agrigento. Extending over two slopes – the present-day **Acropolis** and the **Capo Soprano** area – the town was revived again, after a long period of abandonment, by Frederick II. Today Gela is marred by ugly buildings, industrial plants and a strong anti-Mafia military presence. However, there are the archaeological sites: a long stretch of Greek fortifications built by Timoleon at Capo Soprano and the sacred precinct and ancient Temple of Athena on the **Acropolis**, all good introductions to a visit to the **Museo Archeologico**.

Chiaramonte Gulfi ⓫

Road map E4. ⚔ *8,106.*

THIS TOWN was founded by Manfredi Chiaramonte, the Count of Modica, on the steep slopes of a rise and then developed towards the valley. The **Chiesa del Salvatore** and **Matrice Santa Maria la Nova** are in the centre, while the **Madonna delle Grazie Sanctuary** is on the outskirts.

Vizzini ⓬

Road map E4. ⚔ *8,731.*
ℹ *167-292 942; 0933-962 445.*

THE FASCINATION of Vizzini lies in the small streets and alleys of the old town, which has preserved its atmosphere and town plan – increasingly rare in Sicily because of modern urban growth. Also worth a look is the fine architecture of the **Chiesa Madre di San Gregorio** with its Gothic portal, taken from the destroyed Palazzo di Città.

Palazzolo Acreide ⓭

Road map E4. ⚔ *10,008.*
ℹ *0931-882 000.*

FOUNDED BY the Syracusans and originally named Akrai, this town has some important Baroque churches and buildings – the **Chiesa Madre di San Nicolò, Palazzo Zocco** and the 18th-century **Chiesa dell'Annunziata**. However, the most interesting sight is the peaceful plain with the **excavations of Akrai**.

A Baroque balcony in the centre of Palazzolo Acreide

∩ Excavations at Akrai
2 km (1.2 miles) from the centre.
◯ *9am–5pm.*
This area was inhabited in 664 BC, when the city was founded by the Syracusans. A small **theatre** stands by the entrance. The **acropolis** contains an **agora**, two **latomies** (the Intagliata and Intagliatella quarries), the ruins of the **Temple of Aphrodite** and, after a ten-minute walk, the so-called **Santoni**, 12 rock-hewn statues representing the goddess Cybele.

The theatre at Palazzolo Acreide: the colony dates back to the early 7th century BC

Caltagirone ⑭

Ceramic tile on Ponte San Francesco

IN THE HISTORY of this city, built at the junction of the Erei and Iblei hills, there is one element of continuity – the production of ceramics. Prehistoric pottery has been found on the hills around the Arab *Cal'at Ghiran* (one translation is "castle of vases"). The local potters were world famous in the Middle Ages, and the tradition is maintained today.

San Giuliano, displaying some 20th-century architectural features

Exploring Caltagirone
It is pleasant exploring Caltagirone on foot, walking around the streets and squares, pausing at the local craftsmen's workshops. There is quite a difference in altitude between the lower part and the hill of Santa Maria del Monte, so plan your visit with this in mind.

🏛 Piazza Municipio
The former Piano della Loggia – now Piazza Municipio – is the heart of the city, where the main streets converge. In the piazza are the **Town Hall** and **Palazzo Senatorio**, formerly the city theatre, now home to the Galleria Sturzo.

🏠 Duomo di San Giuliano
The Cathedral is in Piazza Umberto I. The exterior of the church, dedicated to San Giuliano, has a long history: first it was Norman, then Baroque, and was rebuilt in the 20th century (the façade in 1909, the bell tower in 1954). In the interior is a 16th-century wooden crucifix. By going down Via Roma – towards the **San Francesco bridge** – you will come to an open space with the old Bourbon prison and the church of **Sant'Agata**.

🏛 Museo Civico
Via Roma. ◯ 9am–1pm, 4–7pm weekdays (10am–noon Wed). ◉ Mon.
The museum is housed in the former 17th-century Bourbon prison and has prehistoric, Greek and Roman material as well as sculptures and ceramics from the 1500s to the present.

🏠 San Francesco d'Assisi
The Ponte San Francesco, decorated with typical coloured tiles, leads to the church of San Francesco d'Assisi, which was founded in the 12th century and rebuilt in Baroque style after the 1693 earthquake.

🌳 Giardino della Villa
The public gardens can be reached by going down Via Roma. The park was designed in the mid-1800s by Giovanni Battista Basile, and the long balustrade and the bandstand are richly decorated with coverings of ceramic tiles.

🏛 Museo della Ceramica
Via Roma. 📞 0933-21680. ◯ 9am–6:30pm. 🎫
From the Belvedere del Teatrino, in Giardino della Villa, you can visit the Ceramics Museum. There are Bronze Age pots and Greek, Hellenistic and Roman kraters and figurines. The Middle Ages are represented by Arab vases and Sicilian pieces. The collection also has more recent pharmacy jars and glazed vases with religious figures.

🏠 Santa Maria del Monte Stairway
Once back in the centre of town, one of the most impressive sights is the monumental Santa Maria del Monte staircase, with its 142 steps decorated with majolica tiles.

Ponte San Francesco in Caltagirone

Coloured majolica tiles, decorating every step of this staircase

VISITORS' CHECKLIST

Road map D4. 🚗 38,259. **FS**
*from Catania and Gela (0933-
24765).* ℹ️ *AAST, Via Libertini 3
(0933-53809).* 🎉 *24 Jul, Festa
di San Giacomo.*

The flight of steps was built
in 1608 to link the seat of
religious power– the Cathedral – with that of civic
power, the **Palazzo Senatorio**. During the feast day of
San Giacomo (24 July) *(see
p37)* the entire flight of stairs
is illuminated with thousands
of lamps, skilfully arranged
to create interesting patterns
of lighting effects.

🛐 **Santa Maria del Monte**
At the top of the stairway is
the former Cathedral of Caltagirone, built in the mid-1500s
and then rebuilt after the 1693
earthquake. A slender bell
tower, designed by Natale
Bonaiuto, was also added.
    A castle once stood at the
top of the hill. Today, in an
area that was once heavily
fortified, can be found the
Sant'Agostino Convent and
San Nicola, both constructed
in the 18th century.

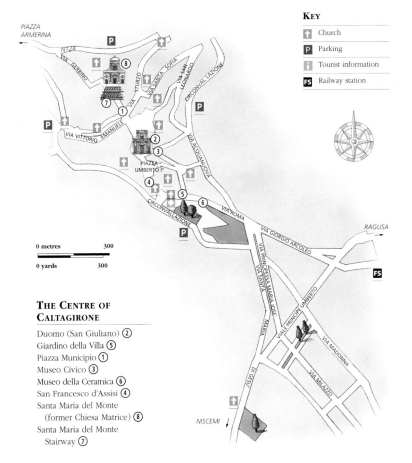

KEY

🛐	Church
🅿	Parking
ℹ️	Tourist information
FS	Railway station

**THE CENTRE OF
CALTAGIRONE**

Duomo (San Giuliano) ②
Giardino della Villa ⑤
Piazza Municipio ①
Museo Civico ③
Museo della Ceramica ⑥
San Francesco d'Assisi ④
Santa Maria del Monte
    (former Chiesa Matrice) ⑧
Santa Maria del Monte
    Stairway ⑦

The Cathedral of Lentini, dedicated to Sant'Alfio, in Piazza Duomo

Lentini **⑮**

Road map E4. **⚘** 27,000. **FS** from Catania, Syracuse & Messina (095-901 122. **ℹ** APT Siracusa, Via San Sebastiano 43/45 (0931-67710 or 461 477). **Museo Archeologico**: Via Museo **[** 095-902 383. **◯** 9am–2pm Tue–Sat; 9am–1pm Sun & hols. **●** Mon. **Digs at Leontinoi**: **◯** 9am– 1 hr before sunset, daily. **✿** Good Friday "Scesa e Cruci"; 1st week of May: Festival of orange trees in bloom.

A N ANCIENT Siculan city originally named *Xuthia*, Lentini was conquered by the Chalcidians in 729 BC and fought against neighbouring Syracuse with the support of Athens. Defeated and then occupied by the Romans, the city went into a period of decline. In the Middle Ages it became an important agricultural centre. The local museum has finds from the ancient city, especially from the Siculan and Greek epochs. The digs at ancient Leontinoi, at the edge of town in the Colle Castellaccio area, can be reached via the ancient Porta Siracusana city gate. The various walls testify to the city's battle-worn history, and there are a number of ancient burial grounds inside the archaeological precinct.

Megara Hyblaea **⑯**

Road map F4. **FS** Augusta station. **ℹ** APT Siracusa, Via San Sebastiano 43/45 (0931-67710 or 461 477). **◯** 9am–1 hr before sunset.

O NE OF THE FIRST Greek colonies in Sicily was founded in 728 BC here at Megara. According to legend, the founders were the followers of Daedalus, who had escaped from Crete. Unfortunately, today the site is surrounded by the oil refineries of Augusta and in such squalid surroundings it is difficult to visit the ruins of the ancient city with a sense of atmosphere. The Megara colonists who founded Megara Hyblaea were soon at war with Syracuse and Leontinoi, and a century later founded the city of Selinunte, in western Sicily *(see pp100–101)*. You should be able to see the ruins of the Hellenistic walls, the Agora quarter, and the remains of some temples, baths and colonnades. The excavations were led by the eminent archaeologist Paolo Orsi and the École Française of Rome. Information display boards will help you to get orientated.

Find from Megara Hyblaea, now in the Museo Archeologico in Syracuse

Ruined foundations in the ancient Greek colony of Megara Hyblaea, founded in the 8th century BC

The Porta Spagnola in Augusta (1681), the old city gate

Augusta ⑰

Road map F4. 🏛 *39,926.* 🚆 *from Catania, Syracuse, Messina (0931-994 100).* 🛈 *APT Siracusa, Via San Sebastiano 43/45 (0931-67710 or 461 477).*

Augusta was founded on an island by Frederick II as a port protected by a castle. Under the Aragonese the city was constantly at war with Turkish and North African pirates. It was almost totally destroyed by the 1693 earthquake. In the early 1900s the city expanded and became a major petrochemical port, and this drastically changed the landscape. You enter the old town through the **Porta Spagnola** city gate, built by the viceroy Benavides in 1681, next to which are the ruins of the old walls. In the centre, the Baroque **Chiesa delle Anime Sante**, the **Chiesa Madre** (1769) and the **Museo delle Armi** (Arms Museum) are worth a look.

Pantalica ⑱

Road map E4 (19 km, 12 miles from Ferla, 45 km, 28 miles from Syracuse).

Rock-cut tombs, dwellings and temples line the steep walls of the limestone gorges at the confluence of the Bottiglieria and Anapo rivers. Pantalica was the heart of the ancient kingdom of Hybla which, in its heyday, used Syracuse as its port. The city was conquered by the Greeks when the coastal colonies became powerful in the 8th century BC, and Pantalica became important again during the early Middle Ages, when Arab invasions and constant wars led the locals to seek refuge in its inaccessible canyons. The cave-dwellings and hermitages date from this period, as do the ruins of a settlement known as the "Byzantine village".

View of the steep gorges surrounding the necropolis of Pantalica

A Walk through Pantalica

This archaeological site – the largest necropolis in Sicily – covers a large area, but the steep gorges mean there are few roads, and the only practical way of getting around is on foot. About 9 km (5 miles) from Ferla stands the Filiporto Necropolis, with more than 1,000 tombs cut out of the cliffs. Next is the North Necropolis; the last place to park is near the

Anaktoron, the megalithic palace of the prince of ancient Hybla dating from the 12th century BC. The road ends 1 km (half a mile) further on. From this point, one path goes down to the Bottiglieria river, where steep walls are filled with rock-cut caves, and another takes you to the so-called "Byzantine village", the rock-hewn church of San Micidiario and the other necropolises in this area. It is not advisable to try to go to Pantalica from Sortino (the northern slope); it is an extremely long walk.

The North Necropolis at Pantalica

NORTHEASTERN SICILY

T HANKS TO *the presence of Mount Etna, the Ionian coast of Sicily has often had to deal with violent volcanic eruptions. One of the most devastating was in 1669, when the molten lava even reached Catania and the sea. The lava flows have formed Etna's distinctive landscape, and flowers, putti and festoons of black lava now adorn many churches and buildings in Catania and Aci Castello.*

In 734 BC the first colonists from Greece landed on this coast and founded Naxos, the first of a series of powerful colonies in Sicily that gave rise to a period of prosperity and cultural sophistication. However, volcanic eruptions and devastating earthquakes have destroyed almost all traces of the splendid Greek cities in this area, with the exception of the ancient theatre in Taormina, which was rebuilt in the Roman era. The panoramic position, mild climate and wealth of architectural beauty have made this coast a favourite with visitors. The first of these were people who undertook the Grand Tour in the 1700s and made their first stop at Messina, just as many modern travellers do. In summer, the Ionian coast is crowded because of the beauty of its beaches and sea. But it is also fascinating in the winter, when the top of Mount Etna is covered with snow and the citrus orchards are heavy with fruit, or in spring, when the air is filled with the scent of orange blossoms and flower gardens in bloom. Another part of northeastern Sicily worth visiting is the archipelago of the unique Aeolian Islands, of volcanic origin.

The old harbour at Catania, still crowded with fishing boats

◁   The awe-inspiring sight of an erupting Mount Etna at night

Exploring Northeastern Sicily

THE PEARL OF THE IONIAN COAST is Taormina, famous for its stupendous panoramic views, but this area has many other fascinating sights too – from the fishing villages of Aci Trezza and Aci Castello to the Baroque splendour of Catania, as well as Mount Etna, the largest active volcano in Europe. You can go up to the edge of its awesome crater by jeep or on foot, or visit the villages on its black lava slopes with the quaint Ferrovia Circumetnea trains. Those who prefer the seaside can visit the beaches of the Aeolian Islands, which also offer unique scenery with volcanic soil and maquis vegetation.

The ravine of the Alcantara River near Taormina

SIGHTS AT A GLANCE

The Monastery of Santa Lucia at Adrano, on the slopes of Etna

SEE ALSO
• *Where to Stay* pp197–9
• *Where to Eat* pp208–209

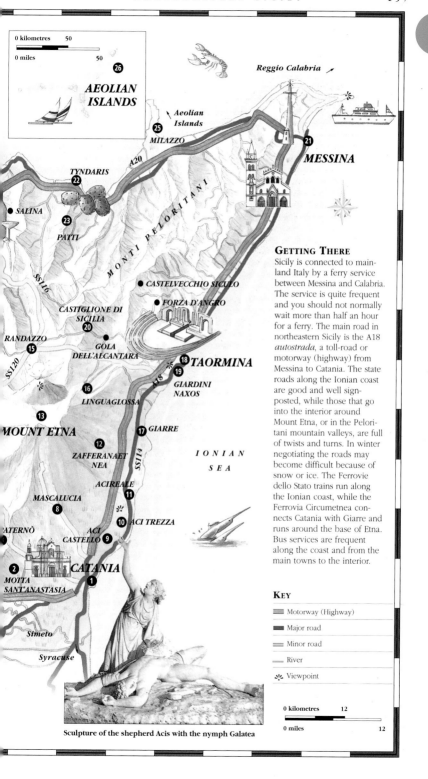

0 kilometres 50
0 miles 50

AEOLIAN ISLANDS 26

Aeolian Islands 25
MILAZZO

Reggio Calabria

21 **MESSINA**

TYNDARIS 22

• SALINA

23
PATTI

SS116

CASTELVECCHIO SICULO

FORZA D'ANGRO

CASTIGLIONE DI SICILIA 20

RANDAZZO 15

SS120

GOLA DELL'ALCANTARA

18 **TAORMINA**
19
GIARDINI NAXOS

16
LINGUAGLOSSA

13
MOUNT ETNA

12
ZAFFERANA ETNEA

17 GIARRE

IONIAN SEA

ACIREALE
11

MASCALUCIA
8

10 ACI TREZZA

ATERNÒ

ACI CASTELLO 9

2 **CATANIA**
1
MOTTA SANT'ANASTASIA

Simeto

Syracuse

Sculpture of the shepherd Acis with the nymph Galatea

GETTING THERE

Sicily is connected to mainland Italy by a ferry service between Messina and Calabria. The service is quite frequent and you should not normally wait more than half an hour for a ferry. The main road in northeastern Sicily is the A18 *autostrada*, a toll-road or motorway (highway) from Messina to Catania. The state roads along the Ionian coast are good and well signposted, while those that go into the interior around Mount Etna, or in the Peloritani mountain valleys, are full of twists and turns. In winter negotiating the roads may become difficult because of snow or ice. The Ferrovie dello Stato trains run along the Ionian coast, while the Ferrovia Circumetnea connects Catania with Giarre and runs around the base of Etna. Bus services are frequent along the coast and from the main towns to the interior.

KEY

▭ Motorway (Highway)
▭ Major road
▭ Minor road
▭ River
� Viewpoint

0 kilometres 12
0 miles 12

Catania ❶

Sᴵᵀᵁᴬᵀᴇᴅ ʙᴇᴛᴡᴇᴇɴ the Ionian Sea and the slopes of Mount Etna, Sicily's second city has always had a close relationship with the volcano, and most of the city's buildings are made from Etna's black lava. According to the historian Thucydides, the city was founded in 729 BC by Greek colonists from Chalcis *(see p152)*. Since then it has been flooded with Etna lava and shaken by earthquakes, most radically in 1693, when it was razed to the ground. The town today is the result of 18th-century rebuilding: broad, straight streets and large, unevenly shaped squares, a precaution against earthquakes.

The Fontana dell'Elefante

CATANIA TOWN CENTRE

Badia di Sant'Agata ④
Castello Ursino ⑨
Cathedral ③
Museo Civico Belliniano ⑤
Museo Verga ⑩
Palazzo Biscari ①
Pescheria ⑥
Piazza Duomo ②
San Nicolò all'Arena ⑪
Roman Theatre ⑧
Via Crociferi ⑦
Via Etnea ⑫

0 metres   550
0 yards   550

🏛 Palazzo Biscari

Via Museo Biscari, Via Dusmet.
This is the largest private palazzo in 18th-century Catania. Construction was begun by Prince Paternò Castello on an embankment of the 16th-century city walls. Work continued for nearly a century and involved some of the leading architects of the time. The most interesting side of the building faces Via Dusmet, with a large terrace decorated with putti, telamons and garlands sculpted by Antonino Amato. The building is partly private and partly used as city administrative offices.

🏛 Piazza Duomo

The heart of city life lies at the crossing of the two main streets, Via Etnea and Via Vittorio Emanuele. The square boasts many fine Baroque buildings: **Palazzo del Municipio** (the Town Hall), the former **Chierici Seminary**, the **Cathedral** and **Porta Uzeda**, the city gate built in 1696 to connect Via Etnea with the port area. In the middle is the **Fontana dell'Elefante**, a well-known fountain sculpted in 1736 by Giovanni Battista Vaccarini. On a pedestal in the basin is an elephant made of lava, on the back of which is an Egyptian obelisk with a

VISITORS' CHECKLIST

Road map E3. 357,000.
✈ Aeroporto Fontanarossa (at
Fontanarossa) (095-578 392 or
578 298). FS Piazza Giovanni
XXIII (095-532 710 or 531 625).
AST, Via Luigi Sturzo 220
(095-281 280).
i AAST, Corso Italia 302 (095-
373 084). (antiques) Sun am
in Piazza Carlo Alberto.
Feb: Festa di Sant'Agata;
Jul–Sep: Catania Musica Estate;
Aug–Sep: International Jazz
Festival; Oct: symphony and
chamber music concerts.

Entrance to the lovely 18th-century Palazzo Biscari

globe on top. The latter, a
late Roman sculpture, has
become the city's symbol.

🏛 Cathedral

Piazza Duomo. 095-320 044.
8am–noon, 4–7pm Mon–Sat;
9–10am, 4:30–6pm Sun &
hols. 8, 10, 11:30am
& 6pm.
The principal church in
Catania is dedicated to
the city's patron saint,
Sant'Agata. It still has
its three original
Norman apses
and transept. The
façade, with two
tiers of columns,
is fully Baroque
thanks to the
design of GB
Vaccarini, who
also designed the
left-hand side of the
Cathedral. The majestic
interior has a cupola, a tall
transept and three apses with

lovely columns. On the
second pilaster to the right
is the **Tomb of Vincenzo
Bellini**; on the first one to
the left, a 15th-century stoup.
A door in the right-hand
transept leads to the Norman
Cappella della Madonna,
which contains the remains
of various Aragonese rulers.

🏛 Badia di Sant'Agata

Via Vittorio Emanuele II.
9am–noon.
This masterpiece of Catanian
Baroque architecture was
built in 1735–67 and designed
by Giovanni Battista Vaccarini. The façade is a play of
convex and concave surfaces.
The centrally planned interior,
a triumph of Rococo decoration, is equally impressive.

🏛 Museo Civico Belliniano

Piazza San Francesco 9. 095-715
05 35. 9am–1:30pm.
1 Jan, 1 May, 25 Dec.
Vincenzo Bellini's
birthplace (see p33) is now
a museum with
mementoes, auto-
graphed scores,
musical instruments
and models of
scenes from
some of the
composer's
operas. The
city's theatre,
**Teatro
Bellini**, is also
dedicated to the
Catania composer.

**Detail of the façade of
Teatro Bellini**

🏛 Teatro Bellini

Via Perrotta 12. 095-312 020.

KEY

i	Tourist information
P	Parking
FS	Railway station
	Ferrovia Circumetnea railway
🏛	Church
	Hospital
	Bus station
	Ferry service
✉	Post office and telephones

The Baroque façade of Catania Cathedral, dedicated to Sant'Agata

The lively Mercato della Pescheria (fish market) in Catania

🖾 Pescheria

Situated at the beginning of Via Garibaldi, the **Fontana dell'Amenano** fountain is fed by the waters of the underground Amenano river, which also forms a pool in the Roman theatre. Sculpted in 1867, the fountain is the focal point of a colourful fish market, the **Mercato della Pescheria**, which occupies the nearby streets and small squares every morning. The smells and atmosphere of the market are reminiscent of North Africa and the Middle East. At the end of Via Garibaldi is the monumental **Porta Garibaldi** city gate, built of limestone and lava in 1768 to celebrate the wedding of Ferdinand IV of Sicily.

▥ Via Cruciferi

This street is lined with lavishly decorated Baroque palazzi and churches. The road begins at **Piazza San Francesco**, with the Baroque **San Francesco d'Assisi**. In the interior are the so-called *candelore*, carved and gilded wooden constructions which symbolize the various artisans' guilds in the city. Every February the *candelore* are carried in procession as part of the impressive celebrations honouring Sant'Agata, the city's patron saint. Outside the church is the **Arco di San Benedetto**, an arch connecting the fine **Badia Grande** abbey, designed by Francesco Battaglia, and the **Badia Piccola**, attributed to Giovan Battista Vaccarini. To the left is **San Benedetto**, where the wooden portal carries scenes of the life of St Benedict, and **San Francesco Borgia**, at the top of a double flight of steps flanked by the former **Jesuit College**. Opposite stands **San Giuliano**, a masterpiece of Catanian Baroque architecture designed by Vaccarini.

⌒ Roman Theatre

Via Vittorio Emanuele 226.
☎ 095-715 05 08. ◷ *8am–1 hr before sunset.*
Built of limestone and lava on the southern slope of the acropolis, the theatre had a diameter of 87 m (285 ft) and could seat 7,000 people. Although there was probably a Greek theatre on this site once, the present ruins are all Roman. The theatre was badly damaged in the 11th century, when Roger I authorized the removal of the marble facing and limestone blocks for use as building material for the cathedral. What remains of the theatre today are the cavea, the edge of the orchestra and part of the skene, or backstage area, of the theatre. Next to the theatre is the small semicircular **Odeion**, made of lava and used mainly for competitions in music and rhetoric. It had a seating capacity of 1,500. The entrance to the Odeion is near the top tiers of seats in the Roman theatre.

♣ Castello Ursino

Piazza Federico di Svevia. ☎ 095-345 830. ◷ *9am–6pm Tue–Sun.* ● *Mon, 1 Jan, Easter, 1 May, 15 Aug, 25 Dec.*
This castle was built in 1239–50 by Riccardo da Lentini for Frederick II and is one of the few vestiges of medieval Catania.

The Roman theatre in Catania, now completely surrounded by buildings

Castello Ursino, one of the rare medieval buildings in Catania

The Castello Ursino originally stood on a promontory overlooking the sea and was part of a massive defence system that once included the Motta, Anastasia, Paternò and Adrano castles. Castello Ursino is square, with four corner towers, and was rebuilt in the mid-1500s. On the eastern side of its exterior, above a large window, a five-pointed star with a cabalistic meaning is visible. In a niche on the façade, the Swabian eagle seizing a lamb with its claws is the symbol of Hohenstaufen imperial power. In the inner courtyard, where the kings of Aragon administered justice, there is a display of sarcophagi, columns and other pieces.

The upper rooms house the interesting **Museo Civico**, which has a fine art gallery with important works such as *The Last Judgement* by Beato Angelico, *The Last Supper* by the Spanish painter Luis de Morales, *St John the Baptist* by Pietro Novelli *(see p21)* and a dismantled polyptych by Antonello Saliba of the *Madonna and Child* taken from Santa Maria del Gesù.

⌂ Home and Museum of Giovanni Verga
Via Sant'Anna 8. 📞 095-71 50 598.
⏲ 9am–1pm, 3–6:30pm. ⏲ Sun, Wed, Sat pm.
The apartment where the great Sicilian author Giovanni Verga lived for many years and died in 1922 is on the second floor of a 19th-century building. The house contains period furniture and personal mementoes. At the entrance are displayed reproductions of manuscripts, the originals of which are at the Biblioteca

Universitaria Regionale di Catania. The library in Verga's house boasts over 2,500 books from the author's collection, ranging from works by the Italian Futurist Marinetti to the Russian author Dostoyevsky. The bedroom is quite simple, with a bed, a dressing table, a wardrobe and portraits of Verga painted by his grandson Michele Grita.

San Nicolò, intended to be the largest church in Sicily

⛪ San Nicolò all'Arena
Piazza Dante. ⏲ 9am–1:30pm; (9am–12:30pm hols).
San Nicolò was designed by Roman architect GB Contini

but work on it stopped in 1768. The unfinished state of this massive church is particularly noticeable in the façade. The nave has two aisles, separated from the central section by huge piers. In the transept is one of the largest sundials in Europe, restored in 1996. It was built in the mid-1800s by the German baron Wolfgang Sartorius von Waltershausen and is extremely precise. Twenty-four slabs of inlaid marble show the signs of the zodiac, days of the year and the seasons. At noon, sunlight falls on the spot from an opening in the roof, marking the day and month.

🚏 Via Etnea
Catania's main street goes up a slight incline and connects the most important zones of the city. Partly closed to traffic, Via Etnea has the most elegant shops and cafés in town. Halfway along it lies **Piazza Stesicoro**, with the ruins of the Roman amphitheatre, built in the 2nd century AD. Nearby is the vast **Piazza Carlo Alberto**, where a bustling antiques market is held every Sunday morning. Back on Via Etnea is the **Collegiata**, a chapel built in the early 1700s and one of the most important late Baroque works in the city. The concave façade, designed by Stefano Ittar, is enlivened by columns, statues and niches. Near the end of Via Etnea is the **Villa Bellini**, a public garden with sub-tropical plants and busts depicting famous Sicilians.

The University building on Via Etnea, the most elegant street in Catania

Motta Sant'Anastasia, with its medieval tower dwarfed by Mount Etna

Motta Sant'Anastasia ❷

Road map E3. 👥 7,585.
🚆 *Ferrovia Circumetnea.*
ℹ️ *095-306 281.*

MOUNT ETNA FORMS a constant backdrop to Motta. From the top of the village, with the massive tower of the 12th-century **Norman Castle**, the snow-capped volcano gleams through the winter, gradually darkening in spring and summer. Not far away is the **Chiesa Madre** (Cathedral), also built in the Norman period. At the foot of the old town is the heart of Motta Sant'Anastasia with its *pasticcerie* (pastry shops), Baroque churches and bustling atmosphere, placed as it is on a major route through the Catania region.

Paternò ❸

Road map E3. 👥 44,595. 🚆
Ferrovia Circumetnea (095-842 016).
ℹ️ *095-841 777.* 🎭 *Carnival.*

SURROUNDED by orchards of citrus fruit, this town lies at the foot of a **castle**, which has a stunning view of Mount Etna and the Simeto Valley.

The 12th-century Norman castle, dominating Paternò from above, with its wide-ranging views taking in the Simeto valley and Etna

The massive square castle was built by Roger I in 1073, totally rebuilt in the 14th century and then restored twice in the 20th century. To get to the castle, go up Via Matrice, which will also take you to the **Chiesa Madre**, the Cathedral dedicated to Santa Maria dell'Alto. The church was originally Norman, but it was rebuilt in 1342.

Centuripe ❹

Road map E3. 👥 6,517. 🚆 *from Catenanuova, Romano (0935-74465).* ℹ️ *0935-74755.* 🚌 *Mon.*

KNOWN AS "the balcony of Sicily" because of the wide views, Centuripe is especially pretty in February–March, when snow-capped Mount Etna forms a striking contrast with the blossoms of orange and almond trees. An

---

THE CIRCUMETNEA RAILWAY

The picturesque carriages of the Ferrovia Circumetnea climb up the slopes of Mount Etna, passing through barren stretches of black lava alternating with luxuriant vegetation. This delightful route will take you back to the dawn of tourism, when the pace of travel was much slower than today. It takes about five hours to cover the 90 km (56 miles) or so between Catania and Riposto, the two termini, plus another hour to get back to Catania from Riposto via state rail. However, the rewards are magnificent views of terraced vineyards and almond and hazelnut groves, as well as the awe-inspiring volcano itself.

🚆 **Ferrovia Circumetnea**
Corso delle Provincie 13, Catania.
📞 *095-374 842 or 534 323.*

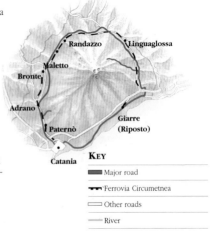

KEY

🟥 Major road

╼╼╼ Ferrovia Circumetnea

▭ Other roads

━━━ River

Agira, perched on a sloping hillside, has preserved its fascinating Arab town plan

important Greek-Roman town, it was destroyed by Frederick II and rebuilt in the 16th century. A long tree-lined avenue leads to a viewing terrace called **Castello di Corradino**, with ruins of an Imperial Roman mausoleum.

Regalbuto ❺

Road map E3. 🕴 *8,197.* 🚌 *from Catania.* ❗ *0935-71099.*

THIS TOWN was destroyed in 1261 by the inhabitants of Centuripe and rebuilt by Manfredi. The heart of Regalbuto is **Piazza della Repubblica**, with its multicoloured paving and **San Rocco**. **San Basilio** and **Santa Maria del Carmine** are also worth a look. Nearby is the **Lake Pozzillo dam**, the largest artificial basin in Sicily, and a **Canadian military cemetery** with the graves of 490 soldiers who were killed in 1943.

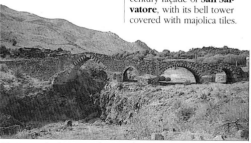

The Saracen bridge on the Simeto river, near Adrano

Agira ❻

Road map D3. 🕴 *9,174.* 🚌 *from Enna.* ❗ *0935-691 001.*

BECAUSE OF its elevated position, Agira is clearly visible from a distance, with Mount Etna rising behind it. The ancient Sicanian town of *Agyron* was colonized by the Greeks in 339 BC, and the ancient historian Diodorus Siculus was born there *(see p21).* The most interesting aspect of Agyron's modern-day counterpart is its Arab layout, with Norman churches and patrician residences with Arab-style portals. Centrally located **Piazza Garibaldi** boasts **Sant'Antonio**, with a 16th-century wooden statue of San Silvestro and a painting on marble of *The Adoration of the Magi*. In the vicinity is **Santa Maria del Gesù**, with a crucifix by Fra' Umile da Petralia. In Piazza Roma is the lovely 16th-century façade of **San Salvatore**, with its bell tower covered with majolica tiles.

Adrano ❼

Road map E3. 🕴 *35,320.* 🚉 *Ferrovia Circumetnea (095-769 30 15).* ❗ *095-769 88 38.* 🎭 *Easter: the "Diavolata".*

A SANCTUARY dedicated to the local deity Adranos stood on a lava plateau facing the Valle del Simeto, where Sicilian hounds *(cirnecos)* were trained as hunting dogs *(see p166).* The city was founded in the Greek period by Dionysius the Elder, who chose this natural balcony to build a military stronghold.

The centre of town is Piazza Umberto I, site of the **Norman Castle**, a massive, quadrilateral 11th-century construction. It houses the **Museo Archeologico**, with a collection of Neolithic pottery, Greek amphoras and millstones. A narrow stair, cut out of the Hohenstaufen wall in the Middle Ages, leads to the upper floors. Two have displays of archaeological items while the third houses the **Art Gallery**. The **Chiesa Madre**, built by the Normans and reconstructed in the 1600s, also stands in the same square.

ENVIRONS: Below the town, a byroad leads to a dirt road that passes through citrus orchards for 1 km (half a mile) to the **Ponte dei Saraceni**, a 14th-century bridge on the Simeto river, with an **archaeological zone** nearby.

Mascalucia ⑧

Road map E3. 🏛 22,494. 🚌 *from Catania.* ℹ 095-727 21 12.

O N THE EASTERN slopes of the volcano, just above Catania, to which it is connected by an uninterrupted series of villages and hamlets, is Mascalucia, a town of largish houses and villas. It is worth stopping here to visit the **Giardino Lavico**, at the Azienda Trinità farmstead, a small green "oasis" surrounded by modern building development on the slopes of Etna. The "lava garden" consists of an organically cultivated citrus grove, a 17th-century house and a garden filled with prickly pears, yuccas and other succulent plants which thrive in the lava soil. The orchard's irrigation canals were inspired by Arab gardens. For helicopter trips over Mount Etna, make inquiries at the Azienda.

🌿 **Giardino Lavico**
Azienda Agricola Trinità, Via Trinità 34. ☎ 095-727 2156. 🗓 *by appt.*

Aci Castello ⑨

Road map E3. 🏛 19,132. ℹ 095-271 020. 🚌 AST (095-281 280). 🗓 15 Jan: Festa di San Mauro.

T HE NAME OF this old fishermen's village, a few kilometres from the centre of Catania, derives from the Norman **Castle** built on the

The castle at Aci Castello, destroyed by Frederick II of Aragon

top of a basalt rock jutting into the sea. It was built in 1076 from black lava and in 1299 was the base for the rebel Roger of Luria. The castle was subsequently destroyed by Frederick II of Aragon *(see p27)* after a long siege. Some rooms in the surviving parts are occupied by the **Museo Civico**, with archaeological and natural history collections relating to the Etna region (temporarily closed). There is also a small **Botanical Garden**. The town, with straight streets and low-rise houses, marks the beginning of the **Riviera dei Ciclopi**: according to Greek mythology, Polyphemus and his friends lived on Etna.

Aci Trezza ⑩

Road map E3. 🗓 24 Jun: San Giovanni Battista.

T HIS PICTURESQUE fishing village, part of Aci Castello, was the setting for Giovanni Verga's novel *I Malavoglia* and for Luchino Visconti's film adaptation, *La Terra Trema (see pp21–2)*. The small harbour faces a pile of basalt rocks, the **Isole dei Ciclopi**, now a nature reserve. On the largest island there is a biology and oceanography station. According to Homer, Polyphemus hurled the rocks at the sea in an attempt to strike the fleeing Ulysses, who had blinded him.

The Aci Trezza stacks, hurled by Polyphemus at Ulysses, according to Greek myth

Acireale ⓫

Road map E3. 🔼 51,249.
FS *Stazione FS (095-605 901).* 🚌
Messina–Catania. 🛈 *095-604 521.*
🎭 *Carnival; Good Friday: Procession
with traditional costumes; Jul: Santa
Venere.*

ACIREALE STANDS ON a lava
terrace overlooking the
Ionian Sea in the midst of
citrus orchards. Since Roman
times it has been famous as a
spa town with sulphur baths.
It is the largest town on the
eastern side of Mount Etna
and has been destroyed time
and again by eruptions and
earthquakes. It was finally
rebuilt after the 1693 earthquake, emerging as a jewel of
Sicilian Baroque architecture.
The heart of town is **Piazza
Duomo**, with its crowded
cafés and ice-cream parlours.
Acireale is dominated by its
Cathedral, built in the late
1500s. The façade has two
cusped bell towers covered
with multicoloured majolica
tiles. The Baroque portal
leads to the vast interior with
its frescoed vaults. In the
right-hand transept
is the **Cappella di
Santa Venera**, the
patron saint of the
town. On the tran-
sept floor is a meri-
dian marked out in
1843 by a Danish
astronomer. Piazza
Duomo also boasts
the **Palazzo Comu-
nale**, with a Gothic
door and a fine
wrought-iron bal-
cony, and **Santi
Pietro e Paolo**,
built in the 17th
century but with an
18th-century façade.
Close by is the **Teatro dei
Pupi**, known for its puppet
shows, and the **Pinacoteca
dell'Accademia Zelantea**,
with works by local painter
Pietro Vasta, whose paintings
also appear in the town's
churches. The main street,
Corso Vittorio Emanuele,
has elegant shops and cafés
and crosses squares such as
Piazza Vigo, with **Palazzo
Pennisi di Floristella** and
San Sebastiano, decorated
with a balustrade and statues.

**Baroque
detail, Acireale**

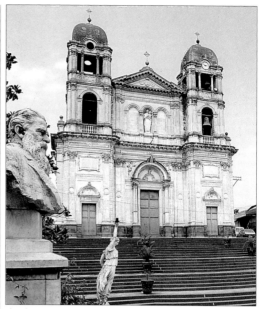

The Chiesa Madre at Zafferana Etnea, on the eastern slopes of Etna

Zafferana Etnea ⓬

Road map E3. 🔼 7,865. 🚌 22 km
(14 miles) from Catania. 🛈 *095-708
28 25.*

ZAFFERANA ETNEA LIES on the
eastern slopes of Mount
Etna and is one of the towns
most frequently affected by
recent lava flows. The most
important eruptions occurred
in 1852, when the lava reached the edge of town, and in
1992. The heart of Zafferana
is its large tree-lined main
square, dominated by the
Baroque **Chiesa Madre**. The
square is also the home of a
permanent agricultural fair
which, besides selling local
wine and produce, has old
farm implements on display.

ENVIRONS: Down the road
towards Linguaglossa is
Sant'Alfio, a town surrounded by vineyards and known
for the huge 2,000 year-old
tree called "Castagno dei
cento cavalli" (Chestnut tree
of 100 horses). According to
legend, the leaves of this
famous tree once protected
Queen Jeanne d'Anjou and
her retinue of 100 knights.

I MALAVOGLIA

Published in 1881 in Milan,
I Malavoglia (The House by
the Medlar Tree) is a masterpiece by novelist Giovanni
Verga *(see p21)* and of Italian
verismo. Set on the Riviera
dei Ciclopi at Aci Trezza, it
describes the harsh life of
fishermen and their constant
struggle with the sea. The
Toscano family, "I Mala-
voglia", are "all good
seafaring people, just the
opposite of their nickname"
(*malavoglia* means ill-will). In 1947 Luchino Visconti made
a film inspired by the book, *La Terra Trema*.

**The beach at Aci Trezza, the
setting for *I Malavoglia* (1881)**

Mount Etna ⓭

MOUNT ETNA is fundamental to Sicily's nature and landscape. The Italian writer Leonardo Sciascia *(see p21)* called it "a huge house cat, that purrs quietly and awakens every so often". Etna is Europe's largest active volcano and dominates the whole of eastern Sicily. Feared and loved, Etna is both snow and fire, lush vegetation and black lava. Around the crater you can still see the remnants of numbers of ancient vents. Further down is the eerie, barren landscape of the Valle del Bove.

Valle del Bove
Many recent lava flows have ended here. The craters Calanna and Trifoglietto I are of very ancient date. This is one of the most fascinating places in the Etna area.

The Sicilian Hound
The Sicilian hound or cirneco is a breed of dog native to the Etna area. In ancient times it was a hunting dog.

Nicolosi

The 1983 eruption was the first that man was able to divert.

Paternò

Catania

Acireale

Zafferana Etnea

THE LARGEST VOLCANO IN EUROPE

Etna, or Mongibello (from the Italian *monte* and the Arab *gebel*, both meaning "mountain"), is a relatively "recent" volcano that emerged two million years ago. It has erupted frequently in known history. Two of the most devastating eruptions were in 1381 and 1669, when the lava reached Catania, and one of the most recent was in the 1920s, when the villages of Cerro and Mascali were destroyed. Eruptions that have occurred in the last 20 years are shown here.

Lowland landscape
The breakdown of volcanic material in the valley below Mount Etna has resulted in very fertile land which supports almonds, olives, grapes, citrus fruit and vegetables below 1,000 m (3,280 ft).

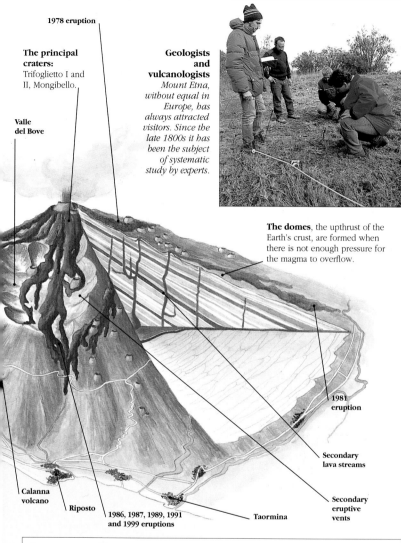

1978 eruption

The principal craters:
Trifoglietto I and II, Mongibello.

Geologists and vulcanologists
Mount Etna, without equal in Europe, has always attracted visitors. Since the late 1800s it has been the subject of systematic study by experts.

Valle del Bove

The domes, the upthrust of the Earth's crust, are formed when there is not enough pressure for the magma to overflow.

1981 eruption

Secondary lava streams

Calanna volcano

Riposto

1986, 1987, 1989, 1991 and 1999 eruptions

Taormina

Secondary eruptive vents

GEOLOGICAL HISTORY OF THE VOLCANO

Over the centuries the appearance of Mount Etna has altered. In 1865 the summit was at 3,313 m (10,867 ft); in 1932 it was 3,263 m (10,703 ft); and today it is 3,342 m (10,962 ft) high. Eruptions in the central crater are rare, but they are frequent in the side vents, and here they create smaller secondary cones.

On the eastern slope of Mount Etna is a huge chasm known as the Valle del Bove, the result of an immense explosion.

First stage, 200,000–100,000 years ago (Monte Calanna)

Second stage, 80,000 years ago (Vulcano Trifoglietto)

Third stage, 64,000 years ago (the cone collapses)

Fourth, current stage (the Mongibello cone)

Exploring Mount Etna

Now a protected area 58,000 ha (143,260 acres) in size, Mount Etna offers numerous opportunities for excursions, and attracts thousands of visitors every year. One of the most popular excursions is from Zafferana to the Valle del Bove, the spectacular hollow whose shape was changed by the 1992 eruptions. The hike up to the large craters at the summit is not to be missed. Start off at the Rifugio Sapienza and Rifugio Citelli refuges and Piano Provenzana. A trip around the mountain is also thrilling: from the Sapienza to the Monte Scavo camp, Piano Provenzana and the former Menza camp. There are also a number of lava grottoes.

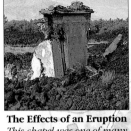

The Effects of an Eruption
This chapel was one of many buildings destroyed in the massive lava flows caused by the 1983 eruptions.

Skiing on Etna
Although there aren't many chair lifts, skiing on Mount Etna is a unique experience. Besides the regular ski runs you can do cross-country skiing or mountain climbing in the snow.

NATURE ON MOUNT ETNA

Despite the many eruptions and the bitter cold that freezes the terrain in winter, many species of plants have succeeded in colonizing the lava soil. At high altitudes you can see small lichens, camomile and soapwort on the slopes. Poplars thrive in the more humid areas. Further down are woods of beech, birch, larch and Corsican pine. Centuries of hunting have reduced the animal population, though there are still rabbits, weasels, wildcats and foxes, while the main bird species are the Sicilian partridge and the *Dendrocopus* woodpecker.

Pine forest on the slopes of Etna

Randaz

• Maletto

MONTE SPA
Grotta del 1,547 m, 5
Burò

• Bronte

Rifugio Monte Scavo

MON
NUNZI
1,803 m,

MONTE RUVOLO
Grotta della 1,410 m, 4,624 ft
Neve

SS284

MONTE TURCHIO
1,295 m, 4,248 ft

Torrente Milia

• Adrano

• Biancavilla

0 kilometres   3

0 miles   3

Rifugio Sapienza

At over 1,800 m (5,904 ft), the Sapienza camp is a base for bikers in the summer and for skiers in winter.

SS120

VISITORS' CHECKLIST

Road map E2, E3, F3.
🚌 095-730 62 66. 🚌 AST (095-746 10 96); SAIS (095-536 168). **FS** Catania (095-730 62 55). 🚆 Ferrovia Circumetnea (095-374 842 or 534 323). **Parco dell'Etna** (095-914 588). **Italian Alpine Club** (095-387 674). **Etna Alpine Guides** (095-911 452). **Rifugio Sapienza** (camp) (095-911 062).

MONTE COLARANDAZZO
▲ 967 m, 3,172 ft

MONTE SANTA MARIA
▲ 1,632 m, 5,353 ft
Grotta dei Lamponi

MONTE ROSSO   MONTE CORRUCCIO
MONTE NERO   ▲ 1,756 m, 5,760 ft   ▲ 1,361 m, 4,464 ft
Lave cordate   ▲ 2,049 m, 6,721 ft

MONTE PIZZILLO
Grotta del gelo   ▲ 2,414 m, 7,918 ft

ONTE FRUMENTO NETTO   Piano Provenzana
2,299 m, 7,541 ft   I DUE MONTI
MONTE DAGALOTTO   MONTE ZAPPINAZZO   ▲ 1,662 m, 5,451 ft
▲ 2,623 m, 8,603 ft   ▲ 1905 m, 6,248 ft

PUNTA LUCIA   Grotta dei ladroni
▲ 2,934 m, 9,623 ft   Rifugio Citelli

MOUNT ETNA (MONGIBELLO)   Lava tunnels
▲ 3,250 m, 10,660 ft

MONTE FRUMENTO SUPINO   Casa Pietracannone
▲ 2,845 m, 9,332 ft

Valle del Bove

Ex Rifugio Menza

Rifugio Sapienza   Zafferana Etnea

anic
den

Eruptions and Lava Flows
The volcano can be visited even when it is active, provided you scrupulously follow instructions. Above, the 1991 eruption.

KEY

ℹ️	Tourist information
═	Major road
🚆	Ferrovia Circumetnea
🚠	Cable car
🏔️	Area of natural beauty, interest
🍴	Restaurant
🎿	Ski run
⛷️	Cross-country skiing
☀️	Viewpoint
– –	Footpath (Trail)

Grotta delle Palombe

Nicolosi •

Craters and Eruptions

At this stage in the history of Mount Etna, most of the eruptions occur in the side vents, while on the summit craters the occasional explosive eruption may take place.

Bronte ❶

Road map E3. 👥 *19,968.*
🚆 *Ferrovia Circumetnea.* ℹ️ *095-
772 28 56.* 🎪 *Oct: Pistachio festival.*

Situated on a terraced lava
slope, Bronte was founded
by Charles V, who wanted to
unify all the villages in the
area around Randazzo. In
1799 Ferdinand IV of Bourbon
gave the town and the estates
in the Valle del Simeto to
Admiral Horatio Nelson, who
had helped him to suppress
the revolts in Naples in 1799.
In 1860, following the success
of Garibaldi's Red Shirts in
Sicily, the peasants of Bronte
rebelled, demanding that
Nelson's land be split up
among them, but their
rebellion was put down by
Garibaldi's men. The episode
was immortalized in a short
story by Verga *(see p21)*. The
eruptions of 1651, 1832 and
1843 struck the centre of
Bronte, which has however
managed to retain its original
character, with stone houses
and steeply rising alleyways.
The 16th-century **Annunziata**
has a sandstone
portal and, inside,
an *Annunciation*
(1541) attributed to
Antonello Gagini
(see p51) as well as
some 17th-century
canvases. In the
village of Piana
Cuntarati, the
**Masseria
Lombardo** farm
has been converted
into an Ethno-
graphic Museum which,
among many interesting
objects, has an Arab paper
mill dating from the year 1000.

**Medieval window in
central Randazzo**

Environs: Around 12 km
(7 miles) from the centre of
town is **Castello di Maniace**,
a Benedictine monastery
founded by Margaret of
Navarre, the mother of
William II, in 1174, on the spot
where the Byzantine general
Maniakes had defeated the
Arabs. Destroyed by the 1693
earthquake, the site became
the property of Horatio
Nelson. It has been restored
and looks like a fortified
farm, with a garden of exotic
plants. Next to the castle is
the medieval **Santa Maria**,
with scenes from the Book
of Genesis sculpted on the
capitals of the columns.

Randazzo ❶

Road map E3. 👥 *11,744.* 🚆
Ferrovia Circumetnea. ℹ️ *095-923
841.* 🎪 *Easter Week, 15 Aug:
Processione della "Vara", Jul–Aug:
medieval festival.* 🚌 *Sun.*

Built of lava stone 765 m
(2,509 ft) above sea level,
Randazzo is the town closest
to the craters of Mount Etna,
but it has never
been inundated
with lava. In the
Middle Ages it was
surrounded by a 3-
km (2-mile) city
wall, some parts of
which have sur-
vived, such as the
Porta Aragonese
gate, on the old
road to Messina.
The major monu-
ment and symbol of
the town is **Santa Maria**, a
basilica built in 1217–39: the
towered apses with the characteristic ribbing are all that is

**The restored Via degli Archi with
its cobbled lava paving**

left of the original Norman
construction, while the
double lancet windows and
portals are Catalan. The nave
with its black lava columns
has multicoloured marble
altars and a marble basin
sculpted by the Gagini
school. **Corso Umberto**, the
main street in Randazzo, leads
to **Piazza San Francesco
d'Assisi**, dominated by the
Palazzo Comunale, once the
monastery of the Minor
Order, which has an elegant
cloister with a cistern.
    The narrow side streets
have many examples of
medieval architecture. The
most characteristic of these
is **Via degli Archi**, which
has a lovely pointed arch
and black lava cobblestone
paving. In **Piazza San Nicolò**
is the church of the same
name, with a late Renaissance
façade made of lava stone. In
the interior there is a fine
statue of San Nicola of Bari
sculpted in 1523 by Antonello
Gagini. The bell tower was
damaged by an earthquake in
1783. Its reconstruction
replaced the original cusp
with a wrought-iron balcony.
After a turn to the left, Corso
Umberto crosses a square
where **San Martino** stands.
It has a beautiful bell tower
with single lancet windows
with two-coloured borders,
and a polygonal spire.

The Castello di Maniace, the property of Lord Nelson's heirs until 1981

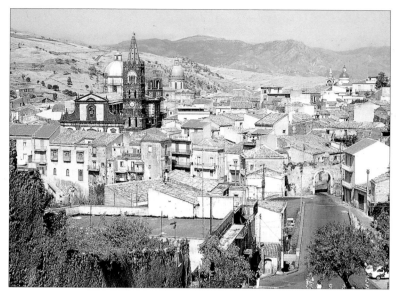

The Randazzo skyline, dominated by the bell tower of San Martino

Opposite is the **Castle**, which was a prison in the 1500s and will be the new home of the **Museo Archeologico Vagliasindi**, with interesting Greek finds from Tissa, such as the famous vase depicting the punishment of the Harpies.

Linguaglossa ⑯

Road map E3. 🏘 5,515. 🚉 Ferrovia Circumetnea. 🛈 095-643 094. 🎉 Last Sun in Aug: Mount Etna festival.

L INGUAGLOSSA is the largest village on the northeastern slopes of Etna as well as the starting point for excursions to the volcano summit and for the ski runs. Its name derives from a 17th-century lava flow that was called *lingua glossa* (big tongue). The town streets are paved with black lava and the houses have small wrought-iron balconies. The **Chiesa Madre**, dedicated to Santa Maria delle Grazie, is well worth a visit for its Baroque decoration and fine coffered ceiling. Linguaglossa also boasts the **Museo delle Genti dell'Etna**, a museum with geological and natural history exhibits as well as everyday objects and craftsmen's tools.

🏛 **Museo delle Genti dell'Etna**
Piazza Annunziata (c/o Pro Loco). 🛈 095-643 094. ◯ 9am–1pm, 4–7:30 pm; 10am–12:30pm Sun & hols. 🎫

Giarre ⑰

Road map F3. 🏘 27,208. 🚉 Ferrovia Circumetnea. 🚌 from Catania. 🛈 095-963 111.

T HIS TOWN lies in the middle of citrus groves extending down to the sea. Giarre is famous for its handmade wrought-iron products. The heart of town is **Piazza Duomo**, dominated by the impressive Neo-Classical **Duomo**, built in 1794 and dedicated to Sant'Isidoro Agricola. The façade has two square bell towers with windows and a tambour. There are many delightful patrician residences made of lava stone in the old town. In the nearby village of Macchia is the **Museo degli Usi e dei Costumi delle Genti dell'Etna**, an ethnographic museum you can visit only by appointment.

One interesting exhibit here is a reproduction of a typical Etna farmhouse, with its old kitchen and bread oven, well and washtub. Also on display are farm implements, looms, clothing, and period photographs and daguerreotypes.

🏛 **Museo degli Usi e dei Costumi delle Genti dell'Etna**
🛈 095-779 17 69.

The rusticated façade of the late 18th-century Neo-Classical Duomo in Giarre

Street-by-Street: Taormina ⑱

Byzantine mosaic

O N A BLUFF above the Ionian Sea, at the foot of Monte Tauro, Taormina is Sicily's most famous tourist resort. Immersed in luxuriant subtropical vegetation, it was a favourite stop for those on the Grand Tour and the preferred summer residence of aristocrats and bankers, from Wilhelm II of Germany to the Rothschilds. In its time the town has been Siculan, Greek and Roman, but its medieval layout gives it today's look.

Piazza IX Aprile
The second largest square in Taormina is home to the churches of San Giorgio and San Giuseppe, the Torre dell'Orologio and the Wünderbar Café.

Porta Catania

Chiesa del Carmine

Badia Vecchia

Convento di San Domenico

Palazzo dei Duchi di Santo Stefano was built in the Norman period with Arab motifs.

Chiesa della Visitazione

San Giorgio

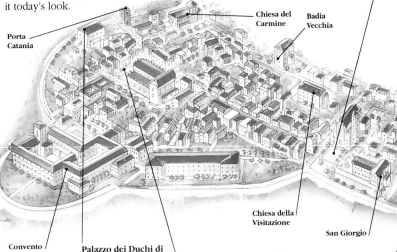

★ Piazza del Duomo
This is the heart of town, at the western end of Corso Umberto I. In the middle of the square is a Baroque fountain, facing the Cathedral of San Nicolò and the Palazzo Comunale (Town Hall).

Villa Comunale
Located on a cliff with a stunning view, this lovely garden was donated to the town by a rich Englishwoman, an aristocrat who had fallen in love with Taormina.

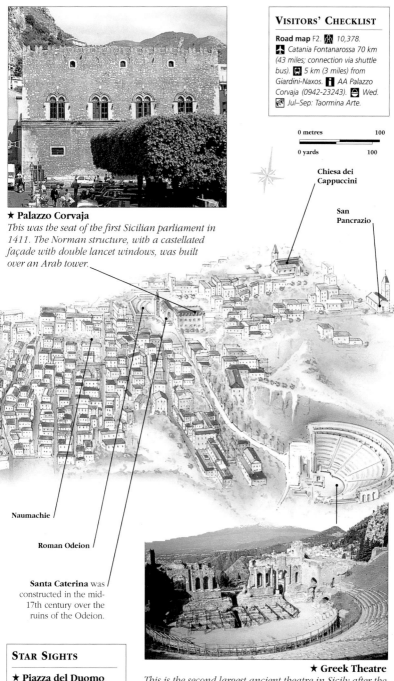

★ **Palazzo Corvaja**
This was the seat of the first Sicilian parliament in 1411. The Norman structure, with a castellated façade with double lancet windows, was built over an Arab tower.

VISITORS' CHECKLIST

Road map F2. 10,378.
Catania Fontanarossa 70 km (43 miles; connection via shuttle bus). 5 km (3 miles) from Giardini-Naxos. AA Palazzo Corvaja (0942-23243). Wed. Jul–Sep: Taormina Arte.

0 metres	100
0 yards	100

Chiesa dei Cappuccini

San Pancrazio

Naumachie

Roman Odeion

Santa Caterina was constructed in the mid-17th century over the ruins of the Odeion.

STAR SIGHTS

★ **Piazza del Duomo**

★ **Palazzo Corvaja**

★ **Greek Theatre**

★ **Greek Theatre**
This is the second largest ancient theatre in Sicily after the one in Syracuse. It was originally built in the Hellenistic age (3rd century BC) and was almost entirely rebuilt by the Romans in the 2nd century AD. The theatre has a magnificent view of the sea and Mount Etna.

Exploring Taormina

FROM EASTER TO OCTOBER Taormina is inundated with visitors, so if you prefer peace and quiet it is probably a good idea to go out of season. The climate is mild here even in the winter. The town is especially delightful in the spring, when the air is filled with the scent of orange and lemon blossoms, the gardens are in bloom and Mount Etna is still snow-capped. A regular shuttle bus links the car park to the centre of town, or you can park at Mazzarò and take the cable car to town.

Corso Umberto I, running the length of the town

🜏 Corso Umberto I

The main street in Taormina begins at **Porta Messina** and ends at **Porta Catania**, a gate crowned by a building showing the municipal coat of arms. The street is lined with shops, *pasticcerie* and cafés famous for their glamorous clientele, like the **Wünderbar**, where you can try the cocktails that Liz Taylor and Richard Burton were so fond of. Halfway down the Corso is **Piazza IX Aprile**, a panoramic terrace with **Sant'Agostino** (now the Municipal Library) and **San Giuseppe**. A short distance away is the **Porta di Mezzo**

The Wünderbar has always been a favourite with film stars

gate with the 17th-century Torre dell'Orologio, or clock tower. Above and below Corso Umberto I there are stepped alleyways and lanes passing through quiet, characterful areas. One such alley leads to the **Naumachie**, a massive Roman brick wall dating back to the Imperial Age with 18 arched niches, which once supported a huge cistern.

🜏 Palazzo Corvaja

Piazza Vittorio Emanuele. **☎** 0942-23243. **○** 8am–2pm, 3–9pm.
Taormina's most important building dates from the 15th century, although it was originally an Arab tower. The austere façade topped by crenellation is made elegant by the three-mullioned windows and the limestone and black lava decorative motifs. The courtyard stairway decorated with reliefs of the *Birth of Eve* and *The Original Sin* takes you to the *piano nobile*, where the Sicilian parliament met in 1411 and where Queen Blanche of Navarre and her retinue lived for a short period. The rooms will be closed until the new Ethnographic Museum is moved here. On the ground floor is the local tourist information bureau. Next to the palazzo are the Baroque **Santa Caterina** and the ruins of the **Odeion**, a small Roman theatre.

⋔ Greek Theatre

Via Teatro Greco. **☎** 0942-23220.
○ 9am to 1 hour before sunset daily. 🜏 🜏
Set in a spectacular position, this theatre is one of the most famous Sicilian monuments in the world. It was built in the Hellenistic age and then almost completely rebuilt in the Roman period, when it became an arena for gladiator combats.

From the cavea, carved from the side of a hill, the view takes in Giardini-Naxos *(see p176)* and Mount Etna. The upper part of the nine-section theatre is surrounded by a double portico. The theatre originally had a diameter of 109 m (358 ft) and a seating capacity of 5,000. Behind the stage area stood a wall with niches and a colonnade. Some of the Corinthian columns are still standing.

The Greek Theatre in Taormina, capable of seating 5,000 spectators

🜏 Villa Comunale

Via Bagnoli Croci. **○** 7am–midnight in summer; 8am–sunset in winter.
Dedicated to Duke Colonna di Cesarò, this public garden was bequeathed to Taormina by an English aristocrat, Florence Trevelyan, who fell in love with the town. Situated on a cliff with a magnificent view of Etna and the coast, the garden is filled with lovely Mediterranean and tropical plants. A characteristic part of the garden is the arabesque-decorated tower, similar to a Chinese pagoda, that the owner used for her favourite hobby, bird-watching.

A view of Piazza del Duomo: in the foreground, the Baroque fountain, which faces the Cathedral

Cathedral

Piazza Duomo. 0942-23123.
8:30am–noon, 3:30–7:30pm
summer; 8:30am–noon, 3:30–6:30pm
winter. 9:30 & 11am, 7 pm (6pm
in winter).

The Cathedral (San Nicolò)
was built in the 13th century
and has been altered over the
centuries. The austere façade
is crowned by crenellation.
The 17th-century portal is
decorated with a medallion
pattern, and over this are a
small rose window and two
windows with pointed arches.
The nave has two side aisles
and a wooden ceiling, as well
as some interesting works of
art: *The Visitation* by Antonio
Giuffrè (15th century), a
polyptych by Antonello Saliba
of the *Virgin Mary and Child*,
and an alabaster statue of the
Virgin Mary by the Gagini
school. In Piazza Duomo, in
the middle of which is a
lovely Baroque fountain, is
the Town Hall, **Palazzo del
Municipio**, with a storey
lined with Baroque windows.

Palazzo dei Duchi di Santo Stefano

Via De Spuches.
9:30am–12:30pm, 4:30–7pm.
This 13th-century building
near Porta Catania was the
residence of the De Spuches,
the Spanish dukes of Santo
Stefano di Brifa and princes
of Galati, two towns on the
Ionian coast near Messina. In
this masterpiece of Sicilian
Gothic architecture the
influence of Arab masons is
clearly seen in the wide black
lava frieze alternating with
rhomboidal white Syracusan
stone inlay. Note the tri-
lobated arches and double
lancet windows on the façade.
The interior has a permanent
exhibition of the works of
sculptor Giuseppe Marzullo.

Castelmola

A winding road of 5 km (3
miles) leads to this village
perched on a rock. Today you
only see the ruins of a
medieval castle, but in
antiquity this may have been
the site of the ancient acropolis of Tauromenion. From
Castelmola you can enjoy
one of the most famous
panoramic views in the world,
especially fine at sunset.

Palazzo dei Duchi di Santo Stefano, built by Arab artisans and masons

View of Isola Bella from the steps that go from Taormina to the beach at Mazzarò

Mazzarò

This small town is virtually Taormina's beach. It can be reached easily by cable car from Taormina or via the road leading to the Catania–Messina state road N144. An alternative is the steps which descend from the centre of Taormina through gardens of bougainvillea in bloom. From the **Bay of Mazzarò**, with its crystal clear water, you can go on excursions to other sights along the coast: **Capo Sant'Andrea**, with the **Grotta Azzurra**, a spectacular marine grotto, can be visited by boat; to the south are the stacks of **Capo Taormina** and the beach at **Villagonia**; and to the north are **Isola Bella**, one of the most exclusive places in the area, partly because of

its clear waters, and the beaches at the **Baia delle Sirene** and the **Lido di Spisone**. Further on is the beach at **Mazzeo**, a long stretch of sand that leads as far as Letoianni and continues up to **Lido Silemi**.

Letojanni

This small seaside resort is 5 km (3 miles) from Taormina. Busy and bustling in the summer, it is perhaps best seen in the spring or autumn. Locals and visitors alike come here to dine out in one of the many good fish restaurants by the water.

Giardini-Naxos ⑲

Road map F3. 8,936. Catania Fontanarossa 66 km (41 miles). 0942-51026). Autolinee Sai (0942-625 301). AA, Via Tysandros 54 (0942-51010).

B ETWEEN Capo Taormina and Capo Schisò, Giardini-Naxos is a seaside resort near what was once the first Greek colony in Sicily. Thucydides relates that Naxos was founded in 735 BC by Chalcidians led by the Athenian Thucles, the first Greek to land on Sicilian soil, and Naxos became the base for all further colonization of the island. Naxos was destroyed by Dionysius of Syracuse in 403 BC. On the headland of Capo Schisò, amid lemon trees and prickly pears, you can visit the **Naxos excavations**.

Of the two phases in the life of the city, the one which yielded the most important (if scarce) archaeological finds dates from the 6th and 5th centuries BC, with remains of the city walls and houses as well as stones from a temple that may have been dedicated to Aphrodite. In the village of **Giardini**, by the beach, there are still some fine mansions on the oldest streets.

Ancient Silenic mask

The sea at Giardini-Naxos, the first Greek colony in Sicily

Castiglione di Sicilia ⑳

Road map F3. 4,229.
Ferrovia Circumetnea. *Giardini di Naxos.* 0942-984 015.

THIS PRETTY VILLAGE lies on a crag dominating the **Alcantara Valley**. It was founded by the Greeks, who built fortifications there. Many years later it became a royal city under the Normans and the Hohenstaufens, and the fief of Roger of Lauria at the end of the 13th century.

Castiglione still retains its medieval layout, the narrow streets converging in central **Piazza Lauria**. From this point, moving up the hill, you will see numerous churches. The first is the **Chiesa Madre**, or San Pietro, which still has its Norman apse; then there are the 17th-century **Chiesa delle Benedettine** and the Baroque **Sant'Antonio** and **Chiesa Della Catena**. At the top of the village is the medieval **Castel Leone**, built by the Normans over the Arab fortifications, where you have a view of the **medieval bridge** on the Alcantara River.

ENVIRONS: The **Alcantara ravine**, 20 m (66 ft) deep, cut out of black basalt by the

The Alcantara River flowing between basalt cliffs

rushing waters of the Alcantara river, are a marvellously compelling sight you should really try to see. If the weather is good, it is worth following the gorge for about 150 m (490 ft), but only if you can manage without raincoats and weatherproof gear. There is also a lift (elevator) that you can take to avoid the long flight of steps that leads from the parking area to the entrance of the ravine.

Forza d'Angrò, a medieval village with a 16th-century castle at the summit

THE PELORITANI MOUNTAINS

The Monti Peloritani form a ridge between two seas peaking in **Monte Poverello** (1,279 m, 4,195 ft) and the **Pizzo di Vernà** (1,286 m, 4,218 ft). It is a marvellous area for excursions, often with stunning views of the sea and Mount Etna, in a landscape of knife-edge ridges and woods. On 4 August a major pilgrimage is made to the **Antennamare Sanctuary**, while 7 September is the day for festivities at the **Sanctuary of the Madonna del Crispino**, above the village of **Monforte San Giorgio**. Many of the mountain villages are interesting from a historical and artistic point of view. **Forza d'Angrò**, dominated by a 16th-century castle; **Casalvecchio Siculo**, with the Arab-Norman Basilica dei Santi Pietro e Paolo; **Savoca**, with Capuchin catacombs and embalmed bodies; **Alì**, which has a strong Arab flavour; **Itala**, overlooking the Ionian Sea, with San Pietro e Paolo, built by Roger I as a thanks offering for a victory over the Arabs; and lastly **Mili San Pietro**, with the basilica-monastery of Santa Maria, which was founded in 1082 by Roger I.

Messina ㉑

T HE POSITION of this ancient city, founded by colonists
from Messenia in Greece, has always been the key
to its importance. Situated between the eastern and
western Mediterranean, and between the two vice-
royalties of Naples and Sicily, Messina has always been
influenced by its role as a meeting point. Over the
centuries it has been populated by Armenians, Arabs,
Jews and other communities from the large maritime
cities of Europe, becoming increasingly important up
to the anti-Spanish revolt of 1674–78, after which the
city fell into decline. Already damaged by the 1783
earthquake, Messina was almost totally razed in 1908.

The votive column at the entrance to the port of Messina

Exploring Messina

The city developed around the harbour and its layout is quite easy to understand if you arrive by sea. The defences of the **Forte San Salvatore** and the **Lanterna di Raineri**, on the peninsula of the same name that protects the harbour to the east, are your introduction to Messina, which lies on the gently sloping sides of the Peloritani Mountains. The main streets are **Via Garibaldi** (which skirts the seafront by the harbour) and **Via I Settembre**, which leads from the sea to the centre of town around **Piazza Duomo**. Interesting attractions such as the **Botanic Garden** and the **Montalto Sanctuary** are located on the hillside above the city.

🏛 Santissima Annunziata dei Catalani

Piazza dei Catalani. ◷ 9:30–11:30am daily (9–11:30am Sun).
Paradoxically, the devastating 1908 earthquake helped to "restore" the original 12th–13th century structure of this Norman period church, as it destroyed almost all the later additions and alterations. The nave has two side aisles and leads to the apse with its austere brick cupola.

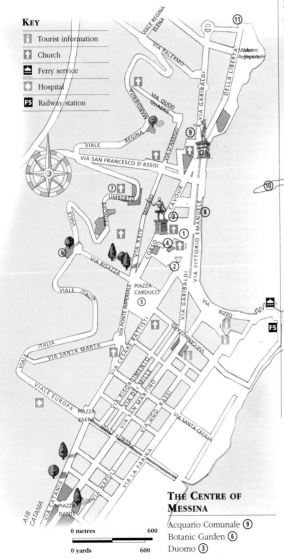

KEY

🛈	Tourist information
🛈	Church
⚓	Ferry service
🛈	Hospital
FS	Railway station

THE CENTRE OF MESSINA

0 metres   600
0 yards   600

Acquario Comunale ⑨
Botanic Garden ⑥
Duomo ③

Fontana di Orione ④
Forte di San Salvatore ⑩
Marina ⑧
Montalto Sanctuary ⑦
Monument to
  John of Austria ②
Museo Regionale ⑪
Santissima Annunziata
  dei Catalani ①
University ⑤

The Orion Fountain, with the Duomo and the Torre dell'Orologio in the background

VISITORS' CHECKLIST

Road map F2. 🏛 *273,570*.
🚢 *SNAV (090-345 422)*.
🚉 *(090-775 234)*. ℹ *AAST, Piazza Cairoli 45 (090-694 780); Azienda Provinciale Incremento Turistico, Via Calabria 301b (090-674 236 or 675 356)*.
🎭 *Carnival: procession of floats with tableaux; Aug: Cavalcata dei Giganti*.

⚜ Monument to John of Austria

In the square in front of the Annunziata church is a statue of John of Austria, the admiral who won the famous Battle of Lepanto, with his foot on the head of the defeated Ottoman commander Alì Pasha. The work was sculpted in 1572 by Andrea Calamech.

The pedestal celebrates the formation of the Holy League and the defeat of the Turks in this historic naval battle. One of the sailors taking part was the great Miguel de Cervantes, author of *Don Quixote*, who recovered from his wounds in a Messina hospital.

🔒 Duomo

The Cathedral is in Piazza Duomo, in the heart of town. Although it was reconstructed after the 1908 earthquake and the 1943 bombings, it has preserved its medieval aspect. It was built by Henry VI Hohen-staufen in 1197. The façade was totally rebuilt but you can still see the original central portal built in the early Middle Ages, decorated with two lions and a statue of the Virgin Mary and Infant Jesus. The side doors are decorated with statues of the Apostles and lovely inlay and reliefs. On the left-hand side of the façade is the large campanile, almost 60 m (197 ft) high, built to house a

unique object – the largest astronomical clock in the world, built by a Strasbourg firm in 1933. Noon is the signal for a number of mechanical figures to move in elaborate patterns, geared by huge cogwheels. Almost all of the impressive interior is the result of fine post-war reconstruction. Some sculptures on the trusses in the central section of the two-aisle nave, a 15th-century basin and the 1525 statue of St John the Baptist by Gagini, are part of the original decoration. The doorways in the right-hand vestibule leading to the Treasury are of note, as is the tomb of Archbishop Palmieri, sculpted in 1195. In the transept is an organ, built after World War II, with five keyboards and 170 stops. The side aisles house many works of art, – especially Gothic funerary monuments – most of which have been reconstructed.

⚜ Orion Fountain

This lovely 15th-century fountain stands next to

One of the two lions on the portal of the Duomo

the Duomo. It incorporates statues representing four rivers: the Tiber, Nile, Ebro and Camaro (the last of which was channelled into Messina via the first aqueduct in the city specifically to supply the fountain with water).

⚜ University

The University is in **Piazza Carducci**. It was founded in 1548, closed by the Spanish in 1679 and reconstructed at last in 1927. Besides the university faculties, the complex also includes the small **Museo Zoologico Cambria**, with its fine collections of vertebrates, shells and insects. Follow Viale Principe Umberto, and you come to the **Botanic Garden** and the **Montalto Sanctuary**, with the *Madonna of Victory*, built after the Battle of Lepanto, standing out against the sky.

THE 1908 EARTHQUAKE

At 5:20am on 28 December 1908, it seemed that nature was intent upon destroying Messina: an earthquake and a tidal wave struck at the same time, bringing over 91 per cent of the buildings to the ground and killing 60,000 people. Reggio Calabria, on the other side of the Straits of Messina, was also destroyed. Reconstruction began immediately.

Some of the remains of the old town were salvaged by being incorporated into a new urban plan, designed by Luigi Borzi. His scheme gives Messina its present-day appearance.

Messina the day after the earthquake

⊞ Marina

After walking along the marina in 1789, the author Frances Elliot wrote: "There is nothing in the world like the Messina seafront. It is longer and more elegant than Via Chiaia in Naples, more vigorous and picturesque than the Promenade in Nice...". Not far away is another focal point in Messina, **Piazza dell'Unità d'Italia**. The buildings that lined the marina before the earthquake were part of the "Palazzata" complex, also known as the **Teatro Marittimo**. The Teatro was a series of buildings that extended for more than a kilometre in the heart of the port area – the centre of commercial transactions – which also included the homes of the most powerful families in Messina.

⚓ Acquario Comunale

The garden of the **Villa Mazzini** is decorated with busts and statues, and is also home to the Municipal Aquarium. Next door is the **Palazzo della Prefettura**, in front of which is the **Fountain of Neptune**, sculpted in the mid-1500s by Giovanni Angelo Montorsoli. The statues are 19th-century copies and the originals are on display in the Museo Regionale.

Madonna and Child, Francesco Laurana

⊞ Forte San Salvatore

Beyond the busy harbour area, at the very tip of the curved peninsula that protects the harbour, is Forte San Salvatore, built in the 17th century to block access to the Messina marina. On top of one of the tall towers in this impressive fort is a statue of the *Madonna della Lettera*: according to tradition, the Virgin Mary sent a letter of benediction to the inhabitants of Messina in AD 42.

On **Via Garibaldi** is the bustling **Stazione Marittima**, the boarding point for the ferry boats that connect Messina to Calabria on the mainland of Italy.

� Museo Regionale

Viale della Libertà. 📞 090-361 292. 🕐 9am–2pm daily (also 3–5:30pm Tue, Thu, Sat); 9am–1pm hols. ♿

This fascinating museum is only 500 m (1,640 ft) from Piazza dell'Unità d'Italia. It boasts an important collection of art works salvaged after the catastrophic 1908 earthquake. In fact, most of the works come from the Civico Museo Peloritano, which was in the now destroyed Monastery of St Gregory. The museum has 12 rooms, which present an overview of the artistic splendour of old Messina and include a number of famous paintings. At the entrance there are 12 18th-century bronze panels depicting the *Legend of the Sacred Letter*. Some of the most important works include paintings from the Byzantine period and fragments from the Duomo ceiling (room 1); the Gothic art in room 2; the examples of Renaissance Messina in room 3; the *Polyptych* that Antonello da Messina *(see p21)* painted for the Monastery of St Gregory

One of the five panels of Antonello da Messina's *St Gregory Polyptych* (1473)

BRIDGING THE STRAITS OF MESSINA

Communications with the mainland have always been a fundamental issue for Sicily, and for over 30 years the question of building a bridge over the Straits of Messina has been debated. There has even been a proposal to build a tunnel anchored to the sea bed. This idea now seems to have been discarded, and work on the design of a bridge is under way. In 1981 the Società Stretto di Messina was established with the aim of designing a single-span suspension bridge over the straits to connect Torre Faro and Punta Pezzo – a distance of 3 km (2 miles). A multitude of problems still needs to be tackled, however, one of which is the constant danger of earthquakes.

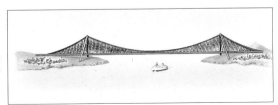

A 1997 design for the planned bridge over the Straits of Messina

(room 4) and, in the same room, a *Madonna and Child* sculpture attributed to Francesco Laurana and a 15th-century oil on panel by an unknown Flemish artist.

Room 9 has two of the "pearls" of the museum, two masterpieces by Caravaggio, executed in 1608–1609: *The Raising of Lazarus* and *The Nativity*. This great artist's sojourn in Messina exerted an influence on other artists, giving rise to a local Caravaggesque school, as can be seen in the canvases by Alonso Rodriguez, *Supper at Emmaus* and *Doubting Thomas*, on view in room 10.

ENVIRONS: By proceeding northwards along the coastline of the Straits, past the Museo Regionale, you will come to **Grotta** and then, about 7 km (4 miles) from Messina, the turn-off to **Ganzirri**. A short drive along the coastal road takes you to the **Pantano Grande** (or Lago Grande), a lagoon that measures 30 ha (74 acres) and is at most 7 m (23 ft) deep. One side of the lagoon consists of a long sandbar and it is connected to the sea by an artificial canal. The Pantano Grande is supplied with fresh water from underground streams and it is used for shellfish farming on a large scale. This point is quite close to the easternmost tip of Sicily: 3 km (2 miles) away is **Torre Faro**, a fishing village known for its excellent swordfish, facing the coast of Calabria. The panorama here is dominated by the pylon and electric

The Pantano Grande lake at Ganzirri, used for shellfish farming

power cable that crosses the Straits of Messina for 3,646 m (11,959 ft) in a single span, from the power stations in Calabria. **Capo Peloro**, a short distance from Torre Faro, is crowned by a 16th-century tower that has been used for centuries as a lighthouse. Further along the coastal road you will come to the second, smaller lagoon of Ganzirri, known as the **Pantano Piccolo**. The lake is a stone's throw away from the Tyrrhenian Sea and is linked to the Pantano Grande.

🏠 **Santa Maria di Mili**
If you head southwards from Messina for about 12 km (7 miles), you will reach the villages of **Mili San Marco** and, higher up in the Peloritani Mountains, **Mili San Pietro**. Not far from the latter, in an area of wild landscape characterized by the deep **Forra di Mili** (ravine), is the **Santa Maria di Mili Sanctuary**. The church is in a convent. It has been rebuilt several times and now has a 17th-century appearance. It was founded in 1090 by Roger I as proof of his recovered religious faith after taking Sicily from the Arabs. The Norman king later chose it as the burial site for his son. The splendid 16th-century marble portal is crowned by a sculpture of the Madonna and Child. Above the two-aisle nave is a finely wrought wooden ceiling that dates from 1411. Once past the three arches marking off the apse area, this ceiling becomes a series of small domes, a characteristic feature of religious architecture of the Norman period.

The church of San Pietro e Paulo in Itala *(see p177)*

Tyndaris ㉒

Road map E2. ☐ 8:30am–1 hr
before sunset, daily. ⊠ 8 Sep:
Pilgrimage of the Madonna Nera.

ANCIENT TYNDARIS was one of the last Greek colonies in Sicily, founded by the Syracusans in 396 BC, when the Romans were already beginning to expand their territory in the Mediterranean. The town also prospered under Roman rule and became a diocese during the early Christian period, after which time it was destroyed by the Arabs. A visit to the archaeological site is fascinating, partly because of the monuments but also because of the many details, which give you an idea of everyday life in the ancient city. The town is laid out in a classical grid plan consisting of two straight and parallel streets *(decumani)* intersected by other streets *(cardines)*. Once you have gone past the walls through the main city gate, not far from the **Madonna di Tindari Sanctuary** (which houses the famous Byzantine *Madonna Nera* or Black Madonna, honoured in a pilgrimage held every 8 September) you will see the **Greek Theatre**, situated on the slope of a rise and facing the sea; it has a diameter of more than 60 m (197 ft). Nearby is the **Agora**, which has, unhappily, been obscured by modern buildings. In the theatre area are the remains of a **Roman villa** and **Roman baths**. If you stroll through the streets of the ancient city you will see storehouses for food and the Greek-era drainage system. A large building known as the **Ginnasio** or **Basilica** was probably used for public meetings during the Imperial Age. Next to the theatre is the **Museo Archeologico**, which has a large model of the Greek theatre stage, as well as Greek statues and vases, a colossal head of the Emperor Augustus and prehistoric finds. One unmissable sight is the marvellous scenery under the **Promontory** of Tyndaris: the **Laguna di Oliveri**, the place celebrated by the poet and Nobel Prize winner Quasimodo *(see p21)*.

THE NEBRODI MOUNTAINS

The Arabs occupied the Nebrodi Mountains for centuries and referred to them as "an island on an island". The name comes from the Greek word *nebros*, or "roe deer", because of the rich wildlife to be found in this mountain range, which separates the Madonie Mountains to the west from the Peloritani Mountains to the east. The Parco Regionale dei Nebrodi is a nature reserve with extensive forests and some pastureland, which is covered with snow in the winter. In the middle of the park is the Biviere di Cesarò lake, a stopover point for migratory birds and an ideal habitat for the *Testudo hermanni* marsh turtle. The tallest peak is Monte Soro (1,850 m, 6,068 ft). Higher up, the maquis is replaced by oak and beech woods.

⚇ Parco Regionale dei Monti Nebrodi
☎ 0921-335 498.

Horses grazing in the Parco Regionale dei Monti Nebrodi

The unusual natural scenery at the Laguna di Oliveri, seen from the Promontory of Tyndaris

The sarcophagus of Roger I's wife Adelaide in Patti Cathedral

Patti

Road map E2. 13,064. from
Messina and Palermo (0941-361 081).
AAST (0941-241 136).

O
N ONE OF THE STRETCHES
where the coastal
scenery is most fascinating,
just past the rocky promontory of **Capo Calavà** on the
slopes overlooking the sea,
is the town of Patti. It was
initially a fief of the Norman
ruler Roger I which was later
destroyed during the wars
with the Angevins and then
frequently pillaged by pirates
from North Africa.

Patti boasts an 18th-century
Cathedral which was built
over the foundations of the
former Norman church. Inside
is a sarcophagus with the
remains of Queen Adelaide,
Roger I's wife, who died in
the town in 1118.

Along the road down to
Marina di Patti are the ruins
of a **Roman villa** which were
brought to light during the
construction of the Messina–
Palermo motorway. This
Imperial Age building measures 20,000 sq m (215,200 sq
ft) and comprises a peristyle,
an apse-like room, thermal
baths and many well-
preserved mosaics. The villa
was destroyed by an earthquake; on the basis of various
archaeological finds, histor-
ians have been able to date
this event at the second half
of the 4th century AD.

⌂ Roman villa at Patti
◻ 9am–12:30pm, 2:30pm–1 hr
before sunset, daily.

Capo d'Orlando ❷⓿

Road map E2. 11,277.
0941-912 611.

F
ORMING PART of a region
known for the intensive
cultivation of citrus fruits, the
Nebrodi Mountains jut out
into the sea at intervals. The
coastal town of Capo
d'Orlando lies at the foot of
the **Rupe del Semaforo** cliff
and the rocky hill after which
the town was named.

A climb of about 100 m
(328 ft) will take you to the
top of the cliff. There, in a
large open space, stand the
remains of a 14th-century
fortress and **Maria Santissima**, a church built in the
late 1500s and now home to a
number of interesting
paintings. However, the main
reward for climbing up the
hill is the panoramic view of
the sea and of the fishing
boats moving about in the
pretty harbour below.

Milazzo ❷⓹

Road map F2. 31,943. from
Messina & Palermo (090-929 60 52).
(090-922 28 65 or 92311).

M
ILAZZO BEGAN to take its
place in written history
when *Mylai* was colonized by
the Greeks in 716 BC. The
Normans later chose it as
their main coastal stronghold.
Frederick II personally
designed the castle built there
in 1239. The town was divided
into three distinct zones in the
Middle Ages – the **walled
town**, the **Borgo** and the
lower town – and it was
expanded in the 1700s. The
Salita Castello leads up to
the **ancient rock**, which
affords access to the walled
town via a covered passageway. A doorway then opens
into **Frederick II's Castle**,
surrounded by a wall with
five round towers and the
great hall of the **Sala del
Parlamento** (Parliament
Hall). On the same rise are
the remains of the old
Duomo, the original 17th-
century cathedral, now in a
state of disrepair. Don't miss
the chance of an excursion to
Capo Milazzo, where you
will be rewarded with towers,
villas and, at the foot of the
18th-century lighthouse, a
marvellous view of the
Aeolian Islands, with Calabria
beyond. This was the site of
the 260 BC naval battle in
which the Romans routed the
Carthaginian fleet. Steps lead
to the place where St Anthony
is said to have taken refuge
from a storm in 1221.

The castle at Milazzo, strengthened structurally by Alfonso of Aragon

The Aeolian Islands

Three-colour clay vase, 4th century BC

Consisting of strikingly beautiful volcanic cliffs separated by inlets, sometimes quite deep, the Aeolian Islands (in Italian, Isole Eolie) are unique for their extraordinary rock formations and volcanoes, and for their history. The islands attract hordes of visitors every summer who come to bathe and dive, yet despite the crowds, each island somehow manages to preserve its own individual character. Dominating the islands, especially in the winter, is the sea, with migratory birds nesting on the cliffs and frequent storms, which can reinforce a sense of isolation, even in this age of rapid communications.

Filicudi
There are three villages on this island: Val di Chiesa, Pecorini and Filicudi Porto. On the Capo Graziano promontory are the ruins of a prehistoric village.

M a r

Pecorini

Alicudi
The 5 sq km (2 sq miles) of Alicudi do not leave room for many inhabitants. The highest peak is the Filo dell'Arpa – 675 m (2,214 ft).

Lipari
The main island in the archipelago, Lipari has many hot springs and fumaroles, evidence of its volcanic origin. The old town, with a castle and cathedral, is built within walls. There is an important Museo Archeo-logico Eoliano here, with an excellent collection.

Stromboli
The main attraction on this island is the climb up the volcano and the fine view from the "Sciara del Fuoco".

VISITORS' CHECKLIST

FS *Milazzo.* **🚌** *from Catania airport, SAIS (095-536 168); from Messina to Milazzo Giunta (090-679 677).*

⛴ *Shipping companies: Siremar, all year from Milazzo and Naples (091-607 01 86 or 607 01 83); SNAV, all year from Milazzo (081-682 322 or 090 36 21 14). In summer there are also connections from Messina, Palermo, Reggio Calabria, Sant'Agata di Militello, Cefalù, Maratea and Riposto/Giardini.*
Lipari: **🛈** *AST (090-988 00 95).*
Vulcano: **🛈** *(090-985 20 28).*
Salina: **🛈** *at Malfa (090-984 43 26), at Leni (090-980 92 25).*

KEY

⛴ Ferry port

Tirreno

Napoli

Ginostra • Stromboli

Messina

S. Pietro

Malfa
S. Marina Salina
Rinella
Acquacalda
Canneto
Lipari

Porto
Levante

Messina →

Panarea
This is the smallest Aeolian island, surrounded by rocks and small islands. It was inhabited in prehistoric times.

0 kilometres   12

0 miles   12

Milazzo ↘

Vulcano
According to ancient mythology, the fabulous island of Vulcano was the workplace of the god of fire and blacksmiths, Hephaestus.

Salina
The island, consisting of two volcanic cones, is the second largest in the group and was named after the ancient salt mine (salina) *at Lingua, now closed.*

Exploring the Aeolian Islands

Gold ring, 4th century BC

THE BEST starting point for a visit to the varied Aeolian Islands is Lipari, because it is the most important of the islands and the boat service is good. Here you can decide what type of holiday you want – natural history excursions, including Vulcano and Stromboli, the exclusive tourist resort at Panarea among villas and yachts, or the timeless tranquillity of Alicudi.

The summit of the Vulcano crater, an hour's climb from the base

Lipari

Road map E1. 🚶 10,725 (the *municipality of Lipari includes all the other islands, except for Salina*). The main Aeolian island is not large – a little less than 10 km (6 miles) long and barely 5 km (3 miles) wide, culminating in **Monte Chirica**, 602 m (1,974 ft) high. The volcanic activity of the past can be noted here and there in the hot springs and fumaroles. The town of Lipari has two landing places: **Sotto-monastero** for ferry boats and **Marina Corta** for hydrofoils. Inevitably, this is the busiest stretch of the seafront.

The old **Cathedral** is worth a visit. Built by the Normans in the 11th century, it was rebuilt after a barbarous pirate raid completely destroyed the town in 1544. Next door to the Cathedral is the **Museo Archeologico Eoliano**, which takes up part of the **old castle**, built by the Spanish (who incorporated the ancient towers and walls) in order to put an end to the constant pirate raids.

The first rooms in the museum are devoted to prehistoric finds in Lipari. The adjoining rooms have objects from the same period, but from the other islands. Then there is an important section featuring classical archaeological finds, some discovered under water. Part of the museum has volcano-related exhibits, with interesting detailed descriptions of the geological configuration of each island. Three further sights are the **Belvedere Quattrocchi** viewpoint, the ancient **San Calogero thermal baths** and **Acquacalda beach**, which was once used as a harbour for the ships that came to load the local pumice stone. The best way to get about is by scooter or bicycle, both of which can be rented in the town of Lipari.

Ancient theatre mask, Museo Archeologico Eoliano

⚜ **Museo Archeologico Eoliano**
Next to the Cathedral.
📞 090-988 01 74. ⏰ 9am–1:30pm, 4–7pm daily.

Vulcano

Road map E1.
Close to Lipari is the aptly named island of Vulcano. Dedicated to Vulcan, the Roman god of fire and metal-working, Homer described the island as the workshop of Hephaestus, the Greek god of fire. The only landing place is the **Porto di Levante**, from which a paved road leads to the **Faro Nuovo** (new light-house). Vulcano consists of three old craters. The first, in the south between **Monte Aria** and **Monte Saraceno**, has been extinct for centuries; the **Gran Cratere**, on the other hand, is still active, the last eruption occurring in 1890. **Vulcanello**, the third crater, is a promontory on the northeastern tip of the island created almost 2,000 years ago by an eruption. The climb up to the middle crater is particularly interesting, and you can reach the top in less than an hour. Once there, it is worthwhile going down the crater to the Piano delle Fumarole. Bathing and mud baths are available all year round at the spas near Porto di Levante, while hot springs heat the sea around the stack (*faraglione*).

Salina

Road map E1. 🚶 2,406.
The second largest Aeolian island is 7 km (4 miles) long, 5.5 km (3 miles) wide, and 962 m (3,155 ft) high at its highest point, **Monte Fossa delle Felci**. There are three villages: **Santa Maria di Salina**, **Leni** and **Malfa**. Santa Maria overlooks the sea and is not far from a beach; it is connected to the other villages by an efficient mini-bus service which runs until late in the evening in the summer. Salina is also the site

The archaeological zone at Lipari, home to many different cultures

of a nature reserve, created to protect the two ancient volcanoes of **Monte dei Porri** and **Fossa delle Felci**. The dominant vegetation here is maquis, as the inhabitants have almost exterminated the forests that grew here in antiquity. The starting point for a visit to the reserve is the **Madonna del Terzito Sanctuary**, the object of colourful pilgrimages. Salina, and, in particular, the steep walls of the Pizzo di Corvo is also a regular nesting ground for colonies of the rare Eleonora's falcon, which migrate to this spot every year from Madagascar.

Among the best-known local products is a highly prized sweet Malvasia wine.

covered the ruins of a Neolithic village, founded at **Cala Junco**. Interesting finds such as Mycenean pottery, tools and other items are on display in the local museum. A half-hour walk will take you to the village, starting off from **San Pietro** and passing through **Drauto** and the **Spiaggia degli Zimmari** beach. This island now has luxury tourist facilities.

The Stromboli volcano, active for 2,000 years

Stromboli
Road map F1.

The still-active crater of the northeasternmost island in the archipelago has been described by travellers for more than 20 centuries. Italian volcanoes have always been both famous and feared. The ancient Greeks believed that Hephaestus, the god of fire (known as Vulcan to the Romans), lived in the depths of Mount Etna. Boats call either at **Scari** or **Ginostra**, but the island has other villages: **San Vincenzo**, **Ficogrande** and **Piscità**. The characteristic features of Stromboli are its stunning craggy coast (the deep waters are a favourite with swimmers and divers) and its famous volcano. For an excursion to the crater, start off from **Piscità**; you first come to the old **Vulcanological Observatory** and then the top of the **crater**. The best time to

go is around evening, as the eruptions are best seen in the dark. The climb is not always accessible, and the volcano can be dangerous. It is best to go with a guide and to wear heavy shoes (or hiking boots) and suitable clothing. There are also boats offering evening excursions to take visitors close to the **Sciara del Fuoco** lava field for the unforgettable spectacle of lava flowing into the sea.

Filicudi
Road map E1.

Halfway between Salina and Alicudi, this extremely quiet island has three villages: **Porto**, **Pecorini a Mare** and **Val di Chiesa**. You can make excursions into the interior or, even better, take a boat trip around the island and visit the **Faraglione della Canna** basalt stack, **Punta del Perciato**, **Grotta del Bue Marino** and **Capo Graziano**.

Alicudi
Road map D1.

This island was abandoned for the entire Middle Ages and was colonized again only in the Spanish period. Tourism is a relatively recent arrival, and there are no vehicles. The steps and paths are covered on foot, and accommodation can be found in private homes. There is no nightlife, making this an ideal spot for those in search of a peaceful, relaxing break.

Santa Maria di Salina, one of the three villages on the island

Panarea
Road map E1.

The smallest Aeolian island is surrounded by cliffs and stacks. Visitors land at the small harbour of **San Pietro** (the other villages are **Drauto** and **Ditella**). At **Capo Milazzese**, in one of the most fascinating spots in the Aeolian Islands, archaeologists have un-

Typical Aeolian landscape at Cala Junco, on Panarea

TRAVELLERS'
NEEDS

WHERE TO STAY

SICILY HAS a wide range of accommodation available, from simple campsites to refurbished mansions. Many hotels have been converted from old palazzi or farmhouses. You may find a room with a view of the Valle dei Templi in Agrigento or of the multicoloured roofs of the churches of Palermo. The place with the most varied accommodation, in all categories, is Taormina, for over a century a favourite with international clients. The coastline of Sicily is lined with 3- and 4-star hotels, often with a pool or private beach. On the islands off the coast the hotels are often open only in the summer and half-board is obligatory. Alternatively you can stay in private homes or tourist villages. More adventurous visitors might opt for a farm holiday in the interior, which can be good value and often includes good local food. This section and the list of hotels on pages 194–9 provide further information on accommodation in Sicily.

Sign from a historic hotel *(see p199)*

The pool at Les Sables Noires on the island of Vulcano *(see p199)*

HOTEL GRADING AND FACILITIES

IN COMMON WITH the rest of Italy, Sicilian hotels are classified by a star-rating system – from one for family-run pensions with simple, basic facilities to five stars for luxury hotels. The only hotels in Sicily in this latter category are the **Villa Igea** *(see p195)* in Palermo and the **San Domenico** and **Grand Hotel Timeo** in Taormina *(see p199)*. The latter hotel has now been restored to its former splendour.

The four-star category offers first-class service without the very high prices of the luxury hotels. Four-star hotels include some lovely places, such as the **Baglio della Luna** in Agrigento *(see p196)*, the **Villa Sant'Andrea** *(p199)* in Taormina and the **Centrale Palace** in Palermo *(see p194)*.

Visitors are sometimes pleasantly surprised at finding good value for money in 3-star hotels, such as the **Atelier** by the sea at Castel di Tusa *(see p195)*, the **Domus Mariae** *(see p197)* in Syracuse or the **Baglio Santa Croce** *(see p195)* in Erice.

In general, all Sicilian hotels, even two-star ones, have a restaurant, which is usually open to non-residents as well. Along the coast, all the 4-star and most of the 3-star hotels provide a swimming pool or a private beach. Facilities for the disabled and access for people in wheelchairs are usually available only in newer or recently renovated hotels.

HOTEL CHAINS

BESIDES SUCH LARGE international chains as **Best Western** and **Sheraton**, there are Sicilian hotel chains as well. One of these is **Framon Hotels**, which is based in Messina. Their 11 hotels, at different locations throughout Sicily, are known for their good restaurants, as well as other facilities.

PRICES

BY LAW, EVERY HOTEL room in Italy must carry, on the back of the door, the **Ente del Turismo** (Tourist Board) price for the room with the maximum charges during the year; these prices may not be exceeded. The displayed prices, or those quoted by the hotel when you book, usually include taxes and service. Breakfast is generally included as well, but you should check with the hotel beforehand. On the whole, you are expected to take half or full board in hotels on the coast.

Breakfast may be served outside in summer

A room with a view at the Grand Hotel Timeo, Taormina *(see p199)*

Extras are likely to include drinks taken with meals, room service, drinks and food taken from the minibar in your room, and telephone calls. Note, however, that hotel phone charges are usually extremely expensive.

In the off season you could try asking for a special bed and breakfast rate, never available in peak season.

TOURIST SEASON

MOST OF THE HOTELS on the offshore islands are open seasonally, from April to October, so that visiting the Aeolian or Egadi islands in the winter months may be difficult. Hotels in the cities are open all year round.

BOOKING

SHOULD YOU DECIDE to go to Sicily in the summer, you need to book well in advance, especially for July and August and if you want to stay on the coast, as the island gets very busy in peak season. When you book, you will probably be asked to pay a deposit by international money order or by giving the hotel a credit card number.

TOURIST VILLAGES

HOLIDAY VILLAGES give you the chance to enjoy a seaside holiday in a less formal atmosphere than in a hotel. Most villages are sited on the islands and along the Sicilian coast, and many offer inclusive package deals.

Accommodation may vary according to requirements, from rooms in a residence to small apartments with an outside terrace.

Each village offers a range of recreation and sports facilities. Besides one or more swimming pools, villages usually offer tennis courts and windsurfing, diving or sailing lessons. Some even provide baby-sitting. Among the best of these are the **Club Vacanze di Favignana e Pantelleria**, the **Club Méditerranée Kamarina** in the Ragusa area and the **Villaggio Valtur Pollina** in the province of Palermo.

Some villages offer all-inclusive holidays where the price even includes drinks at the bar. Charges in tourist villages are always calculated on a weekly basis.

Alternatively, you may choose to rent an apartment and select and pay for any further recreation and sports facilities as you go along. This enables you to be independent, and at the same time provides a range of possible facilities. For full details concerning the most important tourist villages, make enquiries at a travel agent, or contact the major tour operators who manage these villages, listed on page 193.

CAMPING

SPENDING YOUR HOLIDAY on a camping site is a good way of keeping costs down. Almost all the camping sites in Sicily are on the coast, with direct access to a beach. In the interior there are only a few sites on the slopes of Mount Etna, well situated for excursions to the largest volcano in Europe. Camping outside official sites is prohibited, with camping on beaches particularly frowned upon. If you want to stay on private property you must ask the owner's permission.

In general, campsites are clean and well-managed. Besides an area for tents and/or caravans (trailers), most sites also provide bungalows with private bathrooms and a kitchen area. Facilities often include grocery shops, pizzerias (and, occasionally, restaurants), laundries and organized sports facilities.

For longer stays, book well ahead of time, and in high season, phone in advance even for a one- or two-night stop. If you are touring, start to look for a site by early afternoon. Most campsites are open from Easter to October. The main ones are listed on page 193.

The Hotel Grotta Azzurra in Ustica, built above the grotto *(see p196)*

HOSTELS, REFUGES AND PRIVATE HOMES

THERE ARE VERY FEW youth hostels in Sicily, but they do offer very cheap accommodation (roughly 12,000 lire per night for a bed in a dormitory). A membership card will be needed in order to use hostels affiliated with the **Associazione Italiana Alberghi della Gioventù** (Italian Youth Hostel Federation), listed on page 193.

There are also a few mountain refuges, most of them on Mount Etna, but the **Club Alpino Italiano** has two on the Madonie and Nebrodi mountains. On the Aeolian and Egadi islands, near Taormina and at Scopello, you can rent a room in a private home. You may see road signs indicating such rooms, but you can also ask at the local Pro Loco tourist bureaux or in the bars and cafés.

FARM HOLIDAYS

SPENDING YOUR HOLIDAY on a working farm *(agriturismo)* can be both enjoyable and cheap. You may even be lucky enough to find accommodation in an orange grove with a view of Mount Etna or in a fortified farmstead in the vineyards around Marsala. This kind of holiday offers a good opportunity to become acquainted with local traditions. Farm holidays are not widely available in Sicily, but

The Baglio Santacroce in Erice, with many original features *(see p195)*

accommodation is well-kept and hospitable, even if rooms are by no means as luxurious as the equivalent in Umbria or Tuscany. Besides offering rooms, almost always with a private bathroom, some farms offer small apartments with a bathroom and kitchen area, perhaps in converted stables or buildings once used for wine-making.

Most of these farms offer half- or full-board and in the high season lodging is organized on a week-by-week basis. Meals consist of produce grown on the farm and standards are generally very good. Breakfast might include home-grown honey and jams made from the owners' fruit. Main meals may make use of vegetables from the kitchen garden, home-made cheese, or fish from local fishermen.

Meals are eaten at the owner's table together with the other guests, so that if you are fussy about your privacy, this is not the type of holiday for you. But it is ideal for those who want to relax without the formalities of a hotel and for families with children, who will have space to play in. The owners will be only too happy to suggest the best excursions in the vicinity.

SELF-CATERING (EFFICIENCY APARTMENTS)

RENTING AN apartment for two weeks or a month is undoubtedly the cheapest solution for a family or group of friends who want a reasonably priced holiday by the sea.

If you have children, particularly small ones, self-catering is an excellent solution, as you are not tied in to formal mealtimes. Renting an apartment for one week only is less advantageous economically, as cleaning expenses can be high in proportion to the rent.

The local **Pro Loco** or **Aziende di Soggiorno** information bureau will provide you with full details of addresses for apartment rentals. Another source of information is local **real estate offices** (listed in the Yellow Pages of the telephone directory under *Agenzie Immobiliari*), which also have apartments and villas for short-term rental.

A third possibility, though much more expensive, is to make enquiries through travel agencies or tour operators, who sometimes have lists of residential hotels. In these hotels charges are made on a weekly basis. A week's deposit is always required when making a booking.

If you decide to rent a private apartment, it is always a good idea to find out the actual size of the property beforehand to make sure you will have enough room. In some apartments, the living room is designed to double as a bedroom.

Before coming to any agreement on the rental, be sure to check whether electricity and gas are included in the rent or if they are extras. This also goes for other facilities such as swimming pools or use of gardens.

The tower at the Foresteria Baglio della Luna, Agrigento *(see p196)*

DIRECTORY

TOURIST INFORMATION

Assessorato Regionale del Turismo, delle Comunicazioni e dei Trasporti
Via Notarbartolo 11, Palermo.
☎ 091-696 80 33 or 696 80 93.

HOTEL CHAINS

Framon Hotels
Via Oratorio San Francesco is. 306, Messina.
☎ 090-6780.
FAX 090-661 648.

TOURIST VILLAGE BOOKING

Club Mediterranée
Largo Corsia dei Servi 11, Milan.
☎ 02-77861.

Valtur
Via Milano 42, Rome.
☎ 06-482 10 00.

Vacanze
Via Mentana 150, Parma.
☎ 0521-288 111.

CAMPING

Al Yag
Via Altarellazzo, Pozzillo, Acireale (Catania).
☎ 095-764 17 63.

Baia dei Coralli
Località Punta Braccetto, Santa Croce Camerina (Ragusa).
☎ 0932-918 192.

Baia del Sole
Marina di Ragusa (Ragusa).
☎ 0932-239 844.

Baia di Guidaloca
Scopello, Castellammare (Trapani).
☎ 0924-541 262 (summer); 34878 (winter).

Baia Macauda
Contrada Tranchina, Sciacca (Agrigento).
☎ 0925-997 001 (summer) 091-625 25 64 (winter).

Baia Unzi
Località Canneto, Lipari (Messina).
☎ 090-981 19 09.

Bazia
Contrada Bazia, Furnari (Messina).
☎ 0941-800 130.

Calanovella
Contrada Calanovella, Piraino Gliaca (Messina).
☎ 0941-582 258 (summer) 0336-400 571 (winter).

Capo Passero
Contrada Vigne Vecchie, Portopalo di Capopassero (Syracuse).
☎ 0931-842 333.

Costa Ponente
Contrada Ogliastrillo, Cefalù (Palermo).
☎ 0921-20085 (summer) 21345 (winter).

El Bahira
Contrada MaKari, San Vito Lo Capo (Trapani).
☎ 0923-972 633 (summer) 091-322 696 (winter).

Eurocamping Due Rocche
Contrada Faino, Butera (Caltanissetta).
☎ 0934-349 006.

Eurocamping Marmaruca
Via Leto 8, Letojanni (Messina).
☎ 0942-366 76.

Fontane Bianche
Località Fontane Bianche (Syracuse).
☎ 0931-790 333.

La Roccia
Località Cala Greca, Lampedusa (Agrigento).
☎ 0922-970 964.

Mareneve
Contrada Piano Grande, Milo (Catania).
☎ 095-708 21 63.

Miramare
Contrada Costicella, Favignana (Trapani).
☎ 0923-921 330.

Rais Gerbi
Contrada Rais Gerbi, Pollina Finale (Palermo).
☎ 0921-265 70.

FARM HOLIDAY ASSOCIATIONS

Agriturist
Via Di Giovanni 14, Palermo.
☎ 091-346 046.

Terranostra
Via Cuccia 1, Palermo.
☎ 091-280 000.

Turismo Verde
Via Sandron 63, Palermo.
☎ 091-308 151.

FARM HOLIDAYS

Alcalà
Masseria Alcalà, Misterbianco (Catania).
☎ 095-713 00 29.

Antica Vigna
Contrada Montelaguardia, Randazzo (Catania).
☎ 095-924 003 or 922 766.

Baglio Vajrassa
Contrada Bosco, Marsala.
☎ 0923-968 628.

Borgo degli Olivi
Località Aielli, Tusa (Messina).
☎ 090-719 081.

Casa dello Scirocco
Lentini (Syracuse).
☎ 095-447 709.

Casa Migliaca
Località Migliaca, Pettineo (Messina).
☎ 0921-336 722.

Codavolpe
Località Trepunti, Giarre (Catania).
☎ 095-939 802.

Feudo Tudia
Borgo Tudia, Castellana Sicula (Palermo).
☎ 0934-673 029.

Il Daino
San Piero Patti (Messina).
☎ 0941-661 175.

Il Limoneto
Via Provinciale 195 F, Acireale (Catania).
☎ 095-886 568.

Piccolo
Fattoria di Grenne, Ficarra (Messina).
☎ 0941-582 757.

Savoca
Contrada Polleri, Piazza Armerina (Enna).
☎ 0935-683 078.

Tenuta di Rocadia
Carlentini (Syracuse).
☎ 095-990 362.

Trinità
Via Trinità 34, Mascalucia (Catania).
☎ 095-727 21 56.

Valentina
Contrada Piano Colla, Acate (Ragusa).
☎ 0932-989 09 32.

YOUTH HOSTELS

Associazione Italiana Alberghi della Gioventù
Via Cavour 44, Rome.
☎ 06-487 11 52.

Ostello delle Aquile
Salita Federico II d'Aragona, Castroreale (Messina).
☎ 090-974 63 98.

Ostello Amodeo
2nd km on the Trapani–Erice provincial road.
☎ 0923-552 964.

Ostello Lipari
Via Castello 17, Lipari (Messina).
☎ 090-981 15 40 or 981 25 27.

Ostello Etna
Via della Quercia 7, Nicolosi (Catania).
☎ 095-791 46 86.

Choosing a Hotel

THE HOTELS in this guide have been carefully selected across a wide price range for the quality of service, décor and location. They have been divided into four geographical areas and are listed by place and price category. Palermo hotels are listed according to the city zones shown in the chapter on Palermo.

	Price	Credit Cards	Swimming Pool	Beach	Private Parking	Restaurant
PALERMO						
SOUTH PALERMO: *Massimo Plaza* Via Maqueda 437. ☎ 091-327 657. FAX 091-325 711. An efficiently-run hotel situated in an ancient building close to the Teatro Massimo. The rooms are elegantly furnished. ▨ TV ▤ *Rooms:* 15	₤₤₤	V AE DC			●	
SOUTH PALERMO: *Centrale Palace* Corso Vittorio Emanuele 327. ☎ 091-336 666. FAX 091-334 881. A short distance from the Quattro Canti, in a converted 18th-century palazzo. Breakfast is served on a splendid terrace. ▨ TV ▤ & *Rooms:* 63	₤₤₤₤	V AE DC			●	
NORTH PALERMO: *Villa Archirafi* Via Lincoln 30. ☎ 091-616 88 27. FAX 091-616 86 31. This small, charming hotel near the Botanic Garden is a good alternative to the better known – and costlier – hotels in town. ▨ TV *Rooms:* 32	₤₤	V				
NORTH PALERMO: *Excelsior Palace* Via Marchese Ugo 3. ☎ 091-62 56 176. FAX 091-342 139. An elegant Art Nouveau-style hotel with period furniture. Lovely, spacious rooms and an atmospheric hall. ▨ TV ▤ *Rooms:* 128	₤₤₤₤	V AE DC			●	
NORTH PALERMO: *Grand Hotel et des Palmes* Via Roma 398. ☎ 091-583 933. FAX 091-331 545. The former Ingam-Whitaker palazzo became a hotel in 1874 and was furnished in Art Nouveau style at the turn of the century. Now known for its grand style, it has a beautiful foyer. ▨ TV ▤ & *Rooms:* 187	₤₤₤₤	V AE DC			●	
PALERMO, FURTHER AFIELD: *Casena dei Colli* Via Villa Rosato 20. ☎ 091-688 97 71. FAX 091-688 97 79. Near the Parco della Favorita, in the former residence of Ferdinand of Bourbon's secretary. Pleasantly furnished rooms and a garden where breakfast is served in the summer. ▨ TV ▤ & *Rooms:* 71	₤₤	V AE DC			●	
PALERMO, FURTHER AFIELD: *Villa d'Amato* Via Messina Marine 180. ☎ 091-621 27 67. FAX 091-621 27 67. A renovated villa near the sea, with a fine view from the rooms and the terrace, where breakfast is served. ▨ TV ▤ *Rooms:* 38	₤₤	V AE DC		■	●	
PALERMO, FURTHER AFIELD: *Villa Espeira* Mondello. Viale Margherita di Savoia 53. ☎ 091-684 07 17. FAX 091-684 07 17. The relaxing family atmosphere here makes the Villa Esperia the ideal place for enjoying the sea in an oasis of peace. ▨ TV ▤ *Rooms:* 20	₤₤	V AE DC		■	●	
PALERMO, FURTHER AFIELD: *San Paolo Palace* Via Messina Marine 91. ☎ 091-621 11 12. FAX 091-621 53 00. A modern hotel not far from the centre of Palermo, with spacious rooms and a pool with a panoramic view. ▨ TV ▤ & *Rooms:* 290	₤₤₤	V AE DC	●		●	■
PALERMO, FURTHER AFIELD: *Splendid Hotel La Torre* Mondello. Via Piano Gallo 11. ☎ 091-450 222. FAX 091-450 033. Perched on a cliff, with a lovely garden and seawater swimming pool, rooms with a terrace and view of the sea. ▨ TV ▤ *Rooms:* 179	₤₤₤	V AE DC	●	■	●	
PALERMO, FURTHER AFIELD: *Astoria Palace* Via Monte Pellegrino 62. ☎ 091-637 18 20. FAX 091-637 21 78. Located near the Fiera del Mediterraneo, a favourite with businessmen, thanks to its famous conference centre. ▨ TV ▤ *Rooms:* 326	₤₤₤₤	V AE DC			●	■
PALERMO, FURTHER AFIELD: *Mondello Palace* Mondello. Viale Principe di Scalea 2. ☎ 091-450 001. FAX 091-450 657. Completely renovated in 1981, the Mondello Palace is situated in a park with luxuriant tropical plants, a private beach and access to the famous Art Nouveau bath house. ▨ TV ▤ *Rooms:* 82	₤₤₤₤	V AE DC	●	■	●	

		CREDIT CARDS	SWIMMING POOL	BEACH	PRIVATE PARKING	RESTAURANT

Price categories for a standard double room per night, with tax, breakfast and service included:
Ⓛ under L100,000
ⓁⓁ L100,000–199,000
ⓁⓁⓁ L200,000–299,000
ⓁⓁⓁⓁ L300,000–399,000
ⓁⓁⓁⓁⓁ over L400,000.

SWIMMING POOL
Fully equipped pool at the disposal of hotel guests.

BEACH
Fully equipped beach at the disposal of hotel guests. It may be next to the hotel or within easy reach via a shuttle.

PARKING
Parking facilities with attendant on the premises or in a nearby garage.

RESTAURANT
A particularly good restaurant on the premises, also open to non-residents.

Hotel	Price	Credit Cards	Swimming Pool	Beach	Private Parking	Restaurant
PALERMO, FURTHER AFIELD: *Grand Hotel Villa Igea* — Salita Belmonte 43. ☎ 091-543 744. FAX 091-547 654. In a garden going down to the sea, the former residence of the Floria family is now one of the most atmospheric hotels in Sicily, with its Art Nouveau furniture and décor. 🛏 TV 🍽 ♿ *Rooms:* 116	ⓁⓁⓁⓁⓁ	V AE DC	●		●	

NORTHWESTERN SICILY

Hotel	Price	Credit Cards	Swimming Pool	Beach	Private Parking	Restaurant
CARINI: *Sport Club Portorais* — Via Piraineto 125. **Road map** B2. ☎ 091-869 34 81. FAX 091-869 34 58. Only a few minutes' drive from Palermo airport, this hotel has a first-class fitness centre. Many of the tastefully furnished rooms have a view of the sea. 🛏 TV 🍽 *Rooms:* 44	ⓁⓁ	V AE DC	●	■	●	
CASTEL DI TUSA: *L'Atelier sul Mare* — Via Cesare Battisti 4. **Road map** D2. ☎ 0921-334 295. FAX 0921-334 283. A hotel/museum that gives you the unique opportunity to stay in rooms furnished by contemporary artists. The public areas have sculptures and paintings. A beautiful location. 🛏 🍽 *Rooms:* 40	ⓁⓁ	V AE		■	●	
CASTELLAMMARE DEL GOLFO: *Al Madarig* — Piazza Petrolo 7. **Road map** B2. ☎ 0924-33533. FAX 0924-33790. In the town centre overlooking the harbour, an ideal starting point for trips to the Riserva dello Zingaro. 🛏 TV 🍽 *Rooms:* 33	ⓁⓁ	V AE DC				
CEFALÙ: *Baia del Capitano* — Contrada Mazzaforno. **Road map** D2. ☎ 0921-420 003. FAX 0921-420 163. A handsome white Mediterranean-style building with access to the beach. Comfortable rooms with a view of the sea. 🛏 TV 🍽 *Rooms:* 40	ⓁⓁ	V AE	●	■	●	
CEFALÙ: *Kalura* — Calura. Via Cavallaro 13. **Road map** D2. ☎ 0921-421 354. FAX 0921-423 122. Surrounded by maquis vegetation, this hotel has a splendid view of the sea that you can admire from the spacious rooms. 🛏 TV 🍽 *Rooms:* 65	ⓁⓁⓁ	V AE DC	●	■	●	
ERICE: *Baglio Santa Croce* — Valderice. Contrada Santa Croce. **Road map** A2. ☎ 0923-891 111. FAX 0923-891 192. A converted farm building dating from 1637 whose rooms still have fired brick floors, beamed ceilings, wrought-iron beds and olive wood furniture. The view from the swimming pool is wonderful. 🛏 TV *Rooms:* 25	ⓁⓁ	V AE DC	●		●	■
ERICE: *Elimo* — Via Vittorio Emanuele 73. **Road map** A2. ☎ 0923-869 377. FAX 0923-868 252. This delightful little hotel was once a residence in the old town. Tasteful furnishings and a warm, cosy atmosphere. 🛏 TV *Rooms:* 21	ⓁⓁⓁ	V AE DC			●	
ERICE: *Moderno* — Via Vittorio Emanuele 63. **Road map** A2. ☎ 0923-869 300. FAX 0923-869 139. In an old house in the heart of Erice, this hotel distinguishes itself by its tastefully furnished rooms, with pieces made by local craftsmen. 🛏 TV *Rooms:* 41	ⓁⓁⓁ	V AE DC			●	■
ERICE: *Tonnara di Bonagia* — Bonagia. Piazza Tonnara. **Road map** A2. ☎ 0923-431 111. FAX 0923-592 177. Hotel and residential hotel in a 17th-century maritime quarter near a small port. The rooms are large and are equipped with good facilities. ⬤ Nov–Mar. 🛏 TV 🍽 ♿ *Rooms:* 39	ⓁⓁⓁ	V AE DC	●	■	●	■
FAVIGNANA: *Aegusa* — Via Garibaldi 11–17. **Road map** A2. ☎ 0923-922 440. FAX 0923-922 430. A charming small hotel in the Mediterranean style situated near the harbour. Very quiet and with first-class cooking. ⬤ Nov–Mar. 🛏 TV 🍽 *Rooms:* 11	ⓁⓁ	V AE DC				■

For key to symbols see back flap

<table>
<tr><td colspan="2" rowspan="2">

Price categories for a standard double room per night, with tax, breakfast and service included:
Ⓛ under L100,000
ⓁⓁ L100,000–199,000
ⓁⓁⓁ L200,000–299,000
ⓁⓁⓁⓁ L300,000–399,000
ⓁⓁⓁⓁⓁ over L400,000.

</td><td colspan="5">

SWIMMING POOL
Fully equipped pool at the disposal of hotel guests.
BEACH
Fully equipped beach at the disposal of hotel guests.
It may be next to the hotel or within easy reach via a shuttle.
PARKING
Parking facilities with custodian on the premises or in a nearby garage.
RESTAURANT
A particularly good restaurant on the premises, also open to non-residents.

</td></tr>
</table>

	CREDIT CARDS	SWIMMING POOL	BEACH	PRIVATE PARKING	RESTAURANT
SELINUNTE: *Garzia* ⓁⓁ Marinella. Via Piacafetta 2. **Road map** B3. **[** *0923-46660*. **FAX** *0923-46196*. From the terrace and rooms of this simple 3-star hotel there is a splendid view of the sea and the archaeological area. **⌂ TV ▤** *Rooms:* 61	V		■		
TRAPANI: *Crystal* ⓁⓁⓁ Piazza Umberto I. **Road map** A2. **[** *0923-20000*. **FAX** *0923-25555*. A very central and futuristic hotel with large smoked-glass windows. Spacious rooms, tastefully furnished. **⌂ TV ▤ &** *Rooms:* 70	V AE DC			●	
TRAPANI: *Vittoria* ⓁⓁⓁ Via Crispi 4. **Road map** A2. **[** *0923-873 044*. **FAX** *0923-873 044*. A simple hotel in the centre of town with courteous, efficient staff. Rooms have a fine view of the old town or the sea. **⌂ TV ▤** *Rooms:* 65	V AE DC				
USTICA: *Grotta Azzurra* ⓁⓁⓁ San Ferlicchio. **Road map** B1. **[** *091-844 90 48*. **FAX** *091-844 93 96*. In an enchanting position above the Grotta Azzurra, secluded and peaceful, yet near the town. This elegant, comfortable hotel has a terrace with a great view and a disco. **●** *Nov–Mar.* **⌂ TV ▤** *Rooms:* 52	V AE DC	●	■		
SOUTHWESTERN SICILY					
AGRIGENTO: *Dioscuri Bay Palace* ⓁⓁⓁ Lungomare Akragas 1. **Road map** C4. **[** *090-774 774*. **FAX** *090-661 648*. This hotel is ideally located: the temples of Agrigento and the crystal-clear waters of the small bay below are both within easy reach. **⌂ TV ▤** *Rooms:* 102	V AE DC	●	■	●	■
AGRIGENTO: *Kaos* ⓁⓁⓁ Contrada Cumbo–Villaggio Pirandello. **Road map** C4. **[** *0922-598 622*. **FAX** *0922-598 770*. A lovely complex consisting of centuries-old, renovated mansions a stone's throw from the sea and the archaeological zone. **⌂ TV ▤** *Rooms:* 105	V AE DC	●		●	
AGRIGENTO: *Foresteria Baglio della Luna* ⓁⓁⓁⓁ Valle dei Templi. **Road map** C4. **[** *0922-511 061*. **FAX** *0922-598 802*. Three suites in a 12th-century tower and more rooms, fully equipped, in the main house. The Mediterranean garden and the collection of 17th-century paintings are simply splendid. **⌂ TV ▤ &** *Rooms:* 24	V AE DC			●	■
AGRIGENTO: *Villa Athena* ⓁⓁⓁⓁ Via dei Templi 33. **Road map** C4. **[** *0922-26966*. **FAX** *0922-402 180*. An 18th-century villa near the archaeological area. Luxuriant plants and creepers are everywhere and there is a good view of the ancient temples. **⌂ TV ▤** *Rooms:* 40	V AE DC	●		●	
CALTANISSETTA: *Villa San Michele* ⓁⓁⓁ Via Fasci Siciliani. **Road map** D3. **[** *0934-553 750*. **FAX** *0934-598 791*. An example of "American-style" efficiency. Conference centre, American bar, satellite TV and helipad. **⌂ TV ▤ &** *Rooms:* 136	V AE DC	●		●	■
ENNA: *Sicilia* ⓁⓁ Piazza Colajanni 7. **Road map** D3. **[** *0935-500 850*. **FAX** *0935-500 488*. A lovely hotel in the historic centre. The rooms and foyer were renovated recently; the latter has fine old stained glass. **⌂ TV ▤ &** *Rooms:* 80	V AE DC			●	
LAMPEDUSA: *Syrio* ⓁⓁⓁ Via Antonello da Messina 5. **Road map** B5. **[** *0922-970 401*. **FAX** *0922-970 401*. A small hotel facing the harbour, furnished in the classic seaside colours of yellow and blue. The restaurant is first-rate. **●** *Dec–Feb.* **⌂ TV ▤** *Rooms:* 21	V			■	

LAMPEDUSA: *Gattopardo* ⓁⓁⓁ
Cala Creta. **Road map** B5. 📞 *0922-970 051.* FAX *0922-971 645.*
Here accommodation is in *dammusi,* typical stone houses, in a
quiet seaside setting. ● *Nov–Mar.* 🛏 📋 *Rooms:* 15
V AE DC

PANTELLERIA: *Mursia* ⓁⓁⓁ
Mursia. **Road map** A5. 📞 *0923-911 217.* FAX *0923-911 026.*
An attractive white building on the northwestern coast. Every
room has a terrace. ● *Nov–Mar.* 🛏 📺 📋 (by request). *Rooms:* 74
V AE DC

PIAZZA ARMERINA: *Park Hotel Paradiso* ⓁⓁ
Contrada Ramaldo. **Road map** D4. 📞 *0935-680 841.* FAX *0935-683 391.*
This pleasant hotel is situated near the Villa del Casale and the
main communications routes. Lavish breakfasts are served.
🛏 📺 📋 ♿ *Rooms:* 35
V AE DC

SOUTHERN SICILY

CALTAGIRONE: *Villa San Mauro* ⓁⓁ
Via Porto Salvo 14. **Road map** D4. 📞 *0933-26500.* FAX *0933-31661.*
The balconies offer a splendid panoramic view in a hotel combining
functionality with efficient service. 🛏 📺 📋 ♿ *Rooms:* 92
V AE DC

RAGUSA: *Montreal* ⓁⓁ
Corso Italia 70. **Road map** E5. 📞 *0932-621 133.* FAX *0932-621 133.*
Near the Cathedral of San Giovanni and other Baroque monuments,
this small hotel pays attention to detail. 🛏 📺 📋 ♿ *Rooms:* 50
V AE DC

RAGUSA: *Mediterraneo Palace* ⓁⓁⓁ
Via Roma 189. **Road map** E5. 📞 *0932-621 944.* FAX *0932-623 799.*
Next to the Museo Archeologico Ibleo, this modern hotel offers all the
amenities expected from a first-class establishment. 🛏 📺 📋 ♿ *Rooms:* 92
V AE DC

RAGUSA: *Terracqua* ⓁⓁⓁ
Marina di Ragusa. Via delle Sirene 35. **Road map** E5.
📞 *0932-615 600.* FAX *0932-615 580.*
A Mediterranean-style building on a lovely stretch of the Iblean coast.
The facilities are good and include a business centre. 🛏 📺 📋 *Rooms:* 77
V AE DC

RAGUSA: *Eremo della Giubiliana* ⓁⓁⓁⓁ
Contrada Giubiliana. **Road map** E5. 📞 *0932-669 119.* FAX *0932-623 891.*
A 12th-century monastery *(eremo)* set on a plateau with a splendid
panoramic view. The rooms, furnished in keeping with the spirit of
the place, are in the former cells. Well-run kitchen. 🛏 📺 *Rooms:* 10
V AE DC

SYRACUSE: *Domus Mariae* ⓁⓁⓁ
Via Vittorio Veneto 76. **Road map** F4. 📞 *0931-24854.* FAX *0931-24858.*
Some of the rooms in this delightful hotel run by Ursuline nuns
have a view of the sea. There is a small library. 🛏 📺 📋 *Rooms:* 15
V AE DC

SYRACUSE: *Grand Hotel* ⓁⓁⓁⓁ
Viale Mazzini 12. **Road map** F4. 📞 *0931-464 600.* FAX *0931-464 611.*
Overlooking the sea in Ortygia, this historic hotel has returned to its
former splendour, thanks to intelligent renovation. The foyer, with period
furniture and crystal, is luxurious, as are the rooms. 🛏 📺 📋 ♿ *Rooms:* 58
V AE DC

SYRACUSE: *Villa Lucia* ⓁⓁⓁⓁ
Contrada Isola. Traversa Mondello 1. **Road map** F4.
📞 *0931-721 007.* FAX *0931-888 537.*
A lovely villa with a pink façade stands in a park just a stone's throw from
the sea. The rooms have period furniture and paintings. 🛏 📺 📋 *Rooms:* 13
V

NORTHEASTERN SICILY

CATANIA: *Garden* ⓁⓁⓁ
Trappeto. Via Madonna delle Lacrime 16/b. **Road map** E3.
📞 *095-717 77 67.* FAX *095-717 79 91.*
This hotel, located close to the tollgate of the motorway (highway)
for Messina, stands in its own tropical garden. The rooms have tasteful
furniture and there is a good restaurant. 🛏 📺 📋 *Rooms:* 94
V AE DC

CATANIA: *Nettuno* ⓁⓁⓁ
Viale Ruggero di Lauria 121. **Road map** E3. 📞 *095-712 52 52.* FAX *095-498 066.*
Situated on the Ognina seafront, in a quiet and panoramic position,
ideal both for a relaxing break or a business trip. 🛏 📺 📋 ♿ *Rooms:* 80
V AE DC

For key to symbols see back flap

Price categories for a standard double room per night, with tax, breakfast and service included: Ⓛ under L100,000 ⓁⓁ L100,000–199,000 ⓁⓁⓁ L200,000–299,000 ⓁⓁⓁⓁ L300,000–399,000 ⓁⓁⓁⓁⓁ over L400,000.	**SWIMMING POOL** Fully equipped pool at the disposal of hotel guests. **BEACH** Fully equipped beach at the disposal of hotel guests. It may be next to the hotel or within easy reach via a shuttle. **PARKING** Parking facilities with custodian on the premises or in a nearby garage. **RESTAURANT** A particularly good restaurant on the premises, also open to non-residents.	CREDIT CARDS	SWIMMING POOL	BEACH	PRIVATE PARKING	RESTAURANT
CATANIA: *Baia Verde* ⓁⓁⓁⓁ Cannizzaro. Via Musco 8–10. **Road map** E3. ☎ 095-491 522. **FAX** 095-494 464. A splendid building overlooking the sea and blending in with the lava cliff. Majolica tile pavements, whitewashed walls and luxuriant vegetation add to the Mediterranean atmosphere of this hotel. 🅿 TV ▤ *Rooms:* 127		V AE DC	●	■	●	■
CATANIA: *Excelsior* ⓁⓁⓁⓁ Piazza Verga 39. **Road map** E3. ☎ 095-537 071. **FAX** 095-537 015. For those who want a luxury hotel in the heart of town. The Excelsior faces the Fontana dei Malavoglia and the Palazzo di Giustizia in Piazza Verga. Tastefully furnished. 🅿 TV ▤ *Rooms:* 158		V AE DC			●	■
CATANIA: *Sheraton* ⓁⓁⓁⓁ Cannizzaro. Via Antonello da Messina 45. **Road map** E3. ☎ 095-271 557. **FAX** 095-271 380. A modern building that fits in well with the landscape. Tropical garden with a fountain, courtyard and panoramic external lift (elevator). 🅿 TV ▤ *Rooms:* 170		V AE DC	●	■	●	■
CAPO D'ORLANDO: *La Tartaruga* ⓁⓁⓁ Via Lido San Gregorio 70. **Road map** E2. ☎ 0941-955 012. **FAX** 0941-955 056. In this small seaside hotel attention is paid to every detail, from the furniture in the rooms to the quality of the food. 🅿 TV ▤ ♿ *Rooms:* 38		V AE DC		■	●	
GIARDINI-NAXOS: *Nike* ⓁⓁ Via Calcide Eubea 27. **Road map** F3. ☎ 0942-51207. **FAX** 0942-56315. A splendid position overlooking the sea, with large terraces, solarium, beach with facilities and a small pier for pleasure boats. 🅿 TV ▤ *Rooms:* 51		V AE DC		■	●	
GIARDINI-NAXOS: *Arathena Roxs* ⓁⓁⓁ Via Calcide Eubea 55. **Road map** F3. ☎ 0942-51348. **FAX** 0942-51349. A Mediterranean-style building at the seaside with a seawater swimming pool cut out of the rock. Attractive public areas and rooms – bathrooms have Sicilian tiles. Terrace with a view of the sea. ● *Nov–Feb.* 🅿 TV ▤ *Rooms:* 50		V AE DC	●	■	●	
LIPARI: *Giardino sul Mare* ⓁⓁⓁ Via Maddalena 65. **Road map** E1. ☎ 090-981 10 04. **FAX** 090-988 01 50. Charming three-star hotel in a magnificent position overooking the sea. Fine views from the rooms and terrace/solarium. ● *Nov–Feb.* 🅿 TV ▤ *Rooms:* 41		V AE DC	●	■		
LIPARI: *Villa Meligunis* ⓁⓁⓁⓁ Via Marte. **Road map** E1. ☎ 090-981 24 26. **FAX** 090-988 01 49. This small, luxurious hotel near Marina Corta is a converted 18th-century house. Impeccable service. Three panoramic suites. 🅿 TV ▤ *Rooms:* 32		V AE DC		■		
MESSINA: *Grand Hotel Liberty* ⓁⓁⓁ Via 1 Settembre 15. **Road map** F2. ☎ 090-6503. **FAX** 090-292 10 75. A beautiful hotel in the historic part of town. All the rooms are well-equipped and comfortably furnished, and the service is impeccable. 🅿 TV ▤ *Rooms:* 55		V AE DC			●	■
MESSINA: *Royal Palace* ⓁⓁⓁⓁ Via Cannizzaro 224. **Road map** F2. ☎ 090-6503. **FAX** 090-292 10 75. This hotel in the centre of town is characterized by its large stained glass windows and terraces. Excellent service and facilities. 🅿 TV ▤ *Rooms:* 106		V AE DC			●	■
PANAREA: *La Piazza* ⓁⓁⓁ Via San Pietro. **Road map** E1. ☎ 090-983 176. **FAX** 090-983 003. The rooms in this hotel are comfortable, and some have spectacular views of the sea and surrounding islands. Good value for money. ● *Oct–Mar.* 🅿 TV *Rooms:* 31		V AE DC	●	■		
PANAREA: *Cincotta* ⓁⓁⓁⓁ Via San Pietro. **Road map** E1. ☎ 090-983 014. **FAX** 090-983 211. A Mediterranean building set into the cliff a short distance from the harbour. The rooms have a superb view of the sea. ● *Oct–Mar.* 🅿 TV ▤ ♿ *Rooms:* 31		V DC	●	■		■

PANAREA: *Raya*   (L)(L)(L)
Panarea–Isole Eolie. **Road map** E1. 090-983 029. **FAX** 090-983 013.
The Raya consists of two buildings: the upper one typically Aeolian, set amid
greenery, the lower one jutting out over the sea. Nov–Mar. **Rooms**: 36
V AE DC

SALINA: *L'Ariana*   (L)
Rinella. Strada Rotabile 11. **Road map** E1. 090-980 90 75. **FAX** 090-980 92 59.
A villa dominating the small harbour of Rinella. Spacious rooms, some with a
view. Dinner is served on the terrace in the summer. Nov–Feb. **Rooms**: 15
V AE DC

SALINA: *Signum*   (L)(L)
Malfa. Via Scalo 15. **Road map** E1. 090-984 42 22. **FAX** 090-984 41 02.
The rooms are in typical Aeolian houses, decorated with bougainvillea
and caper plants. View of the islands from the terraces. **Rooms**: 23
V

SAN GIOVANNI LA PUNTA: *Paradiso dell'Etna*   (L)(L)(L)
Strada per Viagrande 37. **Road map** E3. 095-751 24 09. **FAX** 095-741 38 71.
This splendid villa on the slopes of Etna was built in 1927 and elegantly
renovated. Marble, frescoed walls, trompe l'oeil décor, period furniture
and fireplaces create an extremely elegant hotel. **Rooms**: 34
V AE DC

STROMBOLI: *La Sciara Residence*   (L)(L)(L)
Piscità. **Road map** F1. 090-986 005. **FAX** 090-986 121.
A marvellous Aeolian building set in a bougainvillea garden.
The rooms are attractively decorated with period objects and
have a terrace with a view. Nov–Apr. **Rooms**: 62
V AE DC

STROMBOLI: *Park Hotel La Sirenetta*   (L)(L)(L)(L)
Ficogrande. **Road map** F1. 090-986 025. **FAX** 090-986 124.
The Sirenetta is a white building right by the sea on a site opposite
Strombolicchio. Fine restaurant. Nov–Mar. **Rooms**: 56
V AE DC

TAORMINA: *Park Hotel La Plage*   (L)(L)(L)
Mazzarò. Via Nazionale 107. **Road map** F2. 0942-626 095. **FAX** 0942-625 850.
Fifty stone bungalows, five of which are particularly luxurious, spread out in a
pine forest that descends to the sea at Isola Bella. Nov–Feb. **Rooms**: 64
V AE DC

TAORMINA: *Villa Ducale*   (L)(L)(L)
Via Leonardo da Vinci 60. **Road map** F2. 0942-28153. **FAX** 0942-28710.
The owners of this villa treat their clients like friends. The rooms are all
different, with period furniture, wrought-iron beds and terracotta floors.
Good breakfasts, served on the terrace. **Rooms**: 12
V AE DC

TAORMINA: *Caparena*   (L)(L)(L)(L)
Mazzarò. Via Nazionale 189. **Road map** F2. 0942-652 033. **FAX** 0942-36913.
This hotel on the Caparena lido is one of the most luxurious. All
rooms have a view. Good service and cuisine. **Rooms**: 88
V AE DC

TAORMINA: *Grand Hotel San Domenico*   (L)(L)(L)(L)(L)
Piazza San Domenico 5. **Road map** F2. 0942-23701. **FAX** 0942-625 506.
One of the most charming hotels in Sicily, housed in a converted Dominican
convent. Splendid sitting rooms with sea views. **Rooms**: 111
V AE DC

TAORMINA: *Grand Hotel Timeo*   (L)(L)(L)(L)
Via Teatro Greco 59. **Road map** F2. 0942-23801. **FAX** 0942-23838.
Near the Greek theatre, this villa, now converted into a luxury hotel,
stands in a park with ancient magnolia trees. Fine marble and tile
bathrooms and large terraces brimming with flowers. **Rooms**: 56
V AE DC

TAORMINA: *Mazzarò Sea Palace*   (L)(L)(L)(L)
Mazzarò. Via Nazionale 147. **Road map** F2. 0942-24004. **FAX** 0942-626 237.
Modern and functional, yet elegant and comfortable, with exceptional
service and good views of the sea. Nov–Mar. **Rooms**: 87
V AE DC

TAORMINA: *Villa Sant'Andrea*   (L)(L)(L)(L)(L)
Mazzarò. Via Nazionale 137. **Road map** F2. 0942-23125. **FAX** 0942-24838.
This renovated 19th-century villa is a real jewel. Period furniture,
paintings and ceramics lend elegance to the rooms; while flowers
and exotic plants enhance the garden that slopes down to the sea.
The restaurant is excellent. **Rooms**: 67
V AE DC

VULCANO: *Les Sables Noires*   (L)(L)(L)
Porto di Ponente. **Road map** E1. 090-985 010. **FAX** 090-985 24 54.
This superbly restructured hotel blends in with the white houses in the Baia
di Ponente. Rooms with terraces and terracotta floors. **Rooms**: 48
V AE DC

For key to symbols see back flap

WHERE TO EAT

ICILIANS LOVE good food and like nothing better than joining family and friends around a restaurant table, especially if the food is genuinely homemade. Fish is one of the highlights of Sicilian cuisine. Almost all restaurants serve freshly caught fish, grilled or fried according to local recipes, and fish is often an ingredient for pasta sauces as well. Pasta is widely available but so is couscous, an Arab legacy.

A restaurant sign in Cassibile (see p207)

Restaurant opening hours are typical of the southern Mediterranean: in general places open from 1–3:30pm for lunch and from 9–12 midnight for dinner. Most restaurants generally close one day a week and may close for up to a month for annual holidays, so it's a good idea to check ahead to avoid disappointment. The restaurants listed on pages 204–209 have been selected from among the best on the island.

Buffet at the Azienda Agricola Trinità, in Mascalucia (see p164)

BREAKFAST AND SNACKS

BESIDES THE TRADITIONAL croissant, eaten with black coffee (*espresso*) or a milky coffee (*cappuccino*), Sicilians also enjoy croissants stuffed with ice-cream and iced coffee and milk for breakfast. Bars and pastry shops (*pasticcerie*) stock a range of pastries, and Sicilian freshly squeezed fruit juices are excellent. If you are staying in a hotel where breakfast is included, it is likely to consist of coffee or tea with croissants and bread with fruit jam. More luxurious hotels will offer a buffet with yoghurt, breakfast cereal, fresh fruit, sliced ham and salami. For a mid-morning snack, or for lunch, you can go to a bar or *rosticceria*, where you will find a range of sandwiches (*tramezzini*) and filled rolls (*panini*),

arancini (rice and meat balls) and *impanate* (breadcrumb croquettes stuffed with aubergines (eggplant), spinach and cheese, or potatoes and onions). Favourite Palermo snacks are *pane ca meusa* (bread stuffed with spleen) or *pane e panelle* (chick pea fritters). These specialities are also sold in outdoor markets.

TYPES OF RESTAURANT

IN SICILY, EVEN the smallest village is likely to have a trattoria serving local specialities. There is not much difference (in terms of price, cuisine and décor) between a restaurant proper and a trattoria, especially along the coast, where even quite sophisticated establishments are decorated with maritime paraphernalia. *Putie* are typically simple trattorias with home cooking and a set menu; they generally offer good value for money. Pizzerias are widespread and

are ideal for cheap and fast meals. Another typical aspect of Sicilian tradition is the *rosticceria*, serving quick, hot meals from the roasting oven, and *focacceria*, where the Sicilian flat bread *focaccia* is used as a pizza base.

READING THE MENU

PRINTED MENUS are still rare in Sicily, as it is the custom for the waiter to recite the day's list at your table. Good antipasti are vegetables (from olives to aubergines) in oil, seafood and fish salads and seafood soups (with mussels, clams, cuttlefish, squid). The first course is pasta, usually with vegetables or fish and often so hearty that it is as filling as a main course: try *pasta con le sarde*, with sardines; *spaghetti alla Norma*, with tomato, basil, aubergine and ricotta, *cuscus alla trapanese*, couscous with onion, spices and a fish sauce; *pasta n'casciata*, macaroni

The terrace at I Mulini on the island of Pantelleria (p206)

The renowned Wünderbar in Taormina *(see p174)*

pie with meat sauce, sausage, cheese and hard-boiled eggs. The main course is often fish (typically tuna, swordfish, bream), freshly cooked and sold by weight (so ask for a rough price). Fresh fruit or dessert (*cannoli*, ricotta cheese and candied fruit rolls; *cassata*, cake with ricotta cheese, sugar, chocolate and candied fruit; ice-cream) wind up the meal. For vegetarians there are excellent vegetables and a range of pasta dishes.

WINE

MOST RESTAURANTS, even the average ones, have a wine list with a good selection of Sicilian wines. Trattorias on the other hand tend to offer their house wine, locally produced, and inexpensive table wine, usually served in a carafe.

FIXED-PRICE MENUS

NOT MANY Sicilian trattorias and restaurants offer fixed-price menus. In general these are limited to the family-run trattorias which offer only one or two different dishes every day.

PRICES AND PAYING

IN TRATTORIAS a normal three-course meal will cost about 25–30,000 lire. In restaurants, a similar meal will cost up to 40–50,000 lire. Even in a top

restaurant you are unlikely to spend more than a maximum of 100,000 lire per person. Pizza is always good value, and never costs more than about 15–20,000 lire.

Your bill may be a simple total, without the different courses being itemized. If you do have an itemized bill, the total will include a cover charge (2,000–5,000 lire) and a service charge. Tipping is not obligatory, but if you do decide to leave a tip you should calculate 12–15 per cent. Italian law requires all eating establishments to issue a bona fide printed receipt (*ricevuta fiscale*) to clients when they pay. Anything else is illegal. Make sure you get a receipt as you may receive a hefty fine if you cannot produce a *ricevuta fiscale* if requested by a police officer.

Most Sicilian restaurants and trattorias accept a range of credit cards, including Master-Card and Visa. Bars, cafés and smaller, family-run establishments may only accept cash, so check you have enough.

Waiter with a tray of desserts

OPENING HOURS

ALL RESTAURANTS are closed one day during the week, with the possible exception of the high season, in July and August. This closing day is

shown in the listings on pages 204–209. Restaurants and trattorias also close for about one month for annual holidays. In large cities like Palermo this usually occurs in August, whereas on the coast almost all restaurants are closed in the winter months. Island restaurants generally open according to the needs of the tourist season.

MAKING RESERVATIONS

IN THE EVENING, especially in the summer, restaurants often get very crowded and you may find it difficult to get a table. It is always a good idea to book a table in advance, even in trattorias. An alternative is to arrive early, about 8pm, to avoid standing in line.

Phoning ahead is also advisable if you want to make sure that a restaurant's specialities will be available.

CHILDREN

CHILDREN ARE always welcome in restaurants, particularly family-run places which are only too happy to prepare special dishes or half-portions for youngsters. Sophisticated restaurants may be less geared for children, so telephone beforehand.

SMOKING

IN SICILY smoking is allowed virtually everywhere and you will not find designated non-smoking areas.

Sicilian ice-cream, almost always locally made

What is Eat in Sicily

A Sicilian cart loaded with marzipan fruit

SICILIAN CUISINE is a mixture of different traditions, with elements from Greek, Roman and Arab cuisines still used. Fish is the basic ingredient, both as a main course and in soups and sauces. Vegetable dishes are delicious, many of them derived from ancient recipes using capers, olives and herbs. Citrus fruit is very important, and put to a variety of uses – lemons and oranges are even sometimes used in salads. Sicilian ice-cream comes in a wide range of styles and flavours, using fruits, vanilla, cinnamon and even jasmine.

Caponata
Fried aubergine (eggplant) chunks are served in a sweet-sour sauce of tomato with pine nuts, celery, olives and capers.

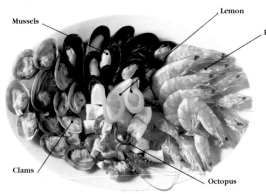

Mussels

Clams

Lemon

Prawns

Octopus

Antipasto di Frutti di Mare
This is a salad of octopus, prawns, clams and mussels with oil, salt, black pepper and lemon dressing. Given the huge portions often served in Sicily, this "antipasto" could be regarded as a complete meal.

Pasta al Nero di Seppia
In this dish, spaghetti is served with a sauce made from the ink sacs of cuttlefish. Salted ricotta cheese may be added.

Pasta con le Sarde
Small macaroni, sardines and wild fennel are the main ingredients of one of the most famous Sicilian dishes.

Arancini
These balls of rice contain a stuffing made with mushrooms, peas, mozzarella cheese and ham.

Pasta alla Norma
Spaghetti is served here with a spicy sauce of tomatoes, fried aubergines and grated, salted ricotta.

Pasta 'ncasciata
This pasta dish contains meat sauce, meat balls, caciocavallo cheese, sausage, hard-boiled eggs and aubergines or peas.

Maccu
This bean soup is made by simmering shelled broad beans with wild fennel until they turn into a purée.

Steamed
semolina

Seafood

Fish
soup

Shellfish

Sfincione
*Focaccia (flat bread) is
covered with onions, tomatoes,
anchovies, caciocavallo cheese,
oregano, oil and breadcrumbs.*

Cuscus alla Trapanese
*This is a traditional North African speciality consisting of couscous
made from semolina, or a special flour made from dried fish paste,
which is steamed and flavoured with fish stock, seafood and shellfish.*

Pesce Spada alla Ghiotta
*A Messina speciality. Swordfish
is cooked in onion and tomato
sauce with potatoes, olives,
capers, celery and black pepper.*

Sarde a Beccafico
*This traditional Palermo dish consists of breaded, fried
sardines stuffed with pine nuts, cinnamon, grapes, raisins,
anchovies and toasted breadcrumbs.*

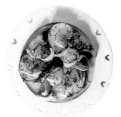

Tonno al Forno
*Sliced tuna (also called "tuna
and onion stew") is marinated
in oil, vinegar, onion, parsley
and red pepper and baked.*

Braciole alla Siciliana
*These marinated pork chops
are grilled and oil, salt, pepper,
oregano and vinegar are
added at the last minute.*

Zuppa di Pesce
*Fish soup Trapani-style – the
main ingredients are types of
bream, eel, cuttlefish, squid and
shellfish, served with croûtons.*

SICILIAN CONFECTIONERY AND ICE-CREAM

Sicilian pastries, based on simple ingredients such as
almonds, pistachios, honey and ricotta cheese, are
among the best in the Mediterranean. *Cassata*, a dessert
of Arab derivation, is made from sponge cake filled
with ricotta, sugar, chocolate and candied fruit (in
the Trapani region it is covered with almond paste).
Ricotta is also the basic ingredient in the filling of
crispy fried pastry *cannoli* rolls. Almonds and sugar
are used to make marzipan fruit. The rich ice-cream,
granite (ices), and lemon, coffee or almond sherbets,
often eaten with croissants, are all first-rate. The best
confectioners are in Palermo, Catania and Messina.

**Cassata, of Arab origin, is the
classic Sicilian dessert**

Choosing a Restaurant

THE RESTAURANTS in this chart have been selected across a wide price range for the high quality of their service and décor and their location. They have been divided into four areas and are listed by price category. Palermo restaurants are listed by price category and according to the city zones shown in the chapter on Palermo.

	CREDIT CARDS	PRIVATE PARKING	FIXED PRICE MENU	GOOD WINE LIST	OUTDOOR TABLES
PALERMO					
SOUTH PALERMO: *Ai Vecchietti* ⓁⓁ Via Paolo Paternostro 28. 📞 *091-585 606.* Brimming with charm and friendliness, a restaurant with first-rate local dishes. The *pappardelle cantalupo* (wide ribbon pasta with prawns and melon) and the prawns and swordfish with mint are unusual and delicious. ● *never.*	V				■
SOUTH PALERMO: *Charleston* ⓁⓁⓁⓁ Piazzale Ungheria 30. 📞 *091-321 366.* An extremely smart restaurant in the heart of Palermo with elegant décor. Classic and Palermitan cuisine, featuring first-class, hot antipasti, the inevitable pasta with sardines and delicious swordfish roulades. In the summer the restaurant moves to the "Terrazze" at Mondello. ● *Sun; Jun–Sep.*	V AE DC			●	
NORTH PALERMO: *Antica Focacceria San Francesco* Ⓛ Via Alessandro Paternostro 58. 📞 *091-320 264.* The oldest *focacceria* in Palermo, featuring local specialities such as *panelle di ceci* (chick pea fritters), tasty *sfinciuni* (stuffed flat-bread pies) and *pani ca' meusa* (bread filled with beef spleen). ● *Mon.*					
NORTH PALERMO: *Shangai* Ⓛ Vicolo dei Mezzani. 📞 *091-589 702.* The name may evoke images of an exotic Chinese setting, but this is a family-run trattoria located opposite the Vucciria market. ● *Sun; Aug.*					
NORTH PALERMO: *Capricci di Sicilia* ⓁⓁ Via Istituto Pignatelli 6, at Piazza Sturzo. 📞 *091-327 777.* This trattoria, situated close to the Politeame Theatre, serves traditional, dishes cooked in a flamboyant style. ● *Mon; 15 days in Aug.*	V AE DC				■
NORTH PALERMO *Santandrea* ⓁⓁ Piazza Sant'Andrea 4. 📞 *091-334 999.* Quite close to the Vucciria market, with excellent, simple cooking. Try the many antipasti, pasta and fish dishes. The wines are first-rate. ● *Tue.*	V AE DC				■
NORTH PALERMO: *Stella (Hotel Patria)* ⓁⓁ Via Alloro 104–Via Aragona 6. 📞 *091-616 11 36.* True home-style Palermitan cooking in a 17th-century palazzo. Specialities include the *pennette alla disgraziata.* ● *Sun; 15 days in Aug.*	V AE DC				■
PALERMO, FURTHER AFIELD: *Al Delfino* ⓁⓁ Sferracavallo. Via Torretta 80. 📞 *091-530 282.* At the Delfino you get surprisingly good value for your money, as well as top quality, especially the antipasti, which alone are worth coming for. ● *Mon; 15 days in Aug.*	V AE DC				■
PALERMO, FURTHER AFIELD: *Bye Bye Blues* ⓁⓁ Mondello. Via del Garofalo 23. 📞 *091-684 14 15.* Not only super-fresh fish, but also seasonal vegetables and mushrooms in the delicious antipasti and pasta dishes. Make sure to leave room for the desserts, all home-made. ● *midday (except Sun & hols); Mon (winter); Jan.*	V			●	■
PALERMO, FURTHER AFIELD: *La Botte* ⓁⓁ Monreale. Contrada Lentizzi 416. 📞 *091-414 051.* This quaint wine shop is also a restaurant offering excellent regional fare that includes both fish and meat dishes. Naturally there is a good wine list available. ● *Mon–Thu; 20 Jun–20 Sep.*	V AE DC	●		●	
PALERMO, FURTHER AFIELD: *Il Ristorantino* ⓁⓁⓁ Piazzale De Gasperi 19. 📞 *091-512 861.* A simple yet elegant restaurant near the Parco della Favorita, one of the best in Palermo for the loving care put into its varied dishes, especially the seafood. Fine wine cellar. Book in advance. ● *Mon; Aug.*	V AE DC	●		●	■

Price categories for a three-course meal, including beverage (except for wine), tax and service.

Ⓛ under L30,000
ⓁⓁ L30,000–50,000
ⓁⓁⓁ L50,000– 70,000
ⓁⓁⓁⓁ L70,000–90,000
ⓁⓁⓁⓁⓁ over L90,000

PRIVATE PARKING
Parking space with a restaurant custodian.

FIXED PRICE MENU
Called menu a prezzo fisso in trattorias and menu degustazione in restaurants.

GOOD WINE LIST
A wide range of specially selected good wines – local, national and international.

OUTDOOR TABLES
Facilities for eating outdoors in summer, in a courtyard, on a terrace (often with a good view) or in a garden.

	CREDIT CARDS	PRIVATE PARKING	FIXED PRICE MENU	GOOD WINE LIST	OUTDOOR TABLES
PALERMO, FURTHER AFIELD: *La Tonnara* ⓁⓁⓁ Arenella. Piazza Tonnara 18. ☎ 091-363 055. Some of the freshest fish in town is prepared in this maritime establishment facing the small Arenella harbour. Try the ravioli filled with grouper or crab meat and the sea bass. The local white wine is good. ● *Wed; 15 days in Aug.*	V AE DC				▣
PALERMO, FURTHER AFIELD: *Sapori di Mare* ⓁⓁⓁ Mondello. Via Mondello 52. ☎ 091-684 06 23. An outstanding fish restaurant in Mondello that offers memorable *linguine* with lobster and exquisite spaghetti with sea urchins. ● *Tue in winter.*	V AE DC				▣
PALERMO, FURTHER AFIELD: *Trattoria da "Franco u Piscaturi"* ⓁⓁⓁ Porticello. Largo Pescheria 26. ☎ 091-957 758. This trattoria is a true temple of seafood: from sea snails to sea urchins, oysters and clams, just off the fishing boats. ● *Mon; Nov.*	V AE DC	●			▣
PALERMO, FURTHER AFIELD: *La Scuderia* ⓁⓁⓁⓁ Via del Fante 9. ☎ 091-520 323. Another pillar of Palermo cuisine. Elegant setting and impeccable service. This is the domain of Sicilian tradition, with the occasional new touch. Try the *merluzzetti* (cod) with tomato and onion sauce. ● *Sun eve; 15 days in Aug.*	V AE DC	●		●	▣
NORTHWESTERN SICILY					
CEFALÙ: *La Brace* ⓁⓁⓁ Via XXV Novembre 10. **Road map** D2. ☎ 0921-423 570. A pleasant and original place near the Cathedral where Sicilian culinary traditions are respected. The aubergines (eggplant) stuffed with pasta are delectable. ● *Mon; Christmas hols.*	V AE DC				
ERICE: *Monte San Giuliano* ⓁⓁⓁ Vicolo San Rocco 7. **Road map** A2. ☎ 0923-869 595. In an alley in the medieval quarter, this restaurant offers top seafood, from Trapani antipasti to mixed fried fish dishes. ● *Mon; Jan.*	V AE DC				▣
FAVIGNANA: *La Bettola* Ⓛ Via Nicotera 47. **Road map** A2. ☎ 0923-921 988. A small but smart trattoria serving dishes typical to the region, such as tunafish, octopus salad and fried squid. Eat outside in the attractive courtyard. ● *Nov.*					▣
FAVIGNANA: *Egadi* ⓁⓁⓁ Via Cristoforo Colombo 17. **Road map** A2. ☎ 0923-921 232. This restaurant has a place in the Pantheon of Sicilian seafood, featuring tuna and other super-fresh fish served raw, cooked or marinated. ● *Oct–Apr.*				●	
LEVANZO: *Paradiso* ⓁⓁ Via Lungomare 8. **Road map** A2. ☎ 0923-924 080. Things get better every year at this little place near the quiet harbour of Levanzo. Fish right off the boats, prepared with passion. ● *Oct–Apr.*					▣
MARETTIMO: *Il Veliero* ⓁⓁ Via Umberto 22. **Road map** A2. ☎ 0923-923 195. A trattoria in the wildest Egadi island features first-class Trapani-style pesto as well as fish couscous and tuna dishes. ● *never.*					
MARSALA: *Villa Favorita* ⓁⓁⓁ Via Favorita 27. **Road map** A3. ☎ 0923-989 100. Next to an old farm, a hall with art deco furniture and superb fish dishes. The *trenette* (ribbon pasta) with salted mullet roe are very good. ● *never.*	V AE DC	●		●	▣
MAZARA DEL VALLO: *Trattoria del Pescatore* ⓁⓁⓁ Via Castelvetrano 191. **Road map** A3. ☎ 0923-947 580. Glorious fish cuisine with a strong Tunisian influence. Besides the fish couscous, try the seafood croquettes (*arancini di mare*). ● *Mon in winter.*	V AE DC	●			

For key to symbols see back flap

<table>
<tr><td>

Price categories for a three-course meal, including beverage (except for wine), tax and service.

Ⓛ under L30,000
ⓁⓁ L30,000–50,000
ⓁⓁⓁ L50,000– 70,000
ⓁⓁⓁⓁ L70,000–90,000
ⓁⓁⓁⓁⓁ over L90,000

</td><td>

PRIVATE PARKING
Parking space with a restaurant custodian.

FIXED PRICE MENU
Called menu a prezzo fisso in trattorias and menu degustazione in restaurants.

GOOD WINE LIST
A wide range of specially selected wines – local, national and international.

OUTDOOR TABLES
Facilities for eating outdoors in summer, in a courtyard, on a terrace (often with a good view) or in a garden.en.

</td></tr>
</table>

	CREDIT CARDS	PRIVATE PARKING	FIXED PRICE MENU	GOOD WINE LIST	OUTDOOR TABLES
SCOPELLO: *Torre Benistra* ⓁⓁⓁ Via Natale di Roma 19. **Road map** B2. ☎ 0924-541 128. There is a genuine family atmosphere in this inn overlooking Scopello and the rocks. Simple, flavoursome cooking. ● *never.*					
SAN VITO LO CAPO: *La Gna Sara* ⓁⓁ Via Abruzzi 6. **Road map** B2. ☎ 0923-972 100. A charming trattoria with typical local dishes. The fish couscous and fresh pasta with Trapani-style pesto are wonderful. ● *Mon; Nov–Feb.*	V			●	
TRAPANI: *Trattoria del Porto* ⓁⓁ Via Ammiraglio Staiti 45. **Road map** A2. ☎ 0923-547 822. This family-run trattoria near the embarkation point for the Egadi islands has perhaps the best fish couscous in the entire region. ● *Mon; Christmas.*	V				
TRAPANI: *Da Peppe* ⓁⓁⓁ Via Spalti 50. **Road map** A2. ☎ 0923-28246. Peppe himself skilfully manages this delightful trattoria, which offers a wide range of veritable masterpieces of Trapani cuisine. If you must make a choice, try the *busiate* (fresh pasta), the *lattume di tonno* (tuna eggs) and the couscous with fish soup. ● *Mon in winter; Jan.*	V AE DC				
USTICA: *Mamma Lia* ⓁⓁⓁ Via San Giacomo 2. **Road map** B1. ☎ 091-844 95 94. In two rooms filled with locally made crafts, Signora Lia serves excellent meals, from marinated prawns to grilled swordfish roulades. ● *Dec–Mar.*	V AE			●	
SOUTHWESTERN SICILY					
AGRIGENTO: *Leon d'Oro* ⓁⓁⓁ San Leone. Via Emporium 102. **Road map** C4. ☎ 0922-414 400. A relaxing restaurant on the road from the Valle dei Templi to the sea. Delicious traditional rustic and seafood dishes. ● *Mon; Nov.*	V AE DC			●	■
AGRIGENTO: *Trattoria del Pescatore* ⓁⓁⓁ Lido di San Leone. Via Lungomare 20. **Road map** C4. ☎ 0922-414 342. It is really worthwhile going a few kilometres beyond the archaeological area to eat superbly prepared fresh fish. ● *Wed in winter.*	V AE DC				■
CALTANISSETTA: *Cortese* ⓁⓁ Viale Sicilia 166. **Road map** D3. ☎ 0934-591 686. A classic restaurant with good regional cooking. Try the *ditalini* (small tubes of pasta) with broad beans and salted ricotta, and *cannoli* as dessert. ● *Mon.*	V AE DC				
ENNA: *Centrale* ⓁⓁ Piazza VI Dicembre 9. **Road map** D3. ☎ 0935-500 963. Situated in a lovely building in the centre and with traditional Sicilian décor, this restaurant offers excellent local dishes. ● *Sat in winter.*	V AE DC				
LAMPEDUSA: *I Gemelli* ⓁⓁⓁⓁ Via Cala Pisana 2. **Road map** B5. ☎ 0922-970 699. The North African coast is close by and the cooking here shows the influences of Tunisian cuisine. The octopus, aubergine (eggplant) and sausage (all very spicy) are remarkably good. ● *midday; Oct–Apr.*	V AE			●	
PANTELLERIA: *I Mulini* ⓁⓁ Contrada Tracino. **Road map** A5. ☎ 0923-915 398. The great virtue of this restaurant is its location: dinner is served on the terrace of a typical *dammuso* house with an unsurpassable view. ● *Jan–Mar.*		●			■
PANTELLERIA: *La Risacca* ⓁⓁⓁ Via Milano 65. **Road map** A5. ☎ 0923-912 975. In a lovely position alongside the harbour you can enjoy genuine island ...es: *caponata*, ravioli with ricotta and mint, couscous. ● *Mon in winter; Oct.*	AE				■

Piazza Armerina: *Al Fogher* ⓁⓁ V AE DC
Contrada Bellia. **Road map** D4. 📞 *0935-684 123.*
There is a positive embarrassment of meat and fish dishes to choose from
at this restaurant. Every dish is of excellent quality. 🌑 *Mon; 15 days in Aug.*

Piazza Armerina: *Del Teatro* ⓁⓁ V
Piazza del Teatro 1. **Road map** D4. 📞 *0935-85662.*
In a romantic small square in the old town. Try the home-made *pappardelle*
(wide ribbon pasta), either *al teatro* or *alla Norma*. Good service. 🌑 *never.*

Sciacca: *Hostaria del Vicolo* ⓁⓁⓁ V AE DC
Via Sammaritano. **Road map** B3. 📞 *0925-23071.*
A good place in the historic centre. Try the fresh tagliatelle with prawns and
courgettes (zucchini), and the angler fish in wine sauce. 🌑 *Sun, Mon eve.*

SOUTHERN SICILY

Augusta: *Donna Ina* ⓁⓁⓁ V AE DC
Faro Santa Croce. **Road map** F4. 📞 *0931-983 422.*
One of the best restaurants on the southeastern coast has a panoramic
view of the sea. Its strong reputation was gained thanks to the chef's
skill and dexterity with grilling fresh fish. 🌑 *midday; Mon.*

Cassibile: *La Vecchia Caserma* ⓁⓁ
Via della Caserma 13. **Road map** F5. 📞 *0931-718 045.*
Located in a converted Carabinieri barracks *(caserma)*, this rustic trattoria
offers home-made cooking using only the freshest produce. 🌑 *Mon.*

Chiaramonte Gulfi: *Majore* ⓁⓁ V AE DC
Via Martiri Ungheresi 12. **Road map** E4. 📞 *0932-928 019.*
This restaurant transforms "humble" products into fine cuisine.
Local cold sliced meats and salami, pork aspic and *risotto alla Majore*
are the specialities. 🌑 *Mon; Jul.*

Modica: *Fattoria delle Torri* ⓁⓁⓁ V AE
Vicolo Napolitano 17. **Road map** E5. 📞 *0932-751 286.*
The owner is a remarkable expert on the history of local recipes, which
he prepares in an imaginative way while respecting tradition. 🌑 *Mon.*

Palazzolo Acreide: *Anapo Da Nunzio* ⓁⓁ V AE
Corso Vittorio Emanuele. **Road map** E4. 📞 *0931-882 286.*
In the historic centre, with good local cooking. Try the provola and
pecorino (buffalo and sheep's milk cheeses) and the ricotta ravioli. 🌑 *Mon.*

Noto: *Del Carmine* ⓁⓁ V
Via Ducezio 1. **Road map** E5. 📞 *0931-838 705.*
Family-run place in the heart of town. Specialities: ricotta ravioli with pork
sauce, tagliatelle and vegetables, rabbit *alla stimpirata* (sweet-sour). 🌑 *Mon.*

Ragusa: *Antica Macina* ⓁⓁⓁ V AE DC
Via Giusti 123. **Road map** E5. 📞 *0932-248 096.*
A converted mill in the middle of Baroque Ibla. Try the *scacce* (quiche) with
vegetables and sausage and the *cavati* (pasta) with pork sauce. 🌑 *Mon; Sep.*

Ragusa: *La Pergola* ⓁⓁⓁ V AE DC
Piazza Luigi Sturzo 6. **Road map** E5. 📞 *0932-255 659.*
A delightful, elegant place. The menu features dishes with delicious
flavour combinations. Of the many treats, the best is the sea bass and
vegetable couscous. 🌑 *Tue.*

Scoglitti: *Sakalleo* ⓁⓁⓁ
Piazza Cavour 12. **Road map** D5. 📞 *0932-871 688.*
The name comes from the boats once used for sponge fishing. The dishes,
all based on fish, also hark back to the old maritime recipes. 🌑 *Wed in winter.*

Syracuse: *La Medusa da Kamel* ⓁⓁ V
Via Santa Teresa 21. **Road map** F4. 📞 *0931-61403.*
Both the cooking and décor in this restaurant at the Fonte Aretusa remind one of
Africa. The imaginative chef Kamel prepares excellent spaghetti *alla mergellina*,
with mussels and prawns, and on Thursday there is couscous. 🌑 *Mon; Sep.*

Syracuse: *Orto di Epicuro* ⓁⓁ V AE DC
Largo della Gancia 5. **Road map** F4. 📞 *0931-464 222.*
A small fish restaurant overlooking the sea at Ortygia. The seafood salad
and risotto *alla pescatora* (also with seafood) are very good. 🌑 *never.*

For key to symbols see back flap

<table>
<tr><td colspan="2">

Price categories for a three-course meal, including beverage (except for wine), tax and service.

Ⓛ under L30,000
ⓁⓁ L30,000–50,000
ⓁⓁⓁ L50,000– 70,000
ⓁⓁⓁⓁ L70,000–90,000
ⓁⓁⓁⓁⓁ over L90,000

PRIVATE PARKING
Parking space with a restaurant custodian.

FIXED PRICE MENU
Called menu a prezzo fisso in trattorias and menu degustazione in restaurants.

GOOD WINE LIST
A wide range of specially selected good wines – local, national and international.

OUTDOOR TABLES
Facilities for eating outdoors in summer, in a courtyard, on a terrace (often with a good view) or in a garden.en.

</td></tr>
</table>

	CREDIT CARDS	PRIVATE PARKING	FIXED PRICE MENU	GOOD WINE LIST	OUTDOOR TABLES
SYRACUSE: *Jonico 'a rutta 'e ciauli* ⓁⓁⓁ Riviera Dionisio il Grande 194. **Road map** F4. ☎ 0931-65540. Perched on a cliff, this restaurant steeped in tradition does not offer only fish specialities. A fine pasta dish is the *a pasta ca muddica*, served with breadcrumbs, anchovies and red peppers. ● Tue.	V AE DC				■

NORTHEASTERN SICILY

	CREDIT CARDS	PRIVATE PARKING	FIXED PRICE MENU	GOOD WINE LIST	OUTDOOR TABLES
ACI TREZZA: *Verga da Gaetano* ⓁⓁⓁ Via Provinciale 119. **Road map** E3. ☎ 095-276 960. Next to the little harbour described by Verga in *I Malavoglia*, this place is famed for its super-fresh fish and pleasant décor. ● Thu; Christmas.	V AE DC				■
ACIREALE: *A'Cumarca* ⓁⓁ Via Simone Zaccanazzo 87. **Road map** E3. ☎ 095-886 200. This restaurant has seating on a terrace offering dramatic views of nearby Etna. The food is traditional, featuring pittas and light snacks. ● Mon.	V AE DC	●			■
CATANIA: *Menza* Ⓛ Viale Mario Rapisardi 143–153. **Road map** E3. ☎ 095-350 606. This rosticceria is a gastronomic centre featuring all the Catanian specialities, from *arancini* (rice balls) to *crispelle* (rice fritters) with honey. ● Mon.	V				
CATANIA: *Trattoria Casalinga* Ⓛ Via Biondi 19. **Road map** E3. ☎ 095-311 319. This restaurant, run by a Mr Mammino, is situated in the heart of the city center. Try the olive salad, or pasta with sword fish and vegetables. ● Sun; 15 days in Aug.	V				
CATANIA: *Al Gabbiano* ⓁⓁ Via Giordano Bruno 128. **Road map** E3. ☎ 095-537 842. A classic Catania trattoria. Great antipasti, from potato fritters to *caponata* and fried *sparacanaci* fish. ● Sun; Aug.					■
CATANIA: *Antica Marina* ⓁⓁ Via Pardo 29 (Pescheria di Catania). **Road map** E3. ☎ 095-348 197. This place is in the middle of the fish market and the fish is superbly prepared. The antipasti and spaghetti with sea urchins are excellent. ● never.	V				
CATANIA: *Sicilia in Bocca* ⓁⓁ Piazza Petro Lupo 16. **Road map** E3. ☎ 095-746 1361. A traditional trattoria specializing in fish dishes. Particularly recommended are the delicious pasta-based meals, with a range of toppings including sword fish, snapper and tomatoes, or chilli peppers. ● Wed; 15 days in Aug.	V				
CATANIA: *Al Rustico* ⓁⓁⓁ San Gregorio. Via Catania 32. **Road map** E3. ☎ 095-717 74 34. Cuisine based on traditional Catanian recipes. The dishes are prepared well and yet are refreshingly simple. ● Tue; Aug.	V AE DC	●			■
CATANIA: *Alioto* ⓁⓁⓁⓁ Via Mollica 24–26. **Road map** E3. ☎ 095-494 444. This is the best fish restaurant in Catania. Enjoy the excellent food, such as fresh shellfish or pasta with lobster, on a terrace by the sea. ● Thu; 15 days in Aug.	V AE DC	●		●	■
CATANIA: *Dell'Hotel Poggio Ducale* ⓁⓁⓁⓁ Via Gaifami 7. **Road map** E3. ☎ 095-330 016. Many rate this as the best restaurant in Catania. The cuisine, based on fish specialities, is varied and has flavoursome combinations. An example of this is the great marriage of shellfish and citrus fruit. ● Sun eve; Aug.	V AE DC	●		●	
CATANIA: *La Siciliana* ⓁⓁⓁⓁ Viale Marco Polo 52/a. **Road map** E3. ☎ 095-376 400. One of the best restaurants in Catania. The *pasta alla Norma* (spaghetti with aubergines) and rice with cuttlefish and ricotta are very good. ● Sun eve; Aug.	V AE DC	●		●	■

FILICUDI: *Nino Santamaria* ⓁⓁ
Filicudi Porto. **Road map** E1. 📞 090-988 99 60.
A terrace over the crystal-clear sea at Filicudi where you can eat octopus salad, pasta with swordfish and fried squid for an absurdly low price. ⬤ *Oct–Mar.*

LIPARI: *E Pulera* ⓁⓁⓁ
Via Diana. **Road map** E1. 📞 090-981 11 58.
Here you eat on a lovely terrace-garden seated at tile-covered tables, each of which represents an island in the archipelago. Truly first-class Aeolian cooking. ⬤ *Oct–May.*

LIPARI: *La Nassa* ⓁⓁⓁⓁ
Via Franza 36. **Road map** E1. 📞 090-981 11 58.
V AE DC
You will find this fine restaurant by going up the hill. It features extremely well-prepared fresh fish. Excellent Malvasia wine. ⬤ *Thu (only in spring); Nov–Mar.*

MESSINA: *Da Piero* ⓁⓁⓁ
Via Ghibellina 121. **Road map** F2. 📞 090-718 365.
V AE DC
This is one of the bulwarks of traditional Messina cuisine which, unlike other local historic establishments, does not feel the need for change and experimentation – perhaps because there is simply no reason to alter the classic dishes. ⬤ *midday; Sun; Aug.*

MESSINA: *Trattoria Anselmo* ⓁⓁⓁ
Ganzirri. Via Lago Grande 29. **Road map** F2. 📞 090-393 225.
V AE DC
One of the few restaurants in the area that has benefitted from rebuilding. Fresh, well-prepared fish, especially the shellfish. ⬤ *Mon in winter.*

PANAREA: *Da Francesco* ⓁⓁ
San Pietro (Porto). **Road map** E1. 📞 090-983 023.
It's hard to find a trattoria like this one on the island where you can eat well at low prices. The view of the port from the terrace is beautiful. ⬤ *Oct–Mar.*

PANAREA: *Da Pina* ⓁⓁⓁ
Via San Pietro 3. **Road map** E1. 📞 090-983 032.
V AE DC
In the splendid and worldly pearl of the Aeolians, Pina is a must for good eating. You can enjoy the specialities, such as *tagliolini* (thin noodles) with lemon, or swordfish roulades. ⬤ *never.*

SALINA: *Porto Bello* ⓁⓁⓁ
Santa Marina. Via Bianchi 1. **Road map** E1. 📞 090-984 31 25.
V AE DC
Aeolian restaurant with many fine dishes such as tuna in oil, baked sea perch with potatoes, and squid with onions and Malvasia wine. ⬤ *Nov.*

SAN GIOVANNI LA PUNTA: *Giardino di Bacco* ⓁⓁⓁ
Via Piave 3. **Road map** E3. 📞 095-751 27 27.
V AE DC
A cheerful, well-kept restaurant in a lovely house on the slopes of Mount Etna. Traditional local fare prepared with passion and great skill. ⬤ *Mon.*

SANT'ALFIO: *Azienda Agricola Case Perrotta* ⓁⓁ
Contrada Perrotta. **Road map** E3. 📞 095-968 928.
A gastronomic society, based in a Benedictine convent. Fine wine cellar and delicious *caponata*, fried *tuma* (local cheese), vegetable soups and roasts. ⬤ *Tue.*

SANTA MARIA LA SCALA: *La Grotta* ⓁⓁⓁ
Via Scalo Grande 46. **Road map** F3. 📞 095-764 81 53.
This small restaurant not far from Acireale was built inside a grotto by the sea. Order any fish dish and you won't go wrong. ⬤ *Tue.*

TAORMINA: *'A Zammara* ⓁⓁⓁ
Via Fratelli Bandiera 15. **Road map** F2. 📞 0942-24408.
V AE DC
In an orange grove you are served typical Sicilian fare such as meatballs wrapped in lemon leaves or country-style roulades. ⬤ *Wed in winter; Jan–Feb.*

TAORMINA: *Nino* ⓁⓁⓁⓁ
Via Rizzo 29, Letojanni. **Road map** F2. 📞 0942-36147 or 651 060.
V AE DC
A short distance from Taormina, this restaurant is an institution. For a great meal, order the bruschetta (toasted bread) with sea urchins and mussels au gratin, spaghetti with sea urchins and Catalan sea bass. ⬤ *Dec–Feb.*

TRECASTAGNI: *Uliveto* ⓁⓁⓁ
Via Perni 4. **Road map** E3. 📞 095-780 69 88.
Fine food at the foot of Mount Etna. Pippo Perni is the owner of this old farmhouse surrounded by olive and fig trees. Delicious macaroni with almonds, and rabbit in sweet-sour sauce. ⬤ *midday; Sun, Mon.*

For key to symbols see back flap

SHOPS AND MARKETS

ALL THE most well-known fashion designer shops can be found in the larger Sicilian cities, together with smart chain stores stocking household articles and furniture. In towns like Palermo, Catania and Syracuse you can buy discount cards which enable you to save up to 40 per cent in many shops. In tourist resorts it is possible to find shops specializing in Sicilian handicrafts, in particular ceramics, although the best items are sold in the

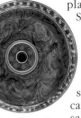

A decorated Sicilian terracotta dish

places where they are made. Sicilian pastry shops sell delicious cakes, *cannoli* pastries, *cassata* cakes and *torroncini* (almond nougat). Keep an eye out for the delicatessens selling local specialities, such as spiced capers, *ventresca* (tuna in oil), salted mullet roe *(bottarga)* and aubergine *caponata*. You can also buy excellent produce such as organic fruit, olive oil, honey and fruit jam at farmhouses offering accommodation for visitors.

A shop specializing in wrought-iron products

OPENING HOURS

GENERALLY, shops, boutiques and department stores are open from 8 or 9am to 1pm, and in the afternoon, opening hours are 4–8pm. In the summer these hours may be extended, particularly in tourist resorts. In the cities, most shops close for two or three weeks in August. Seaside resort towns, on the other hand, usually operate on a seasonal basis, opening only from June to September.

HOW TO PAY

IN THE LARGER CITIES, the leading shops and department stores accept major credit cards, especially Visa and MasterCard, whereas in the towns and villages many shops still prefer cash payment.

A great money-saver available in Palermo, Catania and Syracuse is the **tessera shopping**, a discount card costing L50,000, which is valid at many shops and restaurants for discounts of up to 40 per cent.

HANDICRAFTS

IN CALTAGIRONE, Sciacca and Santo Stefano di Camastra, the main production centres for striking Sicilian ceramics, you can find shops and workshops offering plates, jugs, vases, tiles, mugs and statuettes for sale. The **Laboratorio Branciforti** in Caltagirone makes jugs, vases and dishes with traditional decorative motifs.

At Sciacca, stylish ceramics can be found in the studio of **Giuseppe Navarra**, who has exhibited his works in New York and Montreal. The **Artigianato del Sole** also has a good range: as well as dinner services, jugs and ornamental plates, they make furniture, such as tables made of lava stone, and majolica tiles. Many artisans work in wrought iron. Good workshops can be found near Giarre and Giardini Naxos, such as the **Laboratorio Patanè**.

Two traditional puppet-makers still active in Palermo are **Vincenzo Argento** and **Piero Scalisi**, whose workshops are open to the public.

OPEN-AIR MARKETS

IF YOU WANT to experience the atmosphere of the old quarters of Sicilian towns and buy local produce, you have to go to the outdoor markets. In Palermo, the **Vucciria** market, immortalized by artist Renato Guttuso, is at its most atmospheric in the evening, when it is illuminated by thousands of lights. In Via Argenteria pause at the stall of **Antonino Giannusa**, who offers an amazing range of preserves as well as an excellent Palermo-style pesto sauce. Another market worth visiting is the **Ballarò**, between Piazza del Carmine

Renato Guttuso, *La Vucciria* (1974)

and Piazza Ballarò, which is busiest around noon. Every day, just by the Porta Uzeda, there is an **antiques market** (*mercantino dell'antiquariato*) where furniture sellers and second-hand dealers offer items costing from a few thousand lire to several million. In Catania, by Piazza Duomo, there is a colourful **fish market** every morning (stalls selling vegetables and meat stay open until the evening). On Sundays Piazza Carlo Alberto fills with an **antiques market** with second-hand items as well as rare pieces of Sicilian craftsmanship.

ICE-CREAM PARLOURS AND PASTRY SHOPS

POPULAR pastry shops include **Alba** and **Caflish** in Palermo, **Castorina** in Acireale or **Colicchia** in Trapani, where you can enjoy coffee or an aperitif. Sicilian

pastry shops are a delight for the eye and tastebuds with their *cannoli, cassata* and almond paste cookies. Some cake shops offer their own specialities. These include the marzipan sweets with citron filling at the **Antica Pasticceria del Convento** in Erice; ricotta puff pastries at **Scivoli** in Caltagirone; vanilla- or cinnamon-flavoured chocolate at the **Antica Dolceria Bonaiuto** in Modica; ricotta and pistachio *cannoli* at **Savia** in Catania; chestnuts filled with citrus fruit jam and topped with dark chocolate at the **Caffè Sicilia** in Noto; and nougat at **Geraci**, in Caltanissetta.

Sicily is a paradise for ice-cream buffs. At **Costarelli**, in Acireale, there are fine vanilla ices, semifreddo and sherbet, and ices with coffee, fresh fruit or almonds. In Taormina **Niny Bar** is the place to go, and in Catania it is **Saint Moritz**.

A stall with Sicilian cheese in the varied market in Catania

REGIONAL SPECIALITIES

DELICATESSENS and farms with accommodation (*agriturismo*) are ideal places for regional specialities. Smoked swordfish and tuna in oil can be found at the **Casa del Pesce** in Syracuse; salted mullet roe at **Quartana** in Trapani; on Mount Etna the **Azienda Luigi Conti** sells olive oil, bottled olives, artichokes, cream of artichoke, wild asparagus and pumpkin. The **Azienda Agricola Trinità** has tangerines, olive oil, honey and wine, and the **Azienda Agricola Alcalà** offers a mail order service for all products, including fresh fruit. Both firms are based in Catania.

(Marzipan figure, an Erice speciality)

What to Buy in Sicily

IN GENERAL, Sicilian artisans now concentrate on ceramics and lava stone products. The prices are by no means low, but the objects are often beautifully handcrafted. However, historically, the most classic creations are the traditional Sicilian rod puppets and carts. They have become rarities because there are so few people left who know how to make and repair them. Some shops offer drab reproductions for tourists; but in the antique shops you can still find fine – if expensive – examples of these ancient crafts. When it comes to food and wine, Sicily excels: citrus fruit such as oranges, lemons and grapefruit ripen well in the sunny climate, and you can buy wonderful fruit preserves, wine, nougat, almond paste sweets (candies) and Sicilian pastries such as *cannoli* and *cassata*.

Rococo lamp made by Sicilian artisans in the 18th century

Marzipan fruit

Sicilian oranges

Citrus fruit
Delicious tangerines, blood and navel oranges, grapefruit, lemons and mandarins – superior to those sold elsewhere in Italy – can be purchased in any market. You can also order them directly from the producer, who will send them to your home address.

Sicilian confectionery
You should buy cannoli, *marzipan fruit and* cassata *just before going back home, since they should be eaten within 12 hours.*

Wine
You can buy sweet Passito wine from Pantelleria, sweet Malvasia from Lipari, and dry red or white Corvo from Salaparuta or Bianco d'Alcamo. Buy directly from the producers or from wine shops, which also provide shipment to an onward destination.

Wines from Pantelleria

Tuna and vegetables in oil
Tuna fillets, salted mullet roe, spiced capers in extra virgin olive oil, spiced black olives, aubergines (eggplant) preserved in oil and chilli pepper – are all regional specialities that can be purchased in leading Sicilian delicatessens.

Fillets of tuna

Olive oil
The best comes from the Valle del Belice; it is heavy, almost salty, with a peppery flavour. Ragusa oil is green and fragrant, and Taormina oil is more delicate.

Preserves and honey
Organic fruit jams, prepared on the spot in the "agritourist" farms, have an unmistakeable flavour. The fragrant and rare orange and lemon blossom honey also has therapeutic properties.

SICILIAN CERAMICS

This is probably the most highly appreciated handicrafts product of all. Light blue, yellow and green are the dominant colours in the lovely ceramics made in Caltagirone; they are richly decorated with volutes, flowers and geometric motifs. You can purchase vases, jugs, plates, mugs, jars and statuettes. Terracotta plaques with house numbers are also very much in demand. In the ceramics made in Sciacca – less famous but just as lovely as those from Caltagirone – the lemon is the prevailing decorative motif. Tiles also come in a variety of styles. The multicoloured majolica tiles bear 19th-century motifs and can be used for floors or simply as decorative objects to be set on an elegant table.

Elaborately decorated 19th-century tiles

Ceramic mask

Carts

Once used to transport heavy loads, traditional Sicilian carts – covered with paintings of religious or historical scenes – are now purely decorative objects. There are very few originals left, and sadly this ancient, noble craft is dying out.

Sicilian cart

Jew's harp

Jew's harp
This typical musical instrument consists of an iron frame in the shape of a lyre around a thin flexible metal tongue that produces the sound.

Sicilian puppets

Terracotta pieces

Simple and elegant Sicilian terracotta products – oil jars and huge water storage jars, dishes, jugs and oil cruets – are still made by local craftsmen and can be used as decorative objects for your home.

Traditional Sicilian puppets
The armoured knights errant and the Saracens with round shields and turbans are characters from the puppet plays about Charlemagne. These small masterpieces can be purchased at the few puppet-makers' workshops or in antique shops.

Terracotta jar

ENTERTAINMENT

Bar sign

THE ENTERTAINMENT on offer in Sicily is wide-ranging and varied, and the programmes for cultural, musical and theatrical events are particularly imaginative. In the cities the theatres put on a long and varied winter season, while in the spring and summer the ancient sites become the venues for top-level ancient Greek theatre or symphony concerts. There are also many cultural events connected with artists and personalities who have contributed to the colourful history of Sicily. Added to all this, there are numerous folk festivals and carnival celebrations. Far from being performed for the benefit of tourists, they are genuine expressions of the spirit of Sicily. Easter is a good time to catch some of the more colourful festivals. The nightlife is lively in the major towns, and in the peak of summer the seaside resorts stay active until the small hours.

Programme for the Greek theatre in Syracuse

THEATRE, MUSIC AND OTHER CULTURAL EVENTS

THE THEATRE SEASON in Palermo, which runs from early November to late May, is rich and varied. There is a very interesting programme of opera and ballet at the **Politeama** and **Massimo** theatres *(see p71 and p67 respectively)*. The latter, a historic theatre, has finally been reopened after a long period of restoration work. A centralized ticket office handles booking for both theatres and also offers subscriptions for a limited number of performances. The **Teatro Biondo**, on the other hand, puts on plays, from Greek tragedy to Pirandello, with touring productions by leading Italian and international companies.

In Catania the **Teatro Massimo Bellini** *(see p159)* presents excellent opera and classical music. The Bellini Theatre orchestra and chorus take part in chamber music concerts from October to June and in the same period there is opera and ballet (performed by the theatre ballet company). The **Teatro Stabile** features plays that are directed and performed by Turi Ferro and his son Guglielmo. From roughly May to October many theatrical and music events are held outdoors throughout Sicily.

The **Greek Theatre** in Syracuse is used only for the **Settimana delle Rappresentazioni Classiche**, a week-long programme of ancient drama held every even-numbered year in May. It is organized by the **Istituto Nazionale del Dramma Antico** *(see pp134–5)*.

In odd-numbered years it is **Segesta** *(see p94)* that plays host to classical theatre, from Greek tragedy to classical Japanese theatre.

In the summer the **Valle dei Templi** at Agrigento *(see pp100–101)* is used for ancient theatre and classical music concerts. Agrigento is also the venue for the summer **Rappresentazioni Pirandelliane**, evenings of theatre in front of the house where Pirandello was born. The organizing committee of **Taormina Arte**, in collaboration with the **Azienda Autonoma di Soggiorno e Turismo** (tourist information bureau) organizes important cultural events and festivals all year round in Taormina. The main ones are the **Festival Internazionale di Cinema, Musica, Teatro e Danza**, an international arts festival held in July and August, and **Natale a Taormina**, a Christmas season programme of exhibits, sacred music, and street performances. The **Settimana Internazionale di Musica Medievale e Rinascimentale**, held in late

Outdoor performances, popular in summer

Carnival in Acireale, a week of crowds and colour

July in **Erice**, is a mecca for lovers of medieval and Renaissance music. Each October, artists, writers, composers and film directors head for Palermo to take part in the **Festival sul Novecento** (Festival of the 20th Century), which was first celebrated in 1997. A number of Palermo monuments, some of them closed for years for restoration work, are now open to the public again, thanks to the **Palermo Anno Uno** organization and the Palermo town authorities.

Two unusual and interesting local initiatives worth investigating are **Palermo apre le Porte**, when for one week in May schoolchildren act as guides for tourists around the city's historic sites, and **Palermo Sotterranea**, a visitor tour of the underground sites in the city.

FOLK FESTIVALS AND CARNIVALS

IN FEBRUARY, with spring just around the corner, the town of **Agrigento** greets the blossoming almond trees with the **Sagra del Mandorlo in Fiore**. Together with the **Festival Internazionale del Folklore**, this festival of almond trees in bloom takes place in the magical Valle dei Templi. This is also the carnival season, which is celebrated with gusto in a great number of towns. The major carnivals include the one in **Sciacca**, which dates back to the late 19th century, and the one in **Acireale**, where the celebrations are a blend of history, political satire and dance. There are other folk festivals during the rest of the year: in **Noto**, spring is celebrated with the **Infiorata**, when Via Nicolaci is carpeted with flowers representing figures; and in mid-July the famous long flight of steps with majolica-tiled risers in **Caltagirone** is illuminated by 4,000 candles.

NIGHTLIFE

VIVACIOUS is the word for Sicilian nightlife – in the cities in winter and at the tourist sites in summer. In Catania the evening begins with a sip of *sgroppino* (lemon ice-cream and vodka) at **Mousharabia** in the historic centre, and ends at **Clonezone**, a disco/bar with good music. In the summer you can also dance at **Banaker** amid a maze of plants. At Taormina you can have an aperitif at the historic **Wünderbar** or **Mocambo**, as well as at the more modern **Marrakech**, with Moroccan décor. The trendiest discos are **Giara** and **Tout Va** and, in the summer, **Cabana** and **Marabù** at Giardini-Naxos. Two very attractive spots in Palermo are the multimedia **Grant's Club** and the **Villa Giuditta** disco, in a converted 19th-century palazzo. For summer dancing, go to the outdoor **Quetzal** disco on the beach. Last but not least is the programme of rock music at the **Palasport** in Acireale.

Catania, perhaps the city with the most vivacious nightlife in Sicily

SURVIVAL
GUIDE

PRACTICAL INFORMATION

IN RECENT YEARS, there has been renewed interest in caring for and revitalizing the unique historic, artistic and natural heritage of Sicily, and the island is no longer a destination solely for the adventurous. The Sicilian coastline, one of the most beautiful in Italy, attracts thousands of visitors every year. The island's long history and numerous monuments are as much an attraction – if not a greater one – than its marvellous landscape. Those who are interested in Sicilian history and culture

The Trinacria, ancient symbol of Sicily, now regional coat of arms

would do well to plan their visit for a time other than the crowded – and very hot – months of July and August. But whenever you choose to visit the island known to the ancients as Trinacria, there is always something exciting to explore. Everyone comes expecting to enjoy the island's food and wine, coastline and art treasures. But there are also inland areas to explore, including Mount Etna, the Madonie Mountains and Riserva dello Zingaro nature reserves, as well as sports activities and spas.

Ferry boats, connecting the island of Sicily with mainland Italy

OPENING HOURS

IN SICILY SHOPS are generally open from 8 or 9am until 1pm and then from 3:30 or 4pm (in the winter) or 5pm (in the summer) to 7 or even 8pm from Monday to Saturday. They are closed on Sundays and for one afternoon during the week.

Banks are open from 8:30am to 1:30pm and 3:30 to 4:30pm from Monday to Friday. Restaurants are closed one day a week and for annual holidays, usually in the winter. Off season most hotels, especially those along the coast, will be closed, so that if you travel in the winter months you should book accommodation ahead to avoid complications.

One of the special charac-teristics of Sicilian life is that people dine later than on the

mainland, particularly in the summer when the weather can be very hot. The midday meal may begin as late as 2pm, and evening meals may not be served until 10pm.

MUSEUMS AND MONUMENTS

NORMALLY SICILIAN museums and archaeological sites are open every day in the morning except for Monday – though many sites are also open in the afternoon. Opening hours tend to be longer during the summer. Apart from particularly important places such as Agrigento, admission to the archaeological areas is free.

Entrance fees for museums vary from L2,000 to L8,000. Youngsters and senior citizens are usually either allowed a reduction or enter free of

charge. Church opening hours can be erratic, and you will need both luck and patience if you want to see every interior, especially in smaller villages. Most churches are open to the public during morning and evening mass. Should a church be closed, you can always try asking the priest or sacristan if he will let you in for a brief visit.

COMMUNICATIONS

IT IS EASY ENOUGH to find a post office or phone booth in the larger towns, but they are rare, if not non-existent, in the interior and small villages. You may have problems with reception on a mobile phone, especially on the islands.

Telephone booths, quite rare in the interior of Sicily

NEWSPAPERS

Tʜᴇ ʟᴇᴀᴅɪɴɢ local papers are
Il Mediterraneo and
Giornale di Sicilia in
Palermo, *Gazzetta del Sud* in
Messina, *Gazzettino di Sicilia*
in Syracuse, and *La Sicilia* in
Catania. All are useful for
local events information. The
leading Italian daily news-
papers are sold in Sicily.
English-language newspapers
are sold in the larger towns.

**Italian and foreign daily
newspapers sold in Sicily**

IMMIGRATION
AND CUSTOMS

Eᴜʀᴏᴘᴇᴀɴ ᴜɴɪᴏɴ (ᴇᴜ) resi-
dents and visitors from
the United States, Canada,
New Zealand and Australia,
for example, need no visa for
a stay of up to three months.
Information concerning visas
can be obtained in advance at
your nearest Italian consulate.
Non-EU citizens must carry a
valid passport, while for EU
citizens an ID will suffice. It is
always a good idea to carry
your ID with you at all times,
as it may be needed – during
a road block *(see p220)* for
instance. Any customs
formalities are completed at
the first Italian arrival point
(usually the mainland). Non-
EU citizens can claim back
sales tax (IVA) on purchases
costing over L650,000.

TOURIST
INFORMATION

Tʜᴇ ᴘʀᴏᴠɪɴᴄɪᴀʟ capitals of
Sicily have an official
tourist board, the **Ente
Provinciale per il Turismo**
(it might also be called
**Azienda Autonoma Pro-
vinciale Incremento**

Turistico or **Azienda Provinciale Turismo**), where
information and brochures
are available. Larger towns
have an **Azienda Autonoma
di Soggiorno**. In the small
towns and villages, make
enquiries at the **Pro Loco** or
the Town Hall. You can get
the addresses and phone
numbers of smaller bureaus at
the **Azienda Provinciale
Turismo**. You can obtain
information on how to
organize your trip from the
**Enti Provinciali per il
Turismo** or the **Assessorato
al Turismo della Regione
Sicilia** in Palermo. The web
site www.sicilia.com is useful.

Personal Security and Health

O N THE WHOLE, Sicily is safe for visitors. At busy tourist spots, such as the ferry ports and main stations, it is wise to keep a close eye on your belongings. Also, avoid leaving valuables in your car if the parking lot is unattended. However, in the smaller towns and villages, petty crime is rare. The rural areas are even safer, and if you speak a little Italian, getting to know people will increase your personal security. The summer heat can leave the countryside susceptible to fires. Visitors and residents alike are asked to do all they can to prevent fires from breaking out.

In the event of fire, follow the firemen's instructions carefully

A *carabinieri* patrol boat on duty off the coast of Sicily

PERSONAL PROPERTY

I T IS NOT REALLY a good idea to carry large sums of money on you. Major credit cards such as Visa and Master-Card are accepted by most businesses throughout the island. There are automatic cash dispensers *(bancomat)* in all larger towns and you may choose to buy travellers' cheques in addition.

In general, parking is safe. However, in large cities it is best not to leave your car unattended for too long.

In the event of a theft, make sure you report it immediately to the local police or *carabinieri* stations (you have to do this in order to make an insurance claim).

ROADBLOCKS

G ENERALLY SPEAKING, travelling on Sicilian roads poses no problems whatsoever. However, because of the presence of the Mafia, you may find yourself being stopped at a police or army roadblock *(posto di blocco)*, particularly around the Palermo area. Officers usually check your ID and the vehicle, but it is possible that they might ask to search your car. Simply stay calm and cooperate with the police – there should be no cause for alarm.

IN THE EVENT OF FIRE

S AD TO SAY, FIRES are a scourge in Sicily – and in the rest of Southern Italy, for that matter. Some of them are natural occurrences, some are genuine accidents, but most are cases of arson. Fire can spread rapidly, especially in the dry summer vegetation, and the wind may carry the fire for long distances in a very short time. Firefighting is usually entrusted to the local fire departments and forest rangers, volunteers and specially equipped firefighting planes, which are located at strategic points around the island.

FIRE PREVENTION RULES

1. Don't throw cigarettes out of your car.
2. Never light a fire except in areas where this is explicitly permitted.
3. If you see a fire, call the fire department at once.
4. Do not stop or park your car to watch a fire; you may block the road and interfere with the firefighting operations.
5. Pay attention to the wind direction: it is extremely dangerous to be downwind of a fire, as it may spread rapidly and catch you unawares.

The coastguards at Lampedusa

HEALTH

E MERGENCY MEDICAL CARE is free for all EU citizens in Italy, with an E111 form. The form is available from main post offices in the UK. Emergencies only are covered, and private medical insurance is needed for all other situations. Non-EU citizens should acquire comprehensive medical insurance before their

State policeman   City policeman

Emergency Numbers

General Emergencies
☎ *113.*
Police
☎ *112.*
Fire Department
☎ *115.*
Road Emergencies
☎ *116.*
Telephone Information
☎ *12.*
Nautical Information
☎ *196.*
Mountain Emergencies
☎ *091-684 20 29 or 616 60 85 or 616 79 36.*

arrival. Sicily has a network of hospitals and first-aid stations *(pronto soccorso).* All Sicilian tourist resorts operate seasonal emergency treatment centres *(guardia medica).* Pharmacies are normally open from Monday to Friday at 9am–1pm and 4–7pm and on Saturday morning. However, for emergencies, a list of the night and holiday opening rotas will always be posted on or near the shop door.

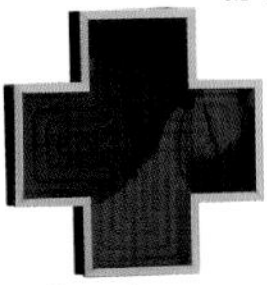

Italian pharmacy sign

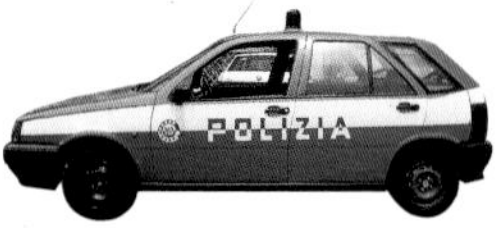

Police car

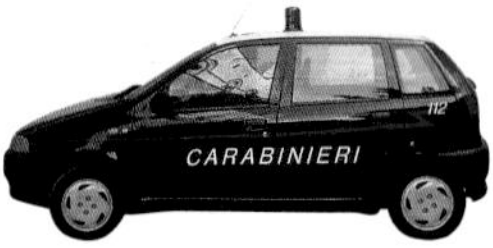

Carabinieri car

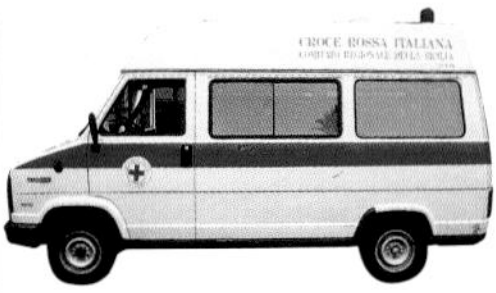

Red Cross ambulance

Safety Outdoors

DURING YOUR STAY in Sicily, whether you go in the summer or winter, you will be spending a good deal of time outdoors, so you must be prepared for the various problems outdoor life can pose in the different seasons. In the summer, whether you are at the seaside or in the interior, do not overdo sunbathing, as it may cause serious burns and sunstroke. The wind can be very deceptive, often making you think the temperature is lower than it actually is.

While exploring among the tumbled stones of the ancient cities of Magna Graecia, or during a hike in the mountains, be on the lookout for snakes, which can be quite common in the summer.

Although camping just anywhere is not allowed, you can make private arrangements with landowners to put up your tent outside an official camp site. Remember, however, that you must take away all rubbish and must not light fires. While on a walk or hiking, keep your distance from the sheepdogs, because they are trained to chase away all intruders. Sicilians are very hospitable but are also reserved, so out of respect you should always ask permission before you cross over private property, go through a gate or a fenced area. On unpaved roads or paths you may come across closed gates or fences. It is always a good idea to ask whether in fact you can go through. Having done so, remember to close the gate or fence so that any animals in the field cannot escape.

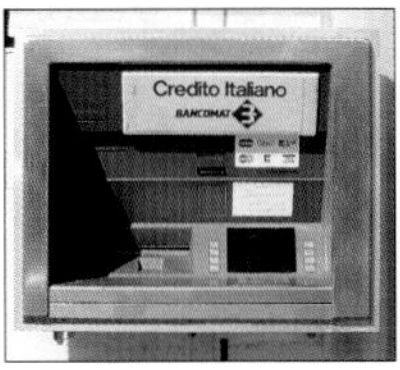

An automatic cash dispenser (ATM)

Currency

You can exchange currency when you arrive at an automatic cash dispenser (ATM), at the airport or at a bank, for example, but it is best to have some Italian money with you beforehand. The best exchange rates are offered by the banks, where commission charges are lower. Italy's currencies are the lira and the euro. Lira bank notes come in denominations of L1,000, L2,000, L5,000, L10,000, L50,000, L100,000 and, rarely, L500,000. The smaller denominations come in handy in bars and small shops. If you prefer travellers' cheques, choose a well-known name or a bank. There is a minimum commission charge for each transaction, so avoid changing small amounts. The euro, a new currency valid in many European countries, has been legal tender in Italy since 1 January 1999.

Bureaux de change operate the same opening hours as shops, which is useful when banks are closed. Credit card holders can draw money directly from the automatic cash dispensers, which can be found throughout Sicily. There is usually a fee.

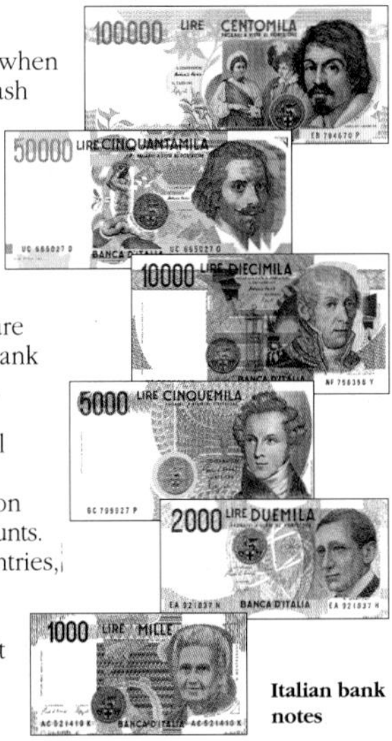

Italian bank notes

Sports and Outdoor Activities

Sport fishing

FOR MOST VISITORS spending their holidays in Sicily, sport is water-based: windsurfing, fishing and diving in the crystal-clear waters of the coast and of the islands. But there are plenty of other outdoor activities to explore, such as hiking along the Madonie and Peloritani mountains or up Mount Etna. In the winter, snowy Etna is also the place to go for downhill and cross-country skiing. Horseback riding, including programmes of organized long-distance trekking, is also becoming popular in Sicily.

SAILING

THE COASTLINE and inlets of Sicily and the islands are a paradise for sailing aficionados. The sport increases in popularity every year, especially along the northern coast. The coming and going of yachts from all over Europe in Sicilian waters has had a positive influence, triggering a vast improvement in the facilities for nautical tourism in the many port towns around the coast.

Sailing, an increasingly popular activity in Sicily in recent years

WINDSURFING

THIS ENERGETIC SPORT can be practised at almost all Sicily's seaside tourist resorts. However, expert windsurfers claim that the ideal places for the sport are the Aeolian Islands and the tip of the Capo Passero area, where the Ionian and Mediterranean seas converge. Virtually every beach in Sicily can offer surfboard rental facilities.

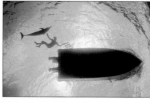

The sea beds of the Aeolian Islands, unequalled in the Mediterranean

SCUBA AND FREE DIVING

THE SEA BEDS in this area are the delight and joy of scuba and free diving buffs, who head in particular for the diving around the offshore islands – especially the Aeolian Islands, which are of volcanic origin. As well as the fish and marine plants, you may well spot some historical objects on the sea bed. Almost all seaside resorts offer basic diving facilities, including refilling your oxygen cylinder. If you are diving independently, make sure someone is aware of your whereabouts and plans.

WALKING, TREKKING AND HORSE RIDING

THERE IS A VAST range of walking itineraries in Sicily. Even though there are mountains, hills and fantastic gorges such as the ones at Pantalica (see p153) and Ispica (see p145), the best hiking spots are in the northeastern region. Mount Etna offers marvellous opportunities for excursions among the lava grottoes and lava fields, and the Madonie and Peloritani mountains offer spectacular panoramas, often quite close to the sea. The most interesting mountains for hikers lie in the network of regional parks and nature reserves, which, thanks to new initiatives, are happily on the increase every year. These parks and reserves include the extensive Parco dell'Etna, the Riserva dello Zingaro, the Parco Regionale dei Monti Nebrodi and the Parco Regionale delle Madonie.

In the interior of Sicily visitors can find a number of sports associations, riding schools and *agriturismo* farms offering trekking holidays. Some of the longer routes take several days. In addition, some of the bigger holiday villages have riding schools. For information on the most important horse riding centres in Sicily, contact the Associazione Nazionale Turismo Equestre (ANTE) in Rome.

Horse riding on the beach in Sicily

The hourly

CONNECT
SMALLER

FERRY SER
off the S
at regular i
well organi
different fe

SKIING

DO NOT EXPECT to find state-of-the-art facilities on the ski runs of Mount Etna. There is no artificial snow (the perennial drought in Sicily precludes anything of the kind), so that the skiing season is from December to March. You can ski on the 25 km (15 miles) of runs on the Rifugio Sapienza and the old Montagnola crater, which drops by about 700 m (2,300 ft) at most. If the weather is good, the panorama is marvellous, the sea at Taormina mirroring the sunlight and the volcano's fumes rising lazily above you. However, Mount Etna is not only for downhill skiing fans, though their numbers grow every year.

A snowboard on the lava field on Vulcano, one of the Aeolian islands

There is also a beaten track near the Grande Albergo, just below the refuge at Rifugio Sapienza, which is ideal for cross-country skiing. Skiing on Mount Etna has become a "classic" for lovers of alpine skiing or telemarking. Finally, a different experience for the sensation-seeker – the uniquely Sicilian sport of travelling down the lava fields of Etna or the slopes of the black volcanoes of the Aeolian islands on a snow-board. But be warned, the dry lava surface is much, much harder than snow.

DIRECTORY

SAILING

Filicudi
Charter and rental
Acquaro Marco Polo
(090-988 98 43.

Lampedusa
Charter and rental
Club Nautico Bolina
(0922-970 826.

Lipari
Harbour Office
(090-981 32 22 or
981 13 20.
Charter and rental
Nauta
(090-982 23 95 or
982 23 06.
Viking
(090-981 25 84.
SEN
(090-981 12 40.
Pignataro Shipping
(090-981 14 17

Pantelleria
Charter and
Quelli di Pant
(0923-918

Salina
Servizi
Dydime v
(090-98
Charter and
Nautica Leva
(090-984

Stromboli
Charter and rental
Strombolania
(090-986 390.
Società di navigazione
(090-984 30 83.

Ustica
Harbour Office
(091-844 90 65.
Marine Reserve
(091-844 94 56.

Vulcano
Charter and rental
Centro Nautico Sabbie N
(090-982 20 41.
Centro Nautico Bai
Levante
(090-9
Club P
(0

Centro Nautico Eoliano
(090-981 24 37.
Diving Center Manta Sub
(090-981 10 04.
Diving Center La Gorgonia
(090-981 20 60.

Panarea
Ricarica ARA
Roberto Buzzelli
(090-983 288.

Pantelleri
Green

Ricarica ARA
Rosaria Ailara
(091-844 91 62.

Vulcano
Vulcano Mare
(090-985 30 51.

TREKKI
H

AIRLINE
INFORM

Air Euro
(Milan
02-671 182

Air Sicili
(Palermo
091-625 05

Alitalia (I
(0171-60.
(0181-74.

Alitalia (I
(800-223

British Ai
(UK)
(0990-444

Continent
(800-231

Delta (US
(800-24

Meridia
(Italy)
Booking
(Mila
02-864 7
(Rome
i Rome
06-478 04

Getting Around Sicily

No-parking
sign

0 - 24

THE HEART OF the largest island in the Mediterranean is rugged and mountainous. You will notice this as soon as you begin to travel around Sicily. Roads become steep and winding the further you go inland. What may look like a short journey on the map may in fact take quite a long time. Networks of railways and buses connect most towns and villages, but you may need a car for the more inaccessible areas. Sicily's rail network includes a full circuit of Mount Etna, a journey that takes five hours.

A fast, straight road crossing a valley in the interior of Sicily

GETTING AROUND BY TRAIN

THE TWO MAJOR railway lines run south from Messina to Catania and Syracuse, and west in the direction of Palermo. A secondary route branches off from the Messina–Palermo line at
~~~~ Bologna, Milan, Pisa, ~~se and goes –
~~rona,~~ summ~~~~gento.
smaller islа~~~~
If you are travе~~~~
~~~he~~ United States, **Tw**
~~~inental~~ and Delta ~~~~
offer direct flights t~~~~
~~~~ere you can catch a ~~~~
~~~~~ight to Sicily.

~~~ay (FS) ~~~
~~~~ugh-
~~~~

GETTING AROUND BY CAR OR MOTORCYCLE

IF YOU WANT TO get to know the real Sicily, travelling around by car, or even by motorcycle if you are brave, is probably the best way. The main roads and motorways linking the major towns are generally in good condition. This includes the Messina–Palermo, Messina–Catania and Catania–Palermo roads. When planning your trip, ~~~~ mind that on some of ~~~~s, including long ~~~ ~~~ southern ~~~ ~~~ may be busy
c~~~~ ~~~erefore
me~~~~ ~~~he
~~~~ e even
BUS SЕ~~~~ it is

GIVEN THE ~~~~ ~~~
~~~~mountainoυ~~~~
of Sicily, not every~~~~ ~~~so accessible by train, ar~~~~ ~~~re there are lines, se~~~~ ~~e slow. In recent ye~~~~ ~~~vestment in infra-
~~~~ has focussed on
~~~~g the roads rather
~~~~ilway. An extensive
~~~~cal bus services
~~~~ the smallest
~~~~e are good
~~~~links to the
~~~~rts.

ARRIVING BY CAR

CAR FERRIES go regularly across the Straits of Messina (see pp224–5), and taking a car to Sicily should not present any particular problems. You need a valid driving licence to drive anywhere in Italy, and it may be a good idea to carry a translation of your licence.

CAR HIRE

ALMOST ALL THE major car hire companies have branch offices throughout Sicily, including the seaports of Palermo and Catania and the airports of Palermo Punta Raisi, Catania Fontanarossa and Trapani Birgi. You can ~~~so find an office in every ~~~vincial capital. If you ~~~ ~~~e a major firm such as ~~~ ~~r Rent a Car (see

~~~e
~~~ port
to
here
rvices
~~ith the
noa,

Directory), check the rental conditions in advance to see what is included and whether you need additional insurance. A number of holiday companies offer budget fly-drive deals, enabling you to pick up your car on arrival at the airport. This is normally cheaper than renting a car on the spot. On some of the offshore islands you can find cars as well as motorcycles and scooters for hire. Island roads are often in poor condition, and you may find travelling by two-wheeled transport is a more comfortable way of getting around.

ROAD REGULATIONS

THE RULES OF THE ROAD are the same as in the rest of Italy, including driving on the right, speed limits (50 km/h, 30 mph in towns) and compulsory seat belts in cars and helmets for motorcyclists. Parking is a real problem in the larger cities (especially Palermo), and also in historic centres. Petrol *(benzina)* is generally expensive.

BICYCLES AND MOUNTAIN BIKES

THE ROADS IN the interior are fairly quiet and are therefore suitable for cycling and even for touring by bicycle. As a result, some travel agencies have begun to offer bike excursions, with the added convenience of vans to carry

Using a rented bicycle, the best way to see the small islands

your luggage for you from place to place. Sicilian drivers are not used to seeing cyclists on the road, however, so stay alert at all times.

Mountain biking is becoming more popular as a sport in Sicily, particularly in the Peloritani, Nebrodi and Madonie mountain areas. Cycling with a group of mountain bike riders is increasingly popular, and it is not uncommon to see a cavalcade on the cattle tracks and paths that run through the various parks and nature reserves on the island.

GETTING AROUND IN THE CITIES

PUBLIC TRANSPORT is quite reliable, and easy to use in the main cities in Sicily – Palermo, Catania and Messina. In other towns such as Trapani, Syracuse and Agrigento and, of course, in the smaller towns, the best way to get around is on foot. Public transport in Palermo is run by the **AMAT** (telephone: 091-222 398) and the service connects all the most interesting sights, including Monreale and Mondello.

Tickets can be purchased at the tobacconists *(tabaccaio)* and news vendors *(giornalaio)*, or in the AMAT kiosks, which also provide maps of the transport network. Tickets are valid for one hour and cost L1,500; it is also possible to buy a ticket that is valid all day. In Catania, all the most

A Palermo transport system tourist ticket

interesting sights can be reached on foot. However, should you need a bus – for example, to go from the centre to the airport or the train station – the network is run by **AMT** (telephone: 095-310 233). Tickets are valid for 90 minutes, but there is also a 24-hour tourist ticket available. In Messina, public transport is handy if you want to visit the Museo Regionale *(see pp178–9)*, which is 45 minutes' walking distance from the centre of town; the stops for buses going in this direction are in Piazza Castronovo, which is also the terminus for buses to Ganzirri (Nos. 78, 79 and 81). Tickets can be purchased from news vendors or tobacconists.

DIRECTORY

CAR HIRE

Avis
(Palermo 091-591 684.
(Catania 095-340 500.

Europcar
(Palermo 091-651 13 93.
(Catania 095-340 252.

Hertz
(General 199 112 211.
(Palermo 091-591 682.
(Catania 095-341 595.

Rent a Car
(Palermo 091-591 681.
(Catania 095-340 594.
(Syracuse 0931-66548.

Buses, the best way of getting around larger cities such as Palermo

General Index

Acknowledgments

DORLING KINDERSLEY WOULD LIKE to thank the following people, museums and organizations, whose contributions and assistance have made the preparation of this book possible. Dorling Kindersley would also like to thank all the people, organizations and businesses, too numerous to mention individually, for their kind permission to photograph their establishments.

Alessandra Arena; Ms Puleo, Assessorato al Turismo Regione Sicilia; AAPT Caltanissetta, Egidio Cacciola; AAST Acireale; Grazia Incorvaia, AAST Agrigento; AAST Caltagirone; AAST Capo D'Orlando; Ms Lidestri, AAST Catania and Acicastello; AAST Cefalù; Ms Petralia, AAST Enna; AAST Giardini Naxos; AAST Messina; AAST Milazzo; Salvatore Giuffrida, AAST Nicolosi; AAST Palermo and Monreale; AAST Patti; Ivana Taschetta, AAST Piazza Armerina; AAST Sciacca; AAST Syracuse; AAST Taormina; Mario Cavallaro, APT Syracuse; Ms Mocata, APT Trapani; Carlo Rigano, Associazione Culturale Sicilia '71 di Mascalucia, Paolo Mazzotta, Biblioteca "E. Vittorietti", Palermo; Barbara Cacciani; Franco Conti, Carthera Aetna; Nicolò Longo; Prof Giorgio De Luca, Istituto Europeo di Scienze Antropologiche; Giorgia Conversi; EPT Agrigento; Nello Musumeci, EPT Catania; Dr Ragno, EPT Messina; Dr Majorca, EPT Palermo; Manilo Peri, Fondazione Culturale Mandralisca, Cefalù; Dr Rosano, Framon Hotels; Galleria Regionale di Sicilia – Palazzo Abatellis (Palermo); Domenico Calabrò, Gazzetta del Sud; Gisella Giarrusso; Ernesto Girardi; Salvo Amato, Giuliano Rotondi Freelance Studio, Acireale; Carmelo Guglielmino; Mr Altieri, Hotel Baglio della Luna; Hotel Baglio Santa Croce; Hotel La Tonnara di Bonagia; Col Girardi; Hotel Villa Paradiso dell'Etna; Luigi Lacagnina and his family; Maggiore Budget Autonoleggi; Prof Gaetano Maltese; Emma Marzullo; Meridiana; Museo Archeologico Regionale Paolo Orsi (Syracuse); Museo Etnostorico dei Nebrodi; Prof Iberia Medici, Museo-Laboratorio Village, Giarre; Ignazio Paternò Castello; Società Aerofotogrammetrica Siciliana (Palermo); Sandro Tranchina; Teatro Massimo (Palermo); Teatro Biondo (Palermo); Prof Amitrano Svarese, Faculty of Anthropological Sciences, University of Palermo; Mara Veneziani; Pia Vesin.

ADDITIONAL ASSISTANCE

Emily Anderson (editorial work); Michelle Clark (proofreading); Giuliano Rotondi (picture research); Mary Sutherland (US consultant).

PICTURE CREDITS

Key: t = top; tl = top left; tlc = top left centre; tc = top centre; trc = top right centre; tr = top right; cla = centre left above; ca = centre above; cra = centre right above; cl = centre left; c = centre; cr = centre right; clb = centre left below; crb = centre right below; cb = centre below; bl = bottom left; br = bottom right; b = bottom; bc = bottom centre; bcl = bottom centre left; bcr = bottom centre right.

Every effort has been made to trace the copyright holders. The publisher apologizes for any unintentional omissions and would be pleased, in such cases, to add an acknowledgment in future editions.

All the photographs reproduced in this book are from the Image Bank, Milan except for the following:

FABRIZIO ARDITO: 2, 3, 15b, 79br, 80, 96tl, 98bl, 106, 109tl, 110tl, 111br, 112tr, 112cl, 113cr, 114tr, 114bl, 115cr, 116tl, 116br, 117br, 118t, 118c, 119tl, 119b, 122cl, 124bl, 125cl, 125clb, 126tl, 127bl, 139tl, 139br, 140br, 145tl, 145br, 149tl, 149cr, 150tl, 152c, 152b, 153br, 162tl, 162cr, 192, 201c, 212br.
ARCHIVIO APT SIRACUSA: 132tl, 133bl, 135br.
ARCHIVIO APT TRAPANI: 82tl, 83b.
ARCHIVIO EPT PALERMO: 105cr.
ARCHIVIO FRAMON HOTELS: 190cl, 191tl, 191br.
FABIO DE ANGELIS: 046tl, 046cl, 046bl, 047cr, 048tl, 048bc, 051br, 053cr, 054tl, 058tr, 058b, 059tr, 059br, 061tr, 063br, 064cr, 065tl, 066br, 067br, 071bl, 072tl, 086c, 203br, 212cl, 218tc, 218br, 219tl, 220cl, 220crb, 220bl, 221tl, 221tr, 221cra, 221crb, 224tc, 224cr, 224br, 226tl.
DORLING KINDERSLEY: 18br, 27bl, 33tr, 33tl, 32–3c, 42tr, 44, 55br, 60, 70cr, 74–5, 142br, 188–9.
CRISTINA GAMBARO–GINO FRONGIA: 67bl, 81, 82bl, 86cl, 87b, 88b, 89tl, 90c, 91, 93bc, 94cl, 94bl, 98tl, 100, 102tl, 102b, 103tl, 113bl, 129, 142c, 173br, 200cr.
NICOLO LONGO: 16crb, 17crb.
RECULEZ: 202–203.
GIULIANO ROTONDI: 3c, 15tr, 20tr, 20cl, 20bc, 21tr, 21cl, 21bc, 22, 23tl, 23tc, 23c, 24, 25tc, 26tr, 26c, 26br, 27tl, 27tc, 27cl, 27br, 28tl, 28cl, 28cb, 28br, 29tl, 29cla, 29bla, 29bl, 30tl, 30ca, 30clb, 30bl, 30bc, 31cr, 31bc, 32tl, 32cl, 32br, 33cr, 33bl, 33br, 34ar, 34cl, 34cla, 34cb, 34bl, 34br, 34clb, 35tl, 35cla, 35cra, 35tr, 35bl, 35br, 43tr, 49c, 49br, 52t, 64tr, 64cl, 65tc, 65cr, 67t, 70bl, 73tl, 88tc, 88c, 90tl, 95tr, 95cl, 98br, 99cr, 99br, 101cr, 102cl, 102cr, 124tr, 124br, 125tr, 125br, 130bc, 141bl, 146tr, 147cr, 148b, 150cl, 150br, 151tl, 152tl, 153cr, 156bl, 159tl, 160tl, 163tl, 163bl, 165br, 168tr, 169tl, 171br, 172bl, 174cl, 179br, 181tr, 181bl, 202tr, 210tc, 212tl, 212tr, 213tr, 213cla, 213cra, 213clb, 213crb, 213b, 214cl, 214br, 215cr, 224cl, 226bl.
SBRIGLIO: 133tl, 134, 138c, 140tl, 140cl, 140bl, 141cr, 141 bl, 142tl, 142tr, 143tr, 143cl, 143br, 144c, 144bl, 156tr.
MARCO SCAPAGNINI: 138tr, 141tr, 143cr, 200tc, 214tc.

DORLING KINDERSLEY SPECIAL EDITIONS

Dorling Kindersley books can be purchased in bulk quantities at discounted prices for use in promotions or as premiums. We are also able to offer special editions and personalized jackets, corporate imprints, and excerpts from all of our books, tailored specifically to meet your own needs.

To find out more, please contact:
(in the United Kingdom) – SPECIAL SALES, DORLING KINDERSLEY LIMITED, 9 HENRIETTA STREET, COVENT GARDEN, LONDON WC2E 8PS; TEL. 020 7753 3572;

(in the United States) – SPECIAL MARKETS DEPARTMENT, DORLING KINDERSLEY, INC., 95 MADISON AVENUE, NEW YORK, NY 10016.

Phrase Book

IN EMERGENCY

Help!	Aiuto!	eye-**yoo**-toh
Stop!	Fermate!	fair-**mah**-teh
Call a doctor.	Chiama un medico.	kee-**ah**-mah oon **meh**-dee-koh
Call an ambulance.	Chiama un' ambulanza.	kee-**ah**-mah oon am-boo-**lan**-tsa
Call the police.	Chiama la polizia.	kee-**ah**-mah lah pol-ee-**tsee**-ah
Call the fire department.	Chiama i pompieri.	kee-**ah**-mah ee pom-pee-**air**-ee
Where is the telephone?	Dov'è il telefono?	dov-**eh** eel teh-**leh**-foh-noh?
The nearest hospital?	L'ospedale più vicino?	loss-peh-**dah**-leh pee-oo vee-**chee**-noh?

COMMUNICATION ESSENTIALS

Yes/No	Sì/No	see/**noh**
Please	Per favore	pair fah-**vor**-eh
Thank you	Grazie	**grah**-tsee-eh
Excuse me	Mi scusi	mee **skoo**-zee
Hello	Buon giorno	bwon **jor**-noh
Goodbye	Arrivederci	ah-ree-veh-**dair**-chee
Good evening	Buona sera	**bwon**-ah **sair**-ah
morning	la mattina	lah mah-**tee**-nah
afternoon	il pomeriggio	eel poh-meh-**ree**-joh
evening	la sera	lah **sair**-ah
yesterday	ieri	ee-**air**-ee
today	oggi	**oh**-jee
tomorrow	domani	doh-**mah**-nee
here	qui	**kwee**
there	la	**lah**
What?	Quale?	**kwah**-leh?
When?	Quando?	**kwan**-doh?
Why?	Perchè?	pair-**keh**?
Where?	Dove?	**doh**-veh?

USEFUL PHRASES

How are you?	Come sta?	**koh**-meh stah?
Very well, thank you.	Molto bene, grazie.	**moll**-toh **beh**-neh **grah**-tsee-eh
Pleased to meet you.	Piacere di conoscerla.	pee-ah-**chair**-eh dee coh-**noh**-shair-lah
See you later.	A più tardi.	ah pee-**oo** tar-dee
That's fine.	Va bene.	va **beh**-neh
Where is/are ...?	Dov'è/Dove sono ...?	dov-**eh**/doveh**soh**-noh?
How long does it take to get to ...?	Quanto tempo ci vuole per andare a ...?	**kwan**-toh **tem**-poh chee voo-**oh**-leh pair an-**dar**-eh ah ...?
How do I get to ...?	Come faccio per arrivare a ...?	**koh**-meh **fah**-choh pair arri-**var**-eh ah ...?
Do you speak English?	Parla inglese?	**par**-lah een-**gleh**-zeh?
I don't understand.	Non capisco.	non ka-**pee**-skoh
Could you speak more slowly, please?	Può parlare più lentamente, per favore?	pwoh par-**lah**-reh pee-oo len-ta-**men**-teh pair fah-**vor**-eh?
I'm sorry.	Mi dispiace.	mee dee-spee-**ah**-cheh

USEFUL WORDS

big	grande	**gran**-deh
small	piccolo	**pee**-koh-loh
hot	caldo	**kal**-doh
cold	freddo	**fred**-doh
good	buono	**bwoh**-noh
bad	cattivo	kat-**tee**-voh
enough	basta	**bas**-tah
well	bene	**beh**-neh
open	aperto	ah-**pair**-toh
closed	chiuso	kee-**oo**-zoh
left	a sinistra	ah see-**nee**-strah
right	a destra	ah **dess**-trah
straight ahead	sempre dritto	**sem**-preh **dree**-toh
near	vicino	vee-**chee**-noh
far	lontano	lon-**tah**-noh
up	su	**soo**
down	giù	**joo**
early	presto	**press**-toh
late	tardi	**tar**-dee
entrance	entrata	en-**trah**-tah
exit	uscita	oo-**shee**-ta
toilet	il gabinetto	eel gab-bee-**net**-toh
free, unoccupied	libero	**lee**-bair-oh
free, no charge	gratuito	grah-**too**-ee-toh

MAKING A TELEPHONE CALL

I'd like to place a long-distance call.	Vorrei fare una interurbana.	vor-**ray far**-eh oona in-tair-oor-**bah**-nah
I'd like to make a reverse-charge call.	Vorrei fare una telefonata a carico del destinatario.	vor-**ray far**-eh oona teh-leh-fon-**ah**-tah ah **kar**-ee-koh dell dess-tee-nah-**tar**-ree-oh
Could I speak to ...	Potrei parlare con...	po-tray par-**lah**-reh con
I'll try again later.	Ritelefono più tardi.	ree-teh-**leh**-foh-noh pee-oo **tar**-dee
May I leave a message?	Posso lasciare un messaggio?	**poss**-oh lash-**ah**-reh oon mess-**sah**-joh?
Hold on.	Un attimo, per favore.	oon **ah**-tee-moh, pair fah-**vor**-eh,
Could you speak up a little, please?	Può parlare più forte?	pwoh par-**lah**-reh pee-oo **for**-teh?
local call	telefonata locale	te-leh-fon-**ah**-tah loh-cah-leh

SHOPPING

How much does this cost?	Quant'è, per favore?	kwan-**teh** pair fah-**vor**-eh?
I would like ...	Vorrei ...	vor-**ray** ...
Do you have ...?	Avete ...?	ah-**veh**-teh..?
I'm just looking.	Sto soltanto guardando.	stoh sol-**tan**-toh gwar-**dan**-doh
Do you take credit cards?	Accettate carte di credito?	ah-chet-**tah**-teh **kar**-teh dee **creh**-dee-toh?
What time do you open/close?	A che ora apre/chiude?	ah keh or-ah **ah**-preh/kee-**oo**-deh?
this one	questo	**kweh**-stoh
that one	quello	**kwell**-oh
expensive	caro	**kar**-oh
cheap	a buon prezzo	ah bwon **pret**-soh
size, clothes	la taglia	lah **tah**-lee-ah
size, shoes	il numero	eel **noo**-mair-oh
white	bianco	bee-**ang**-koh
black	nero	**neh**-roh
red	rosso	**ross**-oh
yellow	giallo	**jal**-loh
green	verde	**vair**-deh
blue	blu	**bloo**

TYPES OF SHOP

antique dealer	l'antiquario	lan-tee-**kwah**-ree-oh
bakery	il forno/ il panificio	eel **forn**-oh/ eel pan-ee-**fee**-choh
bank	la banca	lah **bang**-kah
bookstore	la libreria	lah lee-breh-**ree**-ah
butcher	la macelleria	lah mah-chell-eh-**ree**-ah
cake shop	la pasticceria	lah pas-tee-chair-**ee**-ah
delicatessen	la salumeria	lah sah-loo-meh-**ree**-ah
department store	il grande magazzino	eel **gran**-deh mag-gad-**zee**-noh
pharmacy	la farmacia	lah far-mah-**chee**-ah
fishseller	il pescivendolo	eel pesh-ee-**ven**-doh-loh
florist	il fioraio	eel fee-or-**eye**-oh
greengrocer	il fruttivendolo	eel froo-tee-**ven**-doh-loh
grocery	alimentari	ah-lee-men-**tah**-ree
hairdresser	il parrucchiere	eel par-oo-kee-**air**-eh
ice-cream parlour	la gelateria	lah jel-lah-tair-**ree**-ah
market	il mercato	eel mair-**kah**-toh
newsstand	l'edicola	leh-**dee**-koh-lah
post office	l'ufficio postale	loo-**fee**-choh pos-**tah**-leh
shoe shop	il negozio di scarpe	eel neh-**goh**-tsioh dee **skar**-peh
supermarket	il supermercato	eel su-pair-mair-**kah**-toh
tobacconist	il tabaccaio	eel tah-bak-**eye**-oh
travel agency	l'agenzia di viaggi	lah-jen-**tsee**-ah dee vee-**ad**-jee

SIGHTSEEING

art gallery	la pinacoteca	lah peena-koh-**teh**-kah
bus stop	la fermata dell'autobus	lah fair-**mah**-tah dell **ow**-toh-booss
church	la chiesa/ la basilica	lah kee-eh-zah/ lah bah-**seel**-i-kah
closed for holidays	chiuso per le ferie	kee-**oo**-zoh pair leh **fair**-ee-eh
garden	il giardino	eel jar-**dee**-no
library	la biblioteca	lah beh-leh-oh-**teh**-kah
museum	il museo	eel moo-**zeh**-oh
train station	la stazione	lah stah-tsee-**oh**-neh
tourist information	l'ufficio di turismo	loo-**fee**-choh dee too-**ree**-smoh

STAYING IN A HOTEL

Do you have any vacant rooms?	**Avete camere libere?**	ah-**veh**-teh **kab**-mair-eh **lee**-bair-eh?
double room	**una camera doppia**	oona **kab**-mair-ah **dob**-pee-ah
with double bed	**con letto matrimoniale**	kon **let**-toh mah-tree-moh-nee-**ah**-lee
twin room	**una camera con due letti**	oona **kab**-mair-ah kon **doo**-eh **let**-tee
single room	**una camera singola**	oona **kab**-mair-ah **sing**-goh-lah
room with a bath, shower	**una camera con bagno, con doccia**	oona **kab**-mair-ah kon **ban**-yoh, kon **dot**-chah
porter	**il facchino**	eel fah-**kee**-noh
key	**la chiave**	lah kee-**ah**-veh
I have a reservation.	**Ho fatto una prenotazione.**	oh **fat**-toh oona preh-noh-tah-tsee-**oh**-neh

EATING OUT

Do you have a table for ...?	**Avete una tavola per ... ?**	ah-**veh**-teh oona **tab**-voh-lah pair ...?
I'd like to reserve a table.	**Vorrei riservare una tavola.**	vor-**ray** ree-sair-**vah**-reh oona **tab**-voh-lah
breakfast	**colazione**	koh-lah-tsee-**oh**-neh
lunch	**pranzo**	**pran**-tsoh
dinner	**cena**	**cheh**-nah
The bill, please.	**Il conto, per favore.**	eel **kon**-toh pair fah-**vor**-eh
I am a vegetarian.	**Sono vegetariano/a.**	**soh**-noh **veh**-jeh-tar-ee-**ah**-noh/nah
waitress	**cameriera**	kah-mair-ee-**air**-ah
waiter	**cameriere**	kah-mair-ee-**air**-eh
fixed-price menu	**il menù a prezzo fisso**	eel meh-**noo** ah **pret**-soh **fee**-soh
dish of the day	**piatto del giorno**	pee-**ab**-toh dell **jor**-no
appetizer	**antipasto**	an-tee-**pass**-toh
first course	**il primo**	eel **pree**-moh
main course	**il secondo**	eel seh-**kon**-doh
vegetables	**il contorno**	eel kon-**tor**-noh
dessert	**il dolce**	eel **doll**-cheh
cover charge	**il coperto**	eel koh-**pair**-toh
wine list	**la lista dei vini**	lah **lee**-stah day-ee **vee**-nee
rare	**al sangue**	al **sang**-gweh
medium	**al puntino**	al poon-**tee**-noh
well done	**ben cotto**	ben **kot**-toh
glass	**il bicchiere**	eel bee-kee-**air**-eh
bottle	**la bottiglia**	lah bot-**teel**-yah
knife	**il coltello**	eel kol-**tell**-oh
fork	**la forchetta**	lah for-**ket**-tah
spoon	**il cucchiaio**	eel koo-kee-**eye**-oh

MENU DECODER

l'acqua minerale gassata/naturale	**lab**-kwah mee-nair-**ab**-leh gab-**zab**-tah/nab-too-**rab**-leh	mineral water fizzy/still
aceto	ab-**cheb**-toh	vinegar
aglio	**al**-ee-oh	garlic
l'agnello	lah-**niell**-oh	lamb
al forno	al **for**-noh	baked/roasted
alla griglia	ah-lah **greel**-yah	grilled
l'aragosta	lah-rah-**goss**-tah	lobster
arrosto	ar-**ross**-toh	roast
basilico	bah-**zee**-lee-koh	basil
la birra	lah **beer**-rah	beer
la bistecca	lah bee-**stek**-kah	steak
il brodo	eel **brob**-doh	broth
il burro	eel **boor**-oh	butter
il caffè	eel kah-**feb**	coffee
i calamari	ee kah-lah-**mah**-ree	squid
i carciofi	ee kar-**choff**-ee	artichokes
la carne	la **kar**-neh	meat
la cipolla	la chip-**ob**-lah	onion
i contorni	ee kon-**tor**-nee	vegetables
le cozze	leh **cob**-tzeh	mussels
i fagioli	ee fah-**job**-lee	beans
il fegato	eel **fay**-gah-toh	liver
il finocchio	eel fee-**nok**-ee-oh	fennel
il formaggio	eel for-**mad**-joh	cheese
le fragole	leh **frah**-goh-leh	strawberries
il fritto misto	eel free-toh **mees**-toh	mixed fried dish
la frutta	la **froot**-tah	fruit
frutti di mare	**froo**-tee dee **mab**-reh	seafood
i funghi	ee **foon**-ghee	mushrooms
i gamberi	ee **gam**-bair-ee	shrimp
il gelato	eel jeh-**lab**-toh	ice cream
l'insalata	leen-sab-lab-tah	salad

il latte	eel **laht**-teh	milk
lesso	**less**-oh	boiled
la melanzana	lah meh-lan-**tsab**-nah	aubergine (eggplant)
la minestra	lah mee-**ness**-trah	soup
l'olio	loh-lee-oh	oil
il pane	eel **pab**-neh	bread
le patate	leh pah-**tab**-teh	potatoes
le patatine fritte	leh pah-tah-**teen**-eh **free**-teh	French fries
il pepe	eel **peb**-peh	pepper
la pesca	lah **pess**-kah	peach
il pesce	eel **pesh**-eh	fish
il polipo	eel pob-lee-poh	octopus
il pollo	eel **poll**-oh	chicken
il pomodoro	eel poh-moh-**dor**-oh	tomato
il prosciutto cotto/crudo	eel pro-**shoo**-toh **kot**-toh/**kroo**-doh	ham cooked/cured
il riso	eel **ree**-zoh	rice
il sale	eel **sab**-leh	salt
la salsiccia	lah sal-**see**-chah	sausage
le seppie	leh **sep**-pee-eh	cuttlefish
secco	**sek**-koh	dry
la sogliola	lah **soll**-yoh-lah	sole
i spinaci	ee spee-**nab**-chee	spinach
succo d'arancia/ di limone	**soo**-koh dah-ran-chah/ dee lee-**moh**-neh	orange/lemon juice
il tè	eel **teb**	tea
la tisana	lah tee-**zab**-nah	herbal tea
il tonno	eel **ton**-noh	tuna
la torta	lah **tor**-tah	cake/tart
l'uovo	loo-**ob**-voh	egg
vino bianco	**vee**-noh bee-**ang**-koh	white wine
vino rosso	**vee**-noh **ross**-oh	red wine
il vitello	eel vee-**tell**-oh	veal
le vongole	leh **von**-goh-leh	clams
lo zucchero	loh **zoo**-kair-oh	sugar
gli zucchini	lyee dzu-**kee**-nee	zucchini
la zuppa	lah **tsoo**-pah	soup

NUMBERS

1	**uno**	**oo**-noh
2	**due**	**doo**-eh
3	**tre**	**treb**
4	**quattro**	**kwat**-rob
5	**cinque**	**ching**-kweh
6	**sei**	**say**-ee
7	**sette**	**set**-teh
8	**otto**	**ot**-toh
9	**nove**	**nob**-veh
10	**dieci**	dee-**eb**-chee
11	**undici**	**oon**-dee-chee
12	**dodici**	**dob**-dee-chee
13	**tredici**	**tray**-dee-chee
14	**quattordici**	kwat-**tor**-dee-chee
15	**quindici**	**kwin**-dee-chee
16	**sedici**	**say**-dee-chee
17	**diciassette**	dee-chah-**set**-teb
18	**diciotto**	dee-**cbot**-toh
19	**diciannove**	dee-chah-**nob**-veh
20	**venti**	**ven**-tee
30	**trenta**	**tren**-tab
40	**quaranta**	kwah-**ran**-tah
50	**cinquanta**	ching-**kwan**-tah
60	**sessanta**	sess-**an**-tah
70	**settanta**	set-**tan**-tah
80	**ottanta**	ot-**tan**-tah
90	**novanta**	nob-**van**-tah
100	**cento**	**cben**-toh
1,000	**mille**	**mee**-leh
2,000	**duemila**	**doo**-eh **mee**-lah
5,000	**cinquemila**	ching-kweh **mee**-lab
1,000,000	**un milione**	oón meel-**yob**-neh

TIME

one minute	**un minuto**	oon mee-**noo**-toh
one hour	**un'ora**	oon or-ah
half an hour	**mezz'ora**	medz or-ah
a day	**un giorno**	oon jor-noh
a week	**una settimana**	oona set-tee-**mab**-nah
Monday	**lunedì**	loo-neh-**dee**
Tuesday	**martedì**	mar-teh-**dee**
Wednesday	**mercoledì**	mair-koh-leh-**dee**
Thursday	**giovedì**	job-veh-**dee**
Friday	**venerdì**	ven-air-**dee**
Saturday	**sabato**	**sab**-bah-toh
Sunday	**domenica**	dob-**meb**-nee-kah

TITLES AVAILABLE

THE GUIDES THAT SHOW YOU WHAT OTHERS ONLY TELL YOU

COUNTRY GUIDES

AUSTRALIA • CANADA • FRANCE • GREAT BRITAIN
GREECE: ATHENS & THE MAINLAND • THE GREEK ISLANDS
IRELAND • ITALY • MEXICO • PORTUGAL • SCOTLAND
SOUTH AFRICA • SPAIN • THAILAND

REGIONAL GUIDES

BARCELONA & CATALONIA • CALIFORNIA
FLORENCE & TUSCANY • FLORIDA • HAWAII
JERUSALEM & THE HOLY LAND • LOIRE VALLEY
MILAN & THE LAKES • NAPLES WITH POMPEII & THE
AMALFI COAST • PROVENCE & THE COTE D'AZUR • SARDINIA
SEVILLE & ANDALUSIA • SICILY • VENICE & THE VENETO
GREAT PLACES TO STAY IN EUROPE

CITY GUIDES

AMSTERDAM • BERLIN • BUDAPEST • DUBLIN • ISTANBUL
LISBON • LONDON • MADRID • MOSCOW • NEW YORK
PARIS • PRAGUE • ROME • SAN FRANCISCO
ST PETERSBURG • SYDNEY • VIENNA • WARSAW

TRAVEL MAPS

AUSTRALIA • FRANCE • FLORIDA
GREAT BRITAIN & IRELAND • ITALY • SPAIN

DK TRAVEL GUIDES PHRASE BOOKS

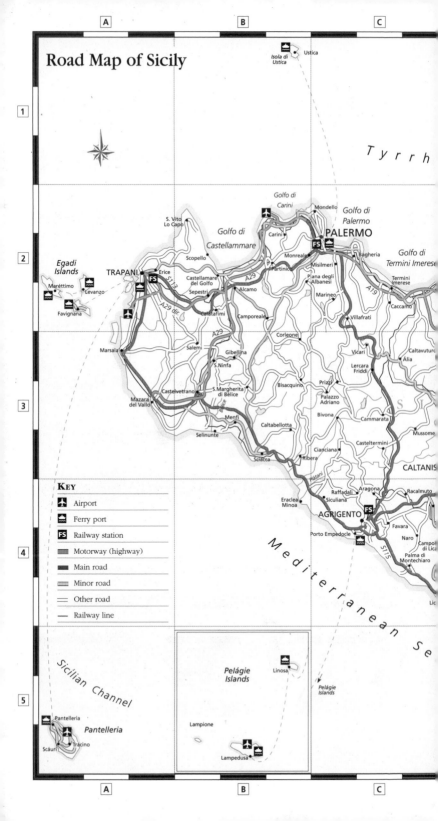